Brian Friel

b.............e.........e..........s greatest .ving playwright, winning ...nternational reputation thi.. .igh such acclaimed works as *Translations* (1980) and *Dancing at Lughnasa* (1990). This collection of specially commissioned essays includes contributions from leading commentators on Friel's work (including two fellow playwrights) and explores the entire range of his career from his 1964 breakthrough with *Philadelphia, Here I Come!* to his most recent success in Dublin and London with *The Home Place* (2005). The essays approach Friel's plays both as literary texts and as performed drama, and provide the perfect introduction for students of both English and Theatre Studies, as well as theatregoers. The collection considers Friel's lesser-known works alongside his more celebrated plays and provides a comprehensive critical survey of his career. This is the most up-to-date study of Friel's work to be published, and includes a chronology and further reading suggestions.

ANTHONY ROCHE is Senior Lecturer in English and Drama at University College Dublin. He is the author of *Contemporary Irish Drama: From Beckett to McGuinness* (1994).

THE CAMBRIDGE
COMPANION TO
BRIAN FRIEL

EDITED BY
ANTHONY ROCHE
University College Dublin

CAMBRIDGE
UNIVERSITY PRESS

CAMBRIDGE UNIVERSITY PRESS
Cambridge, New York, Melbourne, Madrid, Cape Town, Singapore, São Paulo

Cambridge University Press
The Edinburgh Building, Cambridge CB2 2RU, UK

Published in the United States of America by Cambridge University Press, New York

www.cambridge.org
Information on this title: www.cambridge.org/9780521666862

© Cambridge University Press 2006

First published 2006

Printed in the United Kingdom at the University Press, Cambridge

A catalogue record for this publication is available from the British Library

ISBN-13   978-0-521-85399-6 hardback
ISBN-10   0-521-85399-0 hardback

ISBN-13   978-0-521-66686-2 paperback
ISBN-10   0-521-66686-4 paperback

CONTENTS

CONTRIBUTORS

CSILLA BERTHA teaches Irish and English literature at the University of Debrecen, Hungary. She is the author of *A Dramairo Yeats* (*Yeats the Playwright*, 1988), co-author with Donald E. Morse of *Worlds Visible and Invisible: Essays on Irish Literature* (1991), and co-editor of several volumes of essays and journal issues on Irish literature and culture. She has published widely on Irish drama, on the fantastic in literature and the arts, on post-colonial writing, and on parallels between Irish and Hungarian literature. She is currently a member of the Executive Board of IASIL (International Association for the Study of Irish Literatures) and on the Advisory Board of the *Irish University Review*.

PATRICK BURKE teaches in the Department of English at St. Patrick's College, Dublin City University, where he is also Director of the MA in Theatre Studies. He has published widely on Friel, the subject of his Ph.D., as well as on Tom Murphy, T. C. Murray, Shakespeare on film, and on Irish education generally. He has directed plays by Shakespeare, Friel, Murphy, Ibsen and McGuinness. In 1996 he was awarded a scholarship to a world conference on theatre at Salzburg, where he worked with Arthur Miller, Ariel Dorfman and André Brink.

RICHARD ALLEN CAVE is Professor of Drama and Theatre Arts at Royal Holloway, University of London. He has published extensively on aspects of Irish theatre (particularly on Yeats, Wilde, Beckett, Friel, McGuinness); on Renaissance, nineteenth-century and recent English drama; on stage design and theatre history. His special research interest is on dance-drama, physical theatre and the body as a medium of expression. For Penguin Classics, he has edited the plays of W. B. Yeats (1997) and of Oscar Wilde (2000); for Colin Smythe, the plays of T. C. Murray (1998); and for Cornell University Press, the manuscripts of Yeats's *The King of the Great Clock Tower* and *A Full Moon in March* (forthcoming).

NICHOLAS GRENE is Professor of English Literature at Trinity College, Dublin. His books include *Synge: A Critical Study of the Plays* (1975); *Shakespeare, Jonson, Molière: The Comic Contract* (1980); *Bernard Shaw: A Critical View* (1984); *Shakespeare's Tragic Imagination* (1992); *The Politics of Irish Drama* (1999); *Interpreting Synge* (editor, 2000); *Shakespeare's Serial History Plays* (2002). He was the founder Director of the Synge Summer School 1991–2000, and is currently chair of the Irish Theatrical Diaspora project, for which he co-edited *Irish Theatre on Tour* (2005) with Chris Morash.

THOMAS KILROY has written fourteen stage plays. They include *The Death and Resurrection of Mr. Roche, Talbot's Box, Double Cross* and *The Secret Fall of Constance Wilde.* His novel *The Big Chapel* was shortlisted for the Booker Prize and awarded the Guardian Fiction Prize. At *The Irish Times*/ESB [Electricity Supply Board] Theatre Awards in 2004, he was given a Special Tribute award for his contribution to theatre. He is a Fellow of the Royal Society of Literature and Professor Emeritus of Modern English, National University of Ireland – Galway.

HELEN LOJEK is Professor of English at Boise State University, Idaho. She is the author of *Contexts for Frank McGuinness's Drama* (2004) and the editor of *Frank McGuinness: Stages of Mutability* (2002). She has written extensively about Brian Friel, the Charabanc Theatre Company and Northern Irish drama.

FRANK McGUINNESS was born in Buncrana, County Donegal, and is a playwright who lectures in the School of English and Drama at University College Dublin. His plays include *The Factory Girls, Baglady, Observe the Sons of Ulster Marching Towards the Somme, Innocence, Carthaginians, Mary and Lizzie, Someone Who'll Watch Over Me, The Bird Sanctuary, Mutabilitie, Dolly West's Kitchen, Gates of Gold* and *Speaking Like Magpies.* His work has received many awards in Ireland and abroad. His versions of Ibsen, Chekhov, Lorca, Brecht, Sophocles, Euripides, Racine and Pirandello have been performed throughout the English-speaking world.

ANNA McMULLAN is Chair in Drama Studies at Queen's University Belfast. Her book, *Theatre on Trial: Samuel Beckett's Later Drama,* was published in 1993, and she has published many articles on contemporary Irish theatre. She co-edited with Caroline Williams the Contemporary Drama section of the *Field Day Anthology of Irish Writing* volume V (2002) and co-edited with Cathy Leeney *The Theatre of Marina Carr: "Before Rules Was*

Made" (2003) and with Brian Singleton *Performing Ireland* (*Australasian Journal of Drama Studies*, 2003).

GEORGE O'BRIEN was born in Enniscorthy, County Wexford, in 1945, reared in Lismore, County Waterford, and educated at Ruskin College, Oxford, and the University of Warwick. He is the author of *Brian Friel* (1989) and *Brian Friel: A Reference Guide* (1995), as well as three volumes of memoirs. He is Professor of English at Georgetown University, Washington, DC.

MARTINE PELLETIER is a lecturer in English and Irish Studies at the University of Tours. She has published widely on Brian Friel, the Field Day Theatre Company and contemporary Irish and Northern Irish theatre. She is currently working on an updated English version of her book, *Le Théâtre de Brian Friel: Histoire et Histoires*, published by Septentrion in 1997 for Academica Press.

RICHARD PINE is Academic Director of the Durrell School of Corfu and the author of *The Diviner: The Art of Brian Friel* (1999). A graduate of Trinity College, Dublin, he worked in the Irish broadcasting service from 1974 to 1999, and is a former Chair of the Media Association of Ireland and secretary of the Irish Writers' Union. His books include *The Dublin Gate Theatre 1928–1978* (1984); *Laurence Durrell: The Mindscape* (1994/2005); *The Thief of Reason: Oscar Wilde and Modern Ireland* (1995) and *Music and Broadcasting in Ireland* (2005). He is the official historian of the Royal Irish Academy of Music, of which he is an Honorary Fellow.

ANTHONY ROCHE is Senior Lecturer in English and Drama at University College Dublin and Director of the Synge Summer School. He has published widely on the plays of Yeats, Synge and Gregory. His main research interest is in the field of contemporary Irish drama and theatre, where his publications include *Contemporary Irish Drama: From Beckett to McGuinness* (1994) and the chapter on "Contemporary Irish Drama: 1940–2000" in *The Cambridge History of Irish Literature*, edited by Margaret Kelleher and Philip O'Leary. From 1997 to 2002 he was the editor of the *Irish University Review*.

STEPHEN WATT is Professor of English at Indiana University, Bloomington. His most recent books include the co-edited anthologies *A Century of Irish Drama* (2000) and *Ian Fleming and James Bond: The Cultural Politics of 007* (2005), and *Office Hours: Activism and Change in the Academy* (2004, co-authored with Cary Nelson). He is currently completing a book on Samuel Beckett and contemporary Irish and Northern Irish literature.

ACKNOWLEDGMENTS

I would like to express my thanks to all the contributors to this book – for their wholehearted support of the enterprise, for delivering on time and for the quality of their contributions. I am grateful to Richard Pine and to Frank McGuinness for being invaluable sounding boards to me throughout. I wish to thank Ray Ryan, my commissioning editor at Cambridge University Press; the three anonymous readers for their endorsement of what I proposed and for some invaluable suggestions; and to Maartje Scheltens at Cambridge for easing the final stages of delivery. Thanks are also due to Michael Colgan, Marie Rooney and Jenni Rope at the Gate Theatre, Dublin, for advice and support; and to Lyn Haill and her staff in the Print and Publications section of the Royal National Theatre, London, for all of their help. Special thanks are due to Brian Friel himself, in particular for his kind permission to reproduce unpublished material from the Friel Archive at the National Library of Ireland in two of the chapters. My final acknowledgment is my greatest, to my wife Katy Hayes, who helped me in so many ways to see this through.

NOTE ON THE TEXT

The references to *Philadelphia, Here I Come!*, *The Freedom of the City*, *Living Quarters*, *Aristocrats*, *Faith Healer* and *Translations* are to Brian Friel, *Plays One* (London and Boston: Faber and Faber, 1996). The references to *Fathers and Sons*, *Making History*, *Dancing at Lughnasa*, *Wonderful Tennessee* and *Molly Sweeney* are to Brian Friel, *Plays Two* (London: Faber and Faber, 1999). In relation to the following plays, the editions preferred are the most widely available: the Gallery Press edition of *Give Me Your Answer, Do!* and the Faber and Faber editions of *Three Plays After*, *Performances* and *The Home Place*. All of the other references are to the single edition currently in print, either from the Gallery Press or Faber and Faber. Full details of editions used are given in the notes to each chapter.

In quotations from Friel's texts, abbreviations made by the author of the chapter are indicated by square brackets framing three-dotted ellipses [. . .]; unbracketed ellipses are located in Friel's original text.

CHRONOLOGY

1929 Born Brian Patrick Friel on 9 (or 10) January in Killyclogher, near Omagh, County Tyrone, in Northern Ireland; to Sean Friel, a native of Derry and a primary school principal, and Mary McLoone, postmistress, from Glenties, County Donegal.

1939 The Friel family moves to Derry, where Friel's father has a teaching position at the Long Tower school; Friel attended same.

1941 Attends secondary school at St. Columb's College, Derry.

1945 Attends St. Patrick's College, Maynooth, outside Dublin, as a seminarian. Graduates with a BA in 1948 without becoming a priest.

1949 Trains as a teacher in St. Joseph's Training College, Derry.

1950 Teaches at various primary and secondary schools in Derry.

1951 Publishes first short story in *The Bell*.

1954 Marries Anne Morrison. The couple go on to have four daughters and one son.

1958 First radio play *A Sort of Freedom* is produced by the BBC Radio Northern Ireland Home Service (16 January). Another radio play, *To This Hard House*, produced by them on 24 April 1958.

1959 Short story, "The Skelper," appears in the *New Yorker*.

1960 First stage play, *The Francophile*, retitled *A Doubtful Paradise*, premieres at the Group Theatre, Belfast. Leaves teaching to write full time.

1962 Play *The Enemy Within* premieres in Dublin by the Abbey Theatre at the Queen's (6 August). First collection of short stories, *The Saucer of Larks*, published. Begins writing a weekly column for the *Irish Press*.

1963 *The Blind Mice* premieres in Dublin at the Eblana Theatre (19 February). Spends some months in USA at Tyrone Guthrie's invitation to watch rehearsals at the new Guthrie Theatre, Minneapolis.

1964 *Philadelphia, Here I Come!* premiered by Gate Theatre Productions at the Gaiety Theatre during the Dublin Theatre Festival (28 September).

1966 *Philadelphia, Here I Come!* receives American premiere at the Helen Hayes Theater and runs for nine months on Broadway. *The Loves of Cass McGuire* premieres at the Helen Hayes Theater (6 October) and closes after twenty performances. Second collection of short stories, *The Gold in the Sea*, published.

1967 Irish premiere of *The Loves of Cass McGuire* at the Abbey Theatre, running from 10 April to 29 July and from 28 September to 7 October. British premiere of *Philadelphia, Here I Come!* at the Lyric Theatre, London (20 September–4 November). *Lovers* premiered at the Gate Theatre (18 July–30 September).

1968 *Lovers* plays as part of the Lincoln Center Festival in New York (25 July–14 September) before running for over three months at the Music Box there and going on a nationwide tour. *Crystal and Fox* premieres at Gaiety Theatre, Dublin (12 November–6 December).

1969 Moves to live in Muff, County Donegal. British premiere of *Lovers* at the Fortune Theatre, London (25 August–20 September). *The Mundy Scheme* rejected by the Abbey Theatre. Premieres at the Olympia Theatre, Dublin (10 June–28 July) and the Royale Theatre, New York (11 December), where it closes after two performances.

1970 Visiting writer in Magee College, Derry.

1971 *The Gentle Island* premieres at the Olympia Theatre, Dublin (30 November–18 December).

1973 *The Freedom of the City* jointly premieres at Dublin's Abbey Theatre and London's Royal Court Theatre in late February. First meeting with Stephen Rea, who plays Skinner in the Royal Court production. Play produced later in the year at the Goodman Theatre, Chicago (9 October–11 November).

1974 American premiere of *The Freedom of the City* in Washington, DC, at the Eisenhower Theatre, John F. Kennedy Center for the Performing Arts (23 January–9 February) and in New York at the Alvin Theatre, where it closes after nine performances.

1975 Elected as a member of the Irish Academy of Letters. *Volunteers* premiered at the Abbey Theatre (5 March–5 April).

1976 TV plays *Farewell to Ardstraw* and *The Next Parish* screened on BBC TV (Northern Ireland).

1977 *Living Quarters* premiered at the Abbey Theatre (24 March–23 April; and 12 September–5 October during the Dublin Theatre Festival).

1979   *Aristocrats* premiered at the Abbey Theatre (8–31 March; 23 July–25 August). *Faith Healer* premiered in New York at the Longacre Theatre (5 April), where it closes after twenty performances.

1980   Irish premiere of *Faith Healer* at the Abbey Theatre (28 August–27 September). Founds Field Day Theatre Company with Stephen Rea. First production, *Translations*, premieres at Derry's Guildhall (23 September 1980) before touring Ireland, North and South. Subsequently produced worldwide. One-act play, *American Welcome*, premiered by Actors' Theatre of Louisville, Kentucky.

1981   British premiere of *Faith Healer* at the Royal Court. US premiere of *Translations* in New York at Manhattan Theatre Club (14 April–17 May) and British premiere in London at Hampstead Theatre Club (12 May–13 June); latter transfers to the National Theatre at the Lyttelton, where it runs in rep (with seventy-two performances) between August and December. Friel's translation of Chekhov's *Three Sisters*, the year's Field Day production, premieres in Derry on 8 September and then tours.

1982   *The Communication Cord* premieres in Derry on 21 September and then tours. Moves to Greencastle, County Donegal. Elected member of Aosdána (Academy of Irish Artists).

1983   British premiere of *The Communication Cord* at the Hampstead Theatre Club, London (7 May–11 June). RTÉ (Radio Telefís Éireann) TV documentary on Friel and Field Day.

1986   Edits and introduces Charles McGlinchey's *The Last of the Name*, the life-narrative of a Donegal weaver, published in Belfast by the Blackstaff Press.

1987   Appointed to the Irish Senate (until 1989). Adaptation of Turgenev's novel *Fathers and Sons*, premiered in London at the National Theatre at the Lyttelton (9 July); runs in rep until February 1988.

1988   British premiere of *Aristocrats* runs at Hampstead Theatre and subsequently wins *Evening Standard* Drama Award for Best Play. US premiere of *Fathers and Sons* at the Long Wharf Theatre in New Haven (March–April) and Irish premiere at the Gate Theatre (June–July). *Making History* is premiered by Field Day (Friel's last play for them) at Derry's Guildhall on 20 September and then tours.

1989   BBC Radio 3 devotes a six-play season to Friel, the first living playwright to be so honored. US premiere of *Aristocrats* in New York at Manhattan Theatre Club; goes on to win New York Drama Critics' Circle Award for Best New Foreign Play.

1990   *Dancing at Lughnasa* premieres at the Abbey Theatre (24 April). Transfers to the Royal National Theatre, London, at the Lyttelton in

October and goes on to win an Olivier Award for Play of the Year, *Evening Standard* Drama Award and a Writers' Guild Award.

1991   US premiere of *Dancing at Lughnasa* at the Plymouth Theatre, New York, where it runs for a year. The three-volume *Field Day Anthology of Irish Writing* launched in Dublin in December by Taoiseach Charles J. Haughey; Friel attends and makes a rare speech.

1992   Version of Charles Macklin's *The London Vertigo* premiered by the Gate at Andrew's Lane Theatre, Dublin (January). Version of Turgenev's *A Month in the Country* is produced in Dublin at the Gate (4 August). *Dancing at Lughnasa* is nominated for eight Tony Awards in New York and wins three (including Best Play); also wins New York Drama Critics' Circle Award for Best Play.

1993   *Wonderful Tennessee* premieres at the Abbey Theatre (30 June). Production transfers to the Plymouth Theatre, New York, on 24 October and closes after twenty previews and nine performances.

1994   Friel resigns from Field Day. *Molly Sweeney* produced at the Gate Theatre (9 August) and transfers to the Almeida Theatre, London (3 November).

1996   New York premiere of *Molly Sweeney* at the Roundabout Theatre (7 January); goes on to win the Lucille Lortel Award, Outer Critics' Circle Award and the Drama Critics' Circle Award.

1997   *Give Me Your Answer, Do!* premieres at the Abbey Theatre (12 March).

1998   Film version of *Dancing at Lughnasa*, with screenplay by Frank McGuinness. UK premiere of *Give Me Your Answer, Do!* in London at the Hampstead Theatre Club (26 March). Version of Chekhov's *Uncle Vanya* premieres in Dublin at the Gate Theatre.

1999   Seventieth birthday celebrated by a Friel Festival in Dublin, with productions of *Dancing at Lughnasa* and *The Freedom of the City* at the Abbey, *Living Quarters* and *Making History* at the Peacock, *Aristocrats* at the Gate and a visiting RSC production of *A Month in the Country*; talks at the Abbey and a one-day conference at University College Dublin; a special issue of the *Irish University Review* on Friel; and an exhibition at the National Library of Ireland. The Abbey's production of *The Freedom of the City* and the Gate's of *Aristocrats* and *Uncle Vanya* appear as part of the Lincoln Center Festival in New York. US premiere of *Give Me Your Answer, Do!* at the Roundabout Theatre, New York.

2000   Hour-long TV documentary, *Brian Friel*, produced by Ferndale Films, written by Thomas Kilroy, includes participation by Friel.

2001   National Library of Ireland acquires Friel Archive; one-act *The Yalta Game* premieres at the Gate for the Dublin Theatre Festival (2 October–17 November).

2002   Premiere of *The Bear* and *Afterplay* as double bill (entitled *Two Plays After*) at Dublin's Gate Theatre (5 March–20 April); plays in the US at the Spoleto Festival, South Carolina (23 May–9 June); UK premiere of *Afterplay* at London's Gielgud Theatre (10 September–1 December). UK premiere of his version of *Uncle Vanya* at London's Donmar Warehouse (September).

2003   *Performances* premieres at Dublin's Gate Theatre (30 September–25 October).

2005   *The Home Place* premieres at Dublin's Gate Theatre (1 February–2 April); transfers to the Comedy Theatre in London (7 May–13 August); wins the *Evening Standard* Best Play of 2005 Award (30 November).

2006   Elected to the position of Saoi (Wise One), its highest honor, by Aosdána; presented by President Mary McAleese at Dublin's Arts Council (22 February).

I

ANTHONY ROCHE

Introduction

Excepting Beckett (who remains a special case), Brian Friel is the most important Irish playwright in terms both of dramatic achievement and cultural importance to have emerged since the Abbey Theatre's heyday. For all of the Irish Theatre Movement's fame worldwide, the canon of its enduring works is small: J. M. Synge's *The Playboy of the Western World* (1907) and Sean O'Casey's Dublin trilogy. Brendan Behan promised much in the 1950s but the role of Stage Irishman took over and he died young; Samuel Beckett wrote his plays in French and in a context which denied any hint of the local. While other major contemporary Irish playwrights from Friel's generation have made a reputation in their own country (Tom Murphy, Thomas Kilroy, John B. Keane), almost without exception that success has not been replicated abroad. (The exception which proves the rule is Hugh Leonard's *Da*, which won a Tony Award in 1973.) But from Brian Friel's emergence in 1964 with the ground-breaking *Philadelphia, Here I Come!*, which went on from its success at that year's Dublin Theatre Festival to a nine-month run on Broadway, each of the subsequent decades in his writing career has seen at least one of his works achieve critical and worldwide success, notably *Aristocrats* (1979), *Translations* (1980) and *Dancing at Lughnasa* (1990). He has done so with plays which remain resolutely set (for the most part) in the remoteness of County Donegal, in the fictional locale of Ballybeg (from the Gaelic *baile beag* or "small town").

Nor has that international success been achieved at the expense of his status in his own country. As Seamus Heaney puts it, Friel's constant renewal of his dramatic art is a profound record of "what it has been like to live through the second half of the twentieth century in Ireland."[1] The country has undergone a profound transformation in that time, from the economic deprivation of the 1950s through to the Celtic Tiger of the 1990s. The 1960s brought the promise of modernization to Ireland, with the government encouraging US investment; but even at that early stage Brian Friel regarded such "progress" as a mixed blessing, conscious as he is in all his plays of what is being lost alongside what is being gained. The material circumstances of his characters have improved immeasurably over the decades, from the humble fare served at meals in the early (or the history) plays to the point where Terry in 1993's *Wonderful Tennessee* can complain that none of the exotic foods supplied in their picnic hamper is actually edible.

Friel's Irishness is complicated by the fact that he is (as he has described himself) "a member of the [Catholic] minority living in the North."[2] Born in 1929 in Omagh in Northern Ireland, he moved at the age of 10 to a city where he was to grow up and become a teacher, like his father before him. That city bears two names – Derry to the nationalists, Londonderry to the unionists – and to live there is to be acutely aware of linguistic, cultural, religious and political divisions. Summers for Friel were spent in his mother's home county of Donegal, adjacent to and serving as a natural hinterland to Derry, but divided from it by a border established by the Boundary Commission in the 1920s. Over the course of his lifetime Friel (and his family) have gradually moved from Derry into Donegal, progressing along Lough Foyle to near the northernmost tip of the island in Greencastle, where he stares out every day at a scene of incomparable natural beauty and just across the lough to Magilligan, the largest prison for political internees. Brian Friel inhabits the borders of the two Irelands, casting a cold eye on both jurisdictions and their political shortcomings in his plays.

Even before political violence erupted in Northern Ireland in 1969, Friel's plays centered on an attachment to the local, to the small community, to the marginalized and border regions as opposed to the metropolitan center; it is one of the important ways in which he has come to be recognized as a postcolonial writer. His plays dramatize the politics of the tribe, and they do so most often through an obsessive focus on its microcosm, the family. There is always in Friel's small communities a sense of some lost or missing dimension, a context which would give meaning to the isolated and frequently despairing lives of his characters. Yet the plays are also filled with sun, with laughter, with music, with fun. It is this combination in Friel, of a surface gaiety compensating for a great deprivation which can scarcely be named or discussed, which gives his plays their characteristic tone.

Brian Friel is in his late seventies and still writing. In February 2005, a new play, *The Home Place*, premiered at Dublin's Gate Theatre and went on to a three-month run in London's Comedy Theatre. It is an important addition to an extraordinary oeuvre in which there is a good deal to assess. His short stories won him early distinction; many of them were individually published in the *New Yorker*, and two collections appeared in the 1960s. As he himself came to recognize, for all of their qualities, these short stories would never surpass those of a Frank O'Connor. Theatre is the medium on which Brian Friel has concentrated exclusively for the past forty years, the form through which he has realized an extraordinary achievement and secured worldwide recognition. His writing in drama will, accordingly, provide the focus of the *Companion*. What makes Friel a great dramatist is that he seeks (and, in his best plays, finds) a theatrical form adequate to the Irish condition, a form uniquely suited to represent the themes that concern him: the splitting of the protagonist Gar O'Donnell into a public and a private persona in *Philadelphia, Here I Come!*; the use of the four monologues in *Faith Healer* to present conflicting versions of the same event; the conceit in *Translations* by which, even though the native characters speak English, the audience accepts that they are speaking Irish; the eruption of the dance of the five women in *Dancing at Lughnasa*; the image of the head-measuring in *The Home Place*. The tally (to date) is twenty-four original plays and seven translations/versions/adaptations (of the Russian writers Turgenev and Chekhov, mainly). Friel's own plays have been translated into many languages and are performed worldwide; they remain widely in print through Faber and Faber and Peter Fallon's Gallery Press, and feature in university courses on Irish, Postcolonial and Theatre Studies. At least half a dozen of them have been garlanded with awards in London and New York (including the Writers' Guild Award, the *Evening Standard* Best New Play Award three times, the New York Drama Critics' Circle Award twice and a Tony Award).

Friel's plays should not be considered in terms of success only, however. When awarded a Tony for 1990's *Dancing at Lughnasa* as Best Play, he responded by quoting the late Graham Greene to the effect that success is only the postponement of failure. Friel went on to prove (and arguably test) this maxim with the failure of its successor, *Wonderful Tennessee*, which closed on Broadway after nine performances (where *Lughnasa* had run for over a year) in 1993. Friel could be said to encourage the zigzag pattern of his career by reacting against what he sees as a process of simplification when his plays achieve huge success, their deep-felt emotion sentimentalized, their political and historic ironies flattened or removed. The next play he writes is invariably a reaction against this process, often a retaliatory farce where the themes of the previous play are ruthlessly satirized – as in 1982's *The Communication Cord*, which reacted to the success of *Translations* two years earlier. Thomas Kilroy, in the opening essay of this volume, detects this tendency operating from the start in Friel's career, where *Philadelphia, Here I Come!*'s success with Irish America prompted the savage rejoinder of the returned émigré in 1966's *The Loves of Cass McGuire*. And *Wonderful Tennessee* was a more abstract and philosophical meditation on the themes which had so engrossed audiences in *Dancing at Lughnasa*. These subsequent plays may have failed at one level, but they enabled Friel to continue the necessary process of searching out new themes and approaches as a writer. The issues of success and failure are combined in arguably Friel's greatest play, *Faith Healer*, which failed on Broadway in 1979 but has gone on to be one of the most revived and theatrically haunting plays in his canon. This *Companion* looks, therefore, at the entire range of Friel's dramatic output, not just attending to the "successful" plays but wishing to establish the various contexts in which one plays speaks to another, sometimes over decades.

It is instructive in this regard that the first two essays – which examine Friel's plays up to 1971's *The Gentle Island* – are written by two major contemporary Irish playwrights, Thomas Kilroy and Frank McGuinness, both of whom were encouraged in their nascent writerly ambitions by the experience of seeing early Friel plays. McGuinness writes of the risk and amibition of the three plays he considers, of how they lay the groundwork for much of what is to come after. And yet these "early" plays – a term used to cover a prolific period of fifteen years in which Friel secured an international reputation – have not been well served in a number of ways. Faber's *Selected Plays* of 1984 retains only one of the first eight (1964's *Philadelphia, Here I Come!*). This imbalance became even more pronounced in 1996, when *Selected Plays* was redubbed *Plays One* without being recast. Four volumes, not two, of Friel's collected plays are urgently needed for both students and theatrical practitioners: three covering the original plays, and one the versions. If *Selected Plays* has unintentionally narrowed the focus in relation to Friel's drama, Seamus Deane's influential introduction may also have contributed (whether he is responsible for the plays chosen or not). Discussing Friel's "early" career, Deane speaks of the "increasing sentimentality" of the plays written in the six years after 1965 and argues that Irish audiences "gratefully accepted" plays like 1967's *Crystal and Fox* and 1969's *The Mundy Scheme*.[3] The record simply does not bear this out, either in relation to the bleakly unforgiving nature of the plays themselves or their Dublin reception (as Frank McGuinness eloquently demonstrates). Nor is it clear that Friel from the early 1970s (in Deane's words) "cut[s] himself off from his early work."[4] 1971's *The Gentle Island* itself makes a fascinating comparison with *Translations* of almost a decade later. Both have a motherless family of father and sons (sharing some of the same names) and a fidelity to maintaining Gaelic culture which is fatally disrupted by the arrival of two men: in *Translations*, of two British soldiers; in *Gentle Island*, of two gay men from Dublin. His breakthrough play *Philadelphia, Here I Come!* is haunted by the spirit of the five sisters who finally emerge on to the stage twenty-six years later in *Dancing at Lughnasa*.

The *Companion* accordingly looks at the entire range of Friel's dramatic output, mainly through groupings of two to four plays in ways which will enrich understanding of the more acknowledged plays and which chart the fascinating and complex trajectory of his career. The final four essays are designed to broaden the context by considering both the practical staging of the plays and the theoretical issues they raise; nor will these be seen as mutually exclusive but as interacting with and enriching each other. This volume is informed by a keen awareness of the fact that Brian Friel, fron his eyrie in North Donegal, has kept one eye on Ireland and one eye on the world. I am pleased that his signature play, *Translations*, adorns the cover. The two photos are taken from a touring Royal National Theatre production seen throughout the UK in 2005 by packed audiences, many of them young people studying the play for their A level courses. The key term in Friel's theatrical career is "translation" and in particular his plays' ability, while remaining true to the local, to provide a set of dramatic, philosophical and political contexts by which they have been translated worldwide into a rich variety of languages and cultures. His contribution has been one of the most necessary and profound by a living writer in the English language.

NOTES

1. Seamus Heaney, *Friel Festival Programme* (April–August 1999), p. 23.
2. Brian Friel in the TV documentary *Brian Friel* (Ferndale Films, 2000).
3. Seamus Deane, "Introduction," in Brian Friel, *Plays One*, (London and Boston: Faber and Faber, 1996), p. 15.
4. Ibid.

2

THOMAS KILROY

The early plays

The early work of a playwright may display surprising misdirection. But, even then, there may be signals towards the mature work to follow. A playwright of substance creates an alternative world on stage, a world with its own population, its own modes of behavior, its own style and, in particular, its own characteristic stage speech. All of this is constructed with the actor in mind. It is extremely unlikely that such a world will already be in place in the first written plays. There is also the endearing fact that young writers tend to find their own personal experiences of consuming interest and hence the echoes in early work of personal journeys. There is a danger here for the playwright, since plays depend upon an effacement of the personal, a projection of the personal into multiple roles or, as in the case of Shaw or Brecht, upon the assertive expression of personality through a subjective control of the material.

Stephen Greenblatt remarks how Shakespeare, in his first attempt at writing an historical trilogy with *Henry VI* in the 1590s, creates a gang of lower-class rebels from the countryside, led by Jack Cade, who attempt a proletarian revolution.[1] Greenblatt's point is that Shakespeare himself had just recently moved to London from the provinces. He is offering his metropolitan audience a personal version of terror, of the quaking instability beneath the façade of Elizabethan order. Certainly, Cade and his men have the immediacy of closely observed life, of overheard speech, which is not true of the aristocratic characters in those three early plays. There is a comparable reflection of journeying in the first play of another non-metropolitan playwright in George Farquhar's *Love and a Bottle* (1698). Farquhar's journey from Ireland to London was one from the periphery to the center, the typical journey of the outsider from the colony to the center of power and social definition, typical, that is to say, of the journey made by most Anglo-Irish playwrights of the eighteenth and nineteenth centuries. All of this is reflected in the adventures of the young Irish rake Roebuck in this first play.

In contrast, Brian Friel's two early, unpublished but staged plays, *The Francophile* or *A Doubtful Paradise* (1960) and *The Blind Mice* (1963), are firmly located within that northwest corner of the island of Ireland where most of his work is set. In time he was to name this fictionalized locality, with its detailed mirroring of a real place, Ballybeg, thereby absorbing locality into a personal vision. There is, indeed, journeying in Friel's drama, most notably in *Faith Healer* (1979), but the essential image throughout is one of rootedness. Journeys are only made to test the possibilities, or impossibilities, of a return to the home place, which also happens to be the title of his most recent play at the time of writing.

The Francophile is set in Derry and *The Blind Mice* in an unnamed town in the north of Ireland. This specificity is further compounded by the fact that these are family plays. The Logues in the first play and the Carrolls in the second belong to that long line of provincial or rural families which populated the Irish stage through the preceding three decades. The plays, too, are naturalistic, like many Irish plays before them, with just a hint of that poetic movement, the graceful sleights and shifts with which Friel was to break through the naturalistic mode in his later work. What is new in these two plays, compared to other Irish plays of the 1950s, is the quality of the writing and the sharpness of the intelligence. This is clearly a writer who has already a highly developed sense of comedy and characterization, particularly of characters struggling desperately within their given situations in life. One has to remember that Friel's apprenticeship as a writer had ended by the time he came to write plays. As a novice playwright he had already a considerable reputation as a writer of short stories and was to retain the techniques of direct storytelling in many of his plays. These two early plays, despite occasional awkwardness in exposition, also show how skillful he was even then in constructing conventional plays.

Both plays are personal in that they reflect the immediate interests of the young writer, a trained teacher and former seminarian. They are plays about the first generation of fully educated young Irish people in the young Irish state, with parents who never had the same opportunity. In this respect they reflect an important shift in Irish society for someone of Friel's generation, where education became an avenue of moving up in the world. What is interesting is Friel's response to this opportunity. Here is his description of the family in *The Blind Mice*:

> The Carrolls are publicans. The father and mother have no formal education, but because of their money and especially because of their family (Chris is a priest and John is a doctor) they are highly thought of.[2]

Rather like the power of imagination in the mature plays, education is here a very mixed blessing, something transformative but also carrying within it the seeds of bitterness and failure. This is the beginning of a major thematic paradox in Friel, the way that the higher human faculties can yield destruction, how something uplifting can betray the individual even at the very moment of achievement. What is distinctive is that this heavy theme is portrayed through comedy, although, as always with Friel's comedy, there is that cool, unblinking eye observing everything. Specifically, both mothers in the plays, Maggie in *The Francophile* and Lily in *The Blind Mice*, are the carriers of this comedy, innocents from an older generation trying to manage in a new world of new knowledge, new jobs and new social status. There is satire here of social ambition but it is an affectionate kind. Friel likes these two women.

The two sons, Kevin Logue, a barrister, and John Carroll, a doctor, may both be new professionals but their achievement has turned to dust for both of them. Once again this anticipates a certain kind of recurring male figure in the later plays. Logue and Carroll are early examples of those intelligent, articulate, imaginative, antagonistic figures in Friel's work, who help drive the action with a nagging, questioning restlessness. Compared to the two sons, the two fathers are ineffective, one of them dangerously so. Willie Logue, the francophile of the title in the first play, is a wonderful, farcical creation who epitomizes this ambivalent attitude to education. A perennial autodidact, with his mish-mash of learning (at this point in his life a pursuit of all things cultural and French) he is destructive of everyone around him. The hunger for education in this buffoon is like a malignant flowering that envelops everything and everyone. His self-education, it turns out, is but a front for snobbery and social pretension, far more serious defects in the Friel scheme of things. These all-too-human failings violate what is natural. In the complex order of values in Friel's work this is one of the base lines: nature and the natural as a kind of yardstick, a way of measuring human behavior. It is behind the cry of the son Kevin, near to tears, to his parents, at the end of the play, "Why did you not let us grow naturally?"[3]

The Blind Mice is also a Priest Play, one of the reliable genres of Irish theatre which would have been familiar to Friel in the work of Paul Vincent Carroll or Joseph Tomelty. A more interesting comparison might be made, however, between *The Blind Mice* and Bridget Boland's *The Prisoner* (1954). This latter play was based upon the case of Cardinal Mindszenty who was imprisoned by the Hungarian Communist government in 1948. The London production came to Dublin with Alec Guinness in a bravura soutane and cape-swirling performance. Both the Mindszenty case and the Boland play had an impact upon Catholic Ireland of the 1950s, preoccupied as it was with stories of the mission fields, of Communist torture and brainwashing. The prisoner in the Friel play is Chris Carroll, a young Irish missionary priest returned after five years of solitary confinement in Communist China. The predictable communal hysteria which follows his return home, and the bitter twist which, in turn, follows when the young priest shows human weakness, make up the plot of the play. It is a play which finally has too much happening in it but is still a crucial part of the writer's lifelong treatment of the nature of spirituality. The image of Chris "praying" by singing "Three Blind Mice" in his utterly silent cell is not far removed from the "miracle-working" of Frank Hardy in *Faith Healer*. Conventional piety for Friel was and is an irrelevance. The life of the spirit is to be found in other, far less orthodox places, in the singing of a child's nursery rhyme or the patter of an apparent charlatan.

In between these two unpublished plays, Friel wrote another about sanctity and its uncertain place in the world, *The Enemy Within* (1962). This features the famous sixth-century Ulster saint, Columba, and his voluntary exile on the island of Iona. It is worth remarking upon why, of the three early plays, this is the only one Friel has chosen to publish. The setting is a monk's austere cell on the Scottish island, the atmosphere one of the pervasive presence of the elements, of sea and wind, of hard, manual work. It features a group of monks "cut off from the refining influence of women."[4] The men are dressed in natural-colored robes with the charismatic figure of the Abbot in white. This is a setting of great physicality: "the flight of the sail, the swing of the axe, the warm breadth of a horse" (46). It is intensely physical because it is the arena in which the playwright stages the cost of spirituality in a highly physical man, Columba. The external material detail is perfectly set against the interior struggle. All of this was beautifully realized in Ria Mooney's first production of the play for the Abbey in the old Queen's Theatre in 1962 with Ray McAnally, brimming with animality, as the saint. Important Friel themes are set down here for the first time, to be fleshed out in different ways in later plays. The monks' journeying across the Irish Sea and Britain are brighter versions of pilgrimage than the dark journeys of *Faith Healer* but, oddly, the questors and the quests are undeniably connected. Place-names and place-naming, too, have the same currency here as in *Translations* (1980), as signposts of great political significance. Above all, the important subsidiary theme of *The Enemy Within* is the magnetism of the home place and the anguish of exile which would appear and reappear in the body of work in the future, most immediately in *Philadelphia, Here I Come!*

You can see why Friel has preferred this play to the other two early works. Technically, *The Enemy Within* is the first demonstration of his command of form. Each element of the play, with an exactitude of timing, connects with the next, in perfect unity. The twin engines which drive the play to its final moments are Columba's relationships with the young English novice, Oswald, and with two visitors from Ireland, his brother Eoghan and nephew Aedh. These two strands are welded together. Eoghan and Aedh have come to enlist Columba as a military leader in an inter-tribal conflict back home. We have already seen Columba succumb to this temptation in another episode earlier in the play. We have seen him strike Oswald. The anguish which followed this now allows him to break this cycle forever and in doing so he is heartily cursed by brother and nephew. The seductive, corrupting call they brought with them is clearly identified in Columba's words as having come from Ireland herself, significantly a feminine Ireland, the Ireland of *aisling* poetry, a dream woman with a siren call to violent sacrifice. At the very moment when Columba has driven out his own kin, forever, the missing Oswald turns up, a lost child found, a child of the surrogate family of the monastic community. The blow struck by Columba has clearly been absolved. In abandoning blood relationships for those of the spirit, Columba, in the final moments of the play, offers a simple dramatic expression of the priestly vocation.

To turn to the more established plays, *Philadelphia, Here I Come!* (1964), *The Loves of Cass McGuire* (1966) and *Lovers: Winners and Losers* (1967), is to enter fully the characteristic stage world of this playwright. Richard Pine has described them as "Plays of Love," in two senses: the intimate, private love between individuals, and the more public ties which bind people to their native place and the bonds of the tribe.[5] This is literally true, as the titles of two of the works demonstrate. Pine is also following the line of the playwright himself, who once described these early plays as attempted analysis of "different kinds of love."[6] There is, however, another overarching concern here which gives the treatment of love its sense of fragility and evanescence. This is the power of the imagination, more specifically the performative, histrionic imagination and how it operates in calling up an alternative, alluring reality. The flight of imagination is built upon the available bits and scraps of everyday experience. But such is its power that this material reality loses its factuality, its stubborn firmness, when the imagination flows over it. It is this disconnectedness that is potentially so destructive in Friel's plays. A boy talks to himself because he cannot talk to his father; a woman sits in a chair and invents a false perfection; a man looks at nothing through binoculars and dreams of escape. These are heart-rending images of role-playing, of theatre itself; but they serve real human needs, give some hope before human inadequacy, even if the hope is unreal. When the imagination plays upon the material of memory, its potency is even more destructive because the remembered elements already have an inbuilt instability and tendency to drift, unlike the bare facts of ordinary life. Two great human forces of distortion, imagination and memory, become intermingled, one inviting the other towards even greater excesses of unreal invention. The results can be tragic, as in *The Loves of Cass McGuire*. This subject is not unique to Friel in Irish drama (one thinks of the work of George Fitzmaurice, for instance) but his version of it is utterly distinctive. The connection between this imaginative facility at creating alternative personae, alternative narratives, on the one hand, and the art of acting, on the other, is rather obvious. It is the reason why Friel's plays are filled with natural performers, skillful storytellers and masters of the anecdote, monologuists or those craving monologues, mimics with expert actorly timing, characters who desperately need an audience. His plays often include audiences other than those in the theatre itself.

We meet all this, for the first time, in Willie Logue in *The Francophile*. He may be a very early version of this kind of Friel figure. But the double character of Gar O'Donnell in *Philadelphia, Here I Come!* is a much more complex one. The theatricality of this role is dependent upon the fact that Gar is a performer and an audience of his own performance. Sometimes, as well, he is comically critical of that performance: he is a theatre critic, a performer and an audience, all in one. Above all, this theatricality of Gar is cinematic. It is telling that his final memory, to be stored away and endlessly replayed, is in the form of a film. Throughout the play he is the star and the director, where he plays all the lead parts and redirects the life around him in farcical scenarios. He is the great conductor on the podium; the air-force ace, finger on the trigger, zooming out of the sky; the great athlete in the arena; the all-powerful director with his Chinese spies and absurd models on catwalks. There has rarely been such a cascade of colorful images to convey a condition of helplessness. Gar's quality as a performer, and the roles he chooses to play, brilliantly capture his own inner insecurities, his essential innocence and vulnerability before the future that awaits him. They also unveil the unspoken suffering in the relationship with his father. The mixture of hilarity and unspeakable pain is evident in Gar's introduction of the old man:

> And here comes your pleasure, your little ray of sunshine. Ladies and Gentlemen, I give you – the one and only – the inimitable – the irrepressible – the irresistible – County Councillor – S – B – O'Donnell![7]

The counterpoint which follows between the patter, Gar as performer, and the bleak exchanges between father and son, Gar as victim, is one of the finest examples of Friel's control of verbal tone. It is like a linguistic competition between the comic and the painful and the blend is calibrated to a point where comedy can no longer be sustained:

As the following speech goes on all trace of humour fades from PRIVATE's *voice. He becomes more and more intense and it is with an effort that he keeps his voice under control.* (49)

There is the same beautiful formal equilibrium in the separation of father and son, each lost in a memory of momentary happiness together. These are the two emotional moments around which the whole play revolves. Gar's epiphany, which speaks to him now through the language of music, takes place on the blue boat on Lough na Cloc Cor:

> It says that once upon a time a boy and his father sat in a blue boat on a lake on an afternoon in May, and on that afternoon a great beauty happened, a beauty that has haunted the boy ever since, because he wonders now did it really take place or did he imagine it. (89)

The father's glowing moment, which he conveys to Madge, is of a day when he remembers holding a little boy's hand, going to school: "I had to go with him myself, the two of us, hand in hand, as happy as larks" (97). The whole play rests upon these two moments of memory. Any production of the play has to find them, underline them, like two struts supporting the whole structure but never touching one another. Friel's acute sense of form in this play is displayed in this perfect balance of separation.

In a sense all Friel's plays are about love although poor Cass McGuire cannot understand why the playwright has insisted upon calling *her* play *The Loves of Cass McGuire.* Whatever about fulfillment or non-fulfillment, characters in a Friel play convince us of their need for love. This is what is important even if the love object is a shadow or a lost figure. It is this hunger for love which drives through the plays, burning away at indifference, at social and political stupidities, at the imprisoning clutch of family or church. You could read *The Loves of Cass McGuire* as a response to the huge success of *Philadelphia, Here I Come!* in the United States, particularly among Irish-Americans. It is the kind of rejoinder which this writer was to repeat with *The Communication Cord* (1982), which consciously subverts the consolatory, tribal imagery of the preceding play, *Translations.* Friel's portrait of Cass *"shouting in her raucous Irish-American voice"*[8] is not without pity but it is severe. Some of the American audiences that responded with such warmth to young Gar must have felt distinctly uncomfortable with this "returned Yank" Cass with all her fierce, vulgar energy and her experience of the American system at its most pitiless. If *Philadelphia, Here I Come!* is a play about imminent exile, *The Loves of Cass McGuire* is about a doubled exile, the exile who returns home to find herself exiled there, once again. The grim irony of the ending of the play is that the peace which Cass finally achieves is almost narcotic, a peace through withdrawal from reality in the company of the ghostly couple of Trilbe and Ingram through their trance-like games in the winged chair.

The play begins with a naturalistic portrayal of Irish family life. Cass McGuire is such a strong presence, such a memorable voice that, re-reading the play after a gap of thirty odd years, I realize I had forgotten much of that family detail. When Cass makes her entrance it is like a thunderous clap, an irruption into gentility, an outburst against polite speech. She not only disturbs the family, she changes the style of the play, bringing with her a free-wheeling, highly self-conscious type of theatricality, a playing with the medium of theatre itself. The obvious example of this is her direct address to the audience. This isn't simply modish, but rather an access to communication for Cass, a way of giving her anchorage. When she loses it, when she can no longer see out into the auditorium, she is lost. She has given herself to the unreal dreams of Trilbe and Ingram. It is a poignant moment because the audience is intimately involved in this descent into delusion. As audience we share in the loss when her voice can no longer reach us in intimate exchange, across that divide between stage and auditorium. It is a wonderful dramatization of an inner process, a making external of a condition below the surface.

Eden House, the home for the elderly, where the family dump Cass, is built on the site of the old workhouse, a horror which Cass understands all too well, with its evocation of famine and mass emigration of the nineteenth century. In the Ireland of her childhood the workhouse would still have represented an unspeakable fate of absolute poverty. But Eden House is also a kind of theatre, a place where roles are played out, often in desperation, to stave off the reality of aging and death. Since this is the reality of the future, the past is the place offering a retreat. This is Trilbe's temptation to Cass, the private world she and Ingram have created: "we are your only world now. We have the truth for you" (29). Cass fights this retreat to the end, but she finally surrenders to it.

Friel uses the musical term "rhapsody" to describe the flights into unreality shared by Trilbe, Ingram and, in the end, Cass. *The Loves of Cass McGuire* has been criticized for its recourse to music, the suggestion being that the content cannot carry the weight of, say, Wagner.[9] This is mere niggling. In his prefatory note to the printed text, Brian Friel makes perfectly clear how important musical analogy is to the inspiration of the play. The whole structure of the work can only be understood in terms of composition, of fluid movement across time and space and in and out of differing versions of reality. The play is a unity of splinters, or of dissonant passages, and this splintering is a mirroring of the process taking place inside the mind of Cass. This is a play with exchanges of dialogue where there is no exchange at all since the characters are moving on parallel tracks.

> HARRY: And before I say any more I want you to know that the decision I've made is entirely my own. Alice had nothing to do with it.
> CASS: Betty, she has a baby – fourteen months – I seen pictures of it.
> HARRY: In fact she has asked me not to mention this until after Christmas.
> CASS: (*Unable to hold her own line*) So I left a note for momma and one for Connie. . . .
> HARRY: But I said no, definitely no. (24)

This style of dislocation is an aesthetic reflection of the life experience of Cass and of the loosening of her hold upon reality in the course of the play. For Friel, the roots of this dislocation, of the breakdown of personhood, lie in emigration. Cass is, and has always been, a displaced person.

There is a climactic moment just over halfway through *Dancing at Lughnasa* (1990) where death crosses the stage and passes on. It is precipitated by an incident on a lake (recalling *Philadelphia, Here I Come!*) involving a blue boat. The action onstage is put into pause mode, the actors freeze in their positions, and we are told about the future deaths of several of the people onstage. When the action resumes again, the dancing, the music, the love and bonding of the people before us continue but nothing is ever the same again. A great shadow has passed over everything and this gives the end of the play its particular poignancy.

This is a very Frielian moment, a mix, a typical blending of moods, the nearest one can come to illustrating his sense of tragicomedy. It is also the kind of stylistic device which is the basis of the first play, *Winners*, in the diptych *Lovers* (1967). Because of its dominant mood you could say that it colors the second play, *Losers*, as well. In *Winners* the action onstage is framed by two narrators, a man and a woman. Friel calls them "Commentators,"[10] although they are specifically excluded from making comments. Their sole function is to deliver flat information. The whole force of the piece depends upon the connection between these facts, read out from books, and the bubbly exchanges between the two young 17-year-old lovers who live out the last day of their life together, elsewhere on the stage. The contrast is between the immediacy of vibrant life and the cold record of a ledger, between the straining towards life to the full and the implacable assembling of facts. Before the young people leave the stage, racing off to a day of pleasure on the lake, the curtain of death, as in *Dancing at Lughnasa*, is drawn across their path.

The use of narration like this is, of course, a literary device, more common in prose fiction than in the theatre. This reminds us yet again that, before he became a playwright, Friel was a writer of short stories. He was to use such a narrative device once more, to icy effect, in *Living Quarters* (1977) and frequently in the plays characters assume the function of narration. It is clear from both of these two plays, *Lovers* and *Living Quarters*, that Friel is theatricalizing a literary style of narration by making it take on some of the old dramatic function of Fate:

> MAN: At 6.20 William Anthony Clerkin reported to Sergeant Finlay that his boat had been stolen. The Sergeant and Mr. Finlay returned to Lough Gorm and walked around a portion of the south shore. They sighted the upturned boat floating about fifty yards west of the biggest island, Oileán na gCrann.
>
> (28)

Why does Friel call these young people whose lives are to be cut off before they can begin "winners"? Why does he call the middle-aged couple who at least have life ahead of them "losers"? To understand this is to come close to the vision at the heart of all of Friel's plays. There are not many writers who write as vividly about happiness as Friel, as he does here through Mag in *Winners*:

> MAG: But that's the way I feel, Joe. At this moment – here – now – I'm crazy about you – and mad and reckless, so that I want to shout to the whole town: I love Joe Brennan! I'm mad about him! I'd do anything for him!
>
> (30)

She is one of those Friel characters who expresses an electrifying sense of the immediate moment, of grasping that moment with complete abandon. But happiness such as this is always conditional in Friel's work. It is always transient, evanescent, as it is in life, and this is the nature of Friel's realism. Mag's outburst is immediately followed by the dampening down of such abandon by Joe, Mag's lover, her would-be husband and father of her unborn child. Joe is yet another figure from the early Friel who is weighed down by education. His words to Mag are shocking, like a blow to the head. He strikes out at her. He destroys the image of happiness that she has in their future together, a future which they are spared because they are about to die. Hence the grimly ironic significance of the play's title.

Losers is another of those comic sequels which Friel offers as a successor to a more serious piece. Hanna and Andy and the old mother in the bed occupy a kind of cartoon of Irish sex life before the country was transformed. Middle-aged lovers, rosary praying, plaster statues of saints, home-made altars and the like, call up an Ireland that was already on the way out when the play was first performed. The contrast between this play and *Winners*, is, firstly, generational, the love of youth and that of middle age. But in having the same actors play the Commentators in the first play and the middle-aged couple in the second, Friel is suggesting that one play follows the other in a single line. If dying is loss and avoiding death a victory, the only way in which the predicament of Hanna and Andy can be faced is through the laughter of farce. Any other treatment would reveal it as the horror that it is. It is significant that this play, whatever about its title, opens and closes with a man staring through binoculars at a blank wall, a very Beckettian image indeed.

In addition to the value of individual plays Brian Friel occupies an important historical position in the transmission of the Irish oral tradition into twentieth-century Irish drama. Before Yeats and his contemporaries established their theater in the 1890s there was no indigenous Irish drama as such. There was, however, another ancient, histrionic art in traditional Irish life – that of the oral storyteller. A storyteller before an audience, this is a very particular kind of theatre indeed. It is difficult to exaggerate the importance of the storytelling mode in Irish drama because it is so pervasive. The classic example is Synge's *The Playboy of the Western World* (1907), a play about a told story and the extraordinary impact it has upon its listeners. Brian Friel is a key figure in this process of making storytelling theatrical. His finest example of this is to be found in the three storytelling voices of *Faith Healer*. But already in these early plays this process is in place: in the storyteller Cass McGuire; in the anecdotal riffs of the young Gar; and in the monologues of Andy which open and close the second half of *Lovers*. There are many ways in which Friel's plays carry Irish traditional life into the modern theatre. This, perhaps, is the most important one because it has had such an influence upon the style of Irish playwriting, Irish acting and stage productions in the second half of the twentieth century.

NOTES

1. Stephen Greenblatt, *Will in the World* (London: Jonathan Cape, 2004), p. 167.
2. The Brian Friel Papers, National Library of Ireland, MS 37046, Prefatory Note.
3. The Friel Papers, NLI, MS 37043, p. 46.
4. Brian Friel, *The Enemy Within* (Dublin: Gallery Press, 1979), p. 49. Future references are to this edition and will be incorporated in the text.
5. Richard Pine, *Brian Friel and Ireland's Drama* (London and New York: Routledge, 1990), pp. 69–94.
6. Brian Friel, "Plays Peasant and Unpeasant," *Times Literary Supplement*, 17 March 1972, p. 222. This essay is reprinted in Christopher Murray (ed.), *Brian*

Friel: Essays, Diaries, Interviews: 1964–1999 (London and New York: Faber and Faber, 1999), pp. 51–56.

7. Brian Friel, *Philadelphia, Here I Come!*, in *Plays One* (London and Boston: Faber and Faber, 1996), p. 47. All future references are to this edition and will be incorporated in the text.

8. Brian Friel, *The Loves of Cass McGuire* (Dublin: Gallery Press, 1984), p. 14. All future references are to this edition and will be incorporated in the text.

9. See Harry White, "Brian Friel and the Condition of Music," *Irish University Review* 29:1 (1999), pp. 10–12.

10. Brian Friel, *Lovers* (Oldcastle, County Meath: Gallery Press, 1993), p. 11. All future references are to this edition and will be incorporated in the text.

3

FRANK McGUINNESS

Surviving the 1960s: three plays by Brian Friel 1968–1971

Irish playwrights have a dread of one quality, one that should not be mentioned in front of them: stamina. We seem to lack it in our dramatic genetic code. George Farquhar dies impoverished, leaving two important plays, *The Recruiting Officer* (1706) and *The Beaux' Stratagem* (1707), in his slim volume of works. Clever Sheridan knows he will never better *The Rivals* (1775) and *The School for Scandal* (1777) and turns instead to politics, effectively silencing his writerly voice as he did the singing of his wife, Elizabeth – a sad case of cutting off two noses to spite one face. Wilde let himself be martyred by the sexual violence of heterosexual bigotry. Synge died too young, having achieved an extraordinary output. Shaw is the exception that proves the rule. But who would now take that confused master as model? By the 1960s, when Brian Friel, Tom Murphy, Hugh Leonard and Thomas Kilroy were establishing themselves as the dominant presences in the future of Irish playwriting, it was already clear that O'Casey's powerful legacy would reside in the Dublin trilogy of the 1920s. The great novels and plays behind him, Beckett was sliding into the reductive banality of *Breath* (1969). So, the great question posed to the four young dramatists was: How do I go on? In the case of Brian Friel, it was to take stock of his career so far and concentrate on writing exclusively, deliberately, for the Irish stage through the years 1968 to 1971.

This period marked a decisive, crucial shift in Brian Friel's perception of himself as a writer. He had served an accomplished apprenticeship, culminating in the remarkably ambitious *The Enemy Within* (1962), a broadly focused, densely populated, unsettling examination of Columba's exile on Iona, stressing the saint's human failings of family disloyalty, raging temper and racial bias. This Columba is no dove but rather a complex man, ill at ease making history. If he is the first of Friel's displaced heroes, the writer was also sharpening his narrative skills through his short stories. Friel learned early that economy is everything in this genre. In stories such as "The Diviner" and, especially, "Everything Neat and Tidy," the writing thrives on what it does not say, exposing the darkness beneath the polished surface. There is no doubt Friel was emerging as a master of the form but chose instead to develop as an artist in the theatre. He was already the most acclaimed author of his generation: *Philadelphia, Here I Come!* (1964), *The Loves of Cass McGuire* (1966) and *Lovers* (1967) had to differing extents achieved critical and economic success at home and in London and New York. These plays established him as the most intelligent, inventive, subversive and popular playwright Ireland had produced since Sean O'Casey. There can be no doubt an imagination as ambitious and self-aware as Friel's was well aware of his status. He grasped what was next necessary for him to continue experimenting and expanding his theatre. Paradoxically, this would demand a contraction of subject matter. In his next trio of plays he would deal with aspects of exclusively contemporary Irish experience: the Irish artist in *Crystal and Fox* (1968), Irish politics in *The Mundy Scheme* (1969) and Irish sexuality in *The Gentle Island* (1971).

At one level *Crystal and Fox* is a play about theatre, theatre at its most poor and basic: the touring fit-ups that played through rural Ireland up to their end at the time of the play's composition in the late 1960s. The tattered relations to the more ambitious programmes of Anew McMaster's classic texts, the fit-ups survived cinema but television finished them. We'd learned sophistication. These shows could not match that. Glamor was beyond them. Yet they presented plays for punters. They could not imagine themselves being anything but what they knew themselves to be. It is with a deeply knowing comic irony that Friel, the most experimental dramatist of his generation, turned to this world as metaphor of his art. He had superbly brought off the splitting of a character's atom in Gar Public and Gar Private in *Philadelphia, Here I Come!* He exploited the disturbances connecting reality and illusion through the voices operating in *The Loves of Cass McGuire*. He had created a strange hall of distorting mirrors through the correspondences and discrepancies of *Lovers*. In short, Friel was a young writer who throughout his thirties showed himself all too willing and exceptionally able to display a serious virtuosity of narrative styles and psychological complexities in his theatre. It had gained for itself an international reputation. Friel's status was already soundly established, if not quite at the level achieved after *Aristocrats*, *Faith Healer* and *Translations* in the late 1970s and early 1980s.

Then, in *Crystal and Fox*, he turns to what is essentially an entirely Irish theatrical form. Travelling players span the world but the fit-up is specifically our own. It certainly is in this play. Friel from the opening scene insists that historical details be absolutely accurate, placing the action into its precise historical context. These permeate the text. Papa is teased he is in training for the Olympic Games. These have just ended in Mexico in 1968, a few months before the play's premiere. Zambia, the setting of the play-within-the-play, is given its proper new name, transformed into African from the colonial title of Northern Rhodesia. There are also, as does happen in Friel's theatre, sly nods to cinema. The magician, El Cid, recalls the recent Hollywood epic, even if he and his lovely assistant Tanya may be no match to the beauty and drawing power of the film's stars, Charlton Heston and Sophia Loren. Most wicked of all the contemporary references is the title of the play-within-the-play, *The Doctor's Story*, a neat rewrite of *The Nun's Story*, the most successful pious tearjerker outside of biblical blockbusters throughout the late 1950s and 1960s. From the word go, Friel playfully mocks the idea of theatre as vocation, a new religion, its practitioners having made vows that render them in some shape or form as holy. The experiments of Peter Brook based on Grotowski's theory of Poor Theatre, published in *The Empty Space* (1968), the same year as *Crystal and Fox*, get their first rewrite in the Irish play, because like Brook Friel is attempting to demolish what he knows about theatre, his own theatre, and start again.

This shows itself in Fox's love/contempt for his audience. They pay to be entertained. His thanks is to cheat them out of the raffle money. The prize fiver goes to Crystal's Papa under the guise of being Sean O'Sullivan from outside Dublin. Fox refers to the public as "a noisy pack of bailiffs,"[1] takers as well as givers of favors. He holds them in contempt because they fall all the time not merely for the fixed raffle but also for their formulaic pleasures in his art: "All the hoors want is a happy ending" (13). This is not a man impressed by his public. They are pedestrian, predictable; they have ceased to challenge him. Fox feeds them a diet of rotten magicians, rotten jokes and rotten dramatic material. The more they buy it, the more he holds them up to ridicule. Fox Melarkey's fit-up is a theatre that is not so much rough as deadly. It is on its last legs. He shows no stomach for saving it. Fox has grown exhausted with the effort of believing his own creation. His powers of invention are squandered. It is clear from the vestiges of control he can display when he is called on to perform that there is not a single theatrical trick he has not mastered. But he will only draw on that mastery as a last resort – to calm a restless audience, to divert too curious an inquiry, to replace a missing actor. Fox is an old hand, an experienced hand, but also a bored hand. His boredom takes mischievous, dangerous form.

His contempt for El Cid and Tanya shows the rules of his destructive game. El Cid threatens to leave unless he and Tanya get last call. Fox agrees only to break his word, promptly, deliberately, in order to honor "my charming and devoted wife, Crystal Melarkey." El Cid leaves for the rival show of Dick Prospect, despite Tanya's hesitation and Crystal's panic: "You don't want them to leave us too, do you?" Smiling pleasantly, Fox answers enigmatically: "If I knew a simple answer to that, my Crystal, I'd go in for telling fortunes" (20). In his way Fox does tell fortunes, but the crystal he consults is not his wife. He can defeat the future through his own frightening powers of persuasion and contrivance, warped into his determination to destroy himself, all those in contact with him, and his way of life, his craft, his art. This has its comic side. Fox tries to make an actor out of the terrified Pedro. The dog trainer makes near-hysterical protest that acting is beyond him. Fox chooses not to hear Pedro's terror. So deaf is he to poor Pedro's insistence that he cannot do this, there is a sadistic element to Fox's indifference. Yes, the show must go on, but Fox displays a hardness dealing with other human beings that places him apart from everyone else – until the return of the Prodigal Son, the son called Gabriel, a match for his father in meanness. This boy is no angel. He arrives to announce no miracle of life through a divine shaft of light. Instead, he confesses he may well be a murderer. Only Fox is let into that secret. Crystal must, the men believe, be protected. They are mistaken. A psychiatrist has warned Gabriel that Fox is weaker than Crystal. In terms of strategic planning, that is a correct analysis. Years of dealing with the Irish police have toughened the traveller Crystal. She knows precisely how to hide and handle this situation. She too has her ruthless side. Gabriel must be protected, the family must be shielded. Only one factor defeats her: the health of her loved, dying father, Papa.

Fathers do not shine in the theatre of Brian Friel. They particularly do not in the plays of this period. I will return to this in *The Gentle Island*. But in *Crystal and Fox* fathers in their different ways spectacularly falter at crucial moments. Papa can hardly be blamed for taking ill. But it is in his delirium that he blurts out that Gabriel is back in Ireland, allowing the police to track the boy down. His benevolent desire to set eyes on his grandson leads to discovery and disaster. Papa's helplessness brings Gabriel to the savage justice of both British and Irish police, who hound him for his frenzied crime against an old woman shopkeeper. He has suddenly, shockingly, nearly beaten her to death in a fit of psychopathic temper for the sake of a few pounds. Gabriel gets his first hiding of many more to come from the furious policemen. That physical beating is at the center of *Crystal and Fox*, yet in his own fantasy Fox believes himself to be a harder man than anyone else onstage. To prove this he commits the pathetic, revolting act of killing Pedro's gentle, beautiful dog, Gringo.

Whatever the audience reaction to the murder of a dog in 1968, to a contemporary audience this act of lunatic cruelty would alienate Fox Melarkey to such a brutal extent that the play may as well end with his admission of responsibility. He can do no more to be hated. That job is finished. The shedding of the truck and its trappings, the fiction of how he has betrayed his own son, the loss of Crystal, his abandoning of himself to the miserable fate of his own company – all of these he deserves through the killing of the dog. In poisoning the innocent creature he poisons his audience against him. If he is not quite in the same league as Barabas, Christopher Marlowe's *Jew of Malta* (c. 1592), in the numbers removed, Fox equally lacks that play's blackest humor. He offers no such crazed relief.

Yet we stand with Fox to his bitter end, spinning lyrical yarns about his courtship of Crystal, declaring her "the only good part of me" (48) and then inevitably destroying that goodness. Fox and Crystal end at a crossroads where the signpost points to all directions through Ireland on a beautiful summer's day. The business has been sold for a paltry sixty pounds. They have even done well with that. Now they are dependent on the kindness of strangers for transportation, hitching lifts, cursing those who scorn them. They forge a strange connection with Mary and Martin Doul in Synge's *The Well of the Saints* (1905), for Crystal and Fox are about to see the terrible truth about themselves. But now they are giddy and restless, proclaiming renewed love. Fox asks Crystal to marry him again. She agrees and lets him know she knows all that he has done to destroy himself and his trade. She tells him all is forgiven – on one condition. She demands he does not turn on her: "That's all I cared about. And now we're back at the start, my love; just as we began together. Fox and Crystal. To hell with everything else" (60).

Fox will take that reference to hell seriously. It is all now he can take seriously, for he has one more dramatic act to perform. He asks Crystal would she go to hell with him. "There and back" (61), she blithely replies. He takes her to hell and leaves her there, saying it was he who informed on Gabriel for a reward of one hundred pounds – a reward that will be their infernal salvation. It is as if he has taken a gun to her head, killing her sexually, spiritually. She leaves him with the slow, thunderous, terrifying question: "What . . . are . . . you?" (63). In her absence he tries to answer. He does so by claiming all he confessed was a lie, a fiction he could not resist, because he realized for the first time "love alone isn't enough now" (64). This he admits to the wife he has lost. He spins the rickety wheel. For an instant he believes in chance. The belief is short-lived. He knows for certain that it does not make "a damn bit of difference because the whole thing's fixed, my love, fixed – fixed – fixed" (65). And the fixer is the Fox himself. This sly chancer has managed to pull off the remarkable trick of catching himself in his own trap. His yelps of pain do not go unnoticed. They do go unpitied. This lack of pity makes *Crystal and Fox* the stark, unsympathetic play it is. To borrow a description from the ally-enemy, Peter Brook, this is rough theatre, at its roughest.

Friel displays an uncompromising bleakness at the core of *Crystal and Fox*. His next play, *The Mundy Scheme* (1969), has an alternative title: *May We Write Your Epitaph Now, Mr. Emmet?*[2] The implications of this second name could only exclusively be appreciated by those with some knowledge of Irish history. Robert Emmet, the dead darling of Ireland, asked that his epitaph go unwritten until his country took its rightful place among the nations of the earth. In writing that epitaph with this play, Friel is consumed with an outright contempt for Irish government and politicians unmatched in its utter ferocity since it was first staged at Dublin's Olympia Theatre in June 1969. Three years previously, in celebrations for the golden jubilee of the 1916 Easter Rising, learning in our school was limited to the memorization of the Proclamation. Chairman Mao and his Red Guards would have approved of the indoctrination. That orgy of self-congratulatory, self-righteous backslapping feeds the rage that eats through the energy motivating this play, revealing Friel at his most indignant and, paradoxically, at his most controlled.

If there is a happy synchronicity between the theories of Peter Brook and the action of *Crystal and Fox*, Friel in *The Mundy Scheme* looks further back to find parallels between this play and earlier texts. The spirit of Swift touches *The Mundy Scheme*; it would be a better, more dangerous piece of theatre if it touched more deeply. There is also more than a little homage to the master of Jacobean comedy, Ben Jonson. The preposterous Taoiseach (Prime Minister), Francis Xavier Ryan, may be closer in manipulative spirit to Ben Jonson's *Volpone* (1606) than the more self-wounding Fox Melarkey. Characterization in *The Mundy Scheme* corresponds closely to the practice of much Jacobean comedy where laughter is resolutely dependent on exploiting the limitations and predictability of one-dimensional character types. Everything in *The Mundy Scheme* is dictated by its surface. There are no surprises, not even in Ryan's spontaneous duplicities and machinations. He may be a complete mother's boy, but when it comes to political survival, in his cultural context Ryan proves himself capable of manipulating all under him to serve his will. He is nobody's fool, proving his cleverness time and time again, undermining political rivals and blackmailers, bullying and charming media crews to obtain his deepest desire: staying in power. In *Crystal and Fox* Friel displays sufficient detachment to give a neurological analysis of Fox's mental disintegration. That sense of detachment increases in *The Mundy Scheme* because one factor is undeniable: Friel hates everyone in the play. There are a few tender observations to soften the earlier scenes of *Crystal and Fox*. No such sign of sympathy affects the later play. It is not a smell but a stench of corruption that permeates each and every corner of this world. This is appropriate, for – as in the best of Jonsonian comedy – corruption is literally the subject of this extreme theatre.

The actual Mundy scheme itself, brainchild of Irish-American multi-millionaire Homer Mundy, centers on death, the body's corruption and decay, the necessity to hide it, to bury it. And so the "solution" is to turn the whole west of Ireland into one giant graveyard for America, Britain and Europe. Although the country's economy is in meltdown, Ryan patriotically will not sell out the ports or airports to America. Even as he again refuses to devalue the currency, because "England won't let me" (174), he will protect neutrality. But the actual Mundy scheme has one great historical and financial advantage. It rewrites Cromwell's curse on the Irish to go to hell or to Connaught. Hell can now be left out of the equation, since Connaught will be transformed instead into one giant, profitable cemetery. Ryan and his cohorts win the day in cabinet. The scheme is accepted. Church and state give their full support. The blessings of the 1916 leaders are invoked. Heaven tonight will be turned into a festive Croke Park. As a mark of respect the triumphal procession of the first batch of coffins halts at the General Post Office in Dublin's O'Connell Street, the site of the 1916 Easter Rebellion. This bilious mockery, played three years after the 1966 commemorations, is explosive stuff. Friel spares neither fatherland nor faith. He is hellbent on giving maximum offense, butchering even the most sacred cow of the Irish mammy through the hideous, ballbreaking figure of Ryan's mother. She hates any woman who'd target her 50-year-old bachelor son and steal him. She vilifies every visitor to the house as the tinkers whom she loathes. She makes marmalade to feed her boy as if she could smear it on him and stick even more tightly to him. She even hides his medication so she can find it and increase his dependence on her. While Ryan can display the hardness of a leader, he is essentially a Napoleon in nappies, ultimately reduced to the whims of his mother's will.

Friel gleefully exploits the infantile appetites of his play's ciphers. He steadfastly refuses to dignify their actions with anything other than the basest, most obvious hungers. Their greed is their definition. They worship money and more money. As in Jonson's *Volpone*, it devours nearly all of them as they engage in treacherous roguery. Nash, Ryan's private secretary, wishes to cash in on the scheme. He seems to succeed, thinking he knows how to play this game. He believes he can impersonate Ryan in his financial double-dealing as easily as he does issuing statements on his behalf: "All I did [. . .] was to talk the same crap as you" (259). But Nash is an infant at this boyo's game. Ryan sets him up as a drug dealer in the shady confines of the

Imperial Hotel. There, at the Taoiseach's request, the Gardai will pick him up and chastise him for being a naughty boy. The brutality in that particular playpen is left to the imagination. It is the only thing left so in *The Mundy Scheme*.

Friel's intentions are clear in the play. The explicit anger in the writing does not look to debate with its audience nor even to reveal secrets. The play even bites its tongue when the comedy threatens to turn farcical. It is not so much censoring itself as refusing to allow the anarchy of linguistic license or outrageous action to let the play run riot and absolve itself of any serious confrontation. Its structure is remarkably stable and disciplined. Yet that stability and that discipline reinforce the sheer madness, disguised by the steady spin-doctoring of F. X. Ryan in his televised statements to the nation. He is out to convince us of his protection as patriot and patriarch. In that respect, he is strangely prophetic. As I noted earlier, the play was first performed in June 1969. Two months later Derry, Friel's nearest city, explodes in the Battle of the Bogside. The long war in the north of Ireland begins. And in that August the Irish Taoiseach Jack Lynch, leader of Fianna Fáil, the Republican Party, appears on television to tell Northern Catholics: "We will not stand idly by." To use a phrase beloved by Friel in *Faith Healer*, and parodied by him in *The Home Place*, that is another story.

Neither *Crystal and Fox* nor *The Mundy Scheme* have been frequently revived on the professional stage. His next play, *The Gentle Island*, was first performed late in 1971. I myself directed a revival in the Peacock Theatre in 1988. There is a simple reason why managements shy away from these plays, and that is the sheer number of actors required to perform them. Many appear on stage for a few scenes, some for a few moments. Although each of these three Friel plays was performed outside state-subsidized theatres, it is really inconceivable now how even they could afford to stage them. *The Gentle Island* was possible in 1988 because the Abbey Theatre still had a substantial number of actors employed in the repertory company. I had the opportunity to draw on an experienced body of players and so could adequately stage the play's opening scene: the departure from the island of eight inhabitants. The writing here is magnificent, the farewells are light and loaded. But the essence of the scene is its ending: a shocking silence after the hullabaloo of the leave-taking. Only the sea sounds through the theatre, taking strangers to this strange place, changing all on it forever because of what they bring there and because of what they find on Inishkeen.

It is off the coast of Donegal, this place called Inishkeen. To cross from Inishkeen into the English language involves a risk, not there in transcribing the meaning of Friel's usual location Ballybeg into "small town." The risk depends on how you translate the island's name. Is it, as Sarah says, the "Gentle Island"? Or is it a place of lamentation, of keening (from the Irish, *caoin*) and, if so, for what? It is not the land of youth nor the land of heart's desire, despite lying to the west. Instead it is a province of tough people, who have survived hard times. While this island, it must be stressed, is as imaginary as Ballybeg – I do not envy anyone mapping the topography of that village from the evidence of Friel's plays – there is a profound sense that Inishkeen was created by the sea and that it has known war in a particular way. While great powers fought for world destiny, this people turned into a race of scavengers. Whatever the sea delivered, they took from it, making no distinction between Allied or German disasters. All could be exploited for their survival: clocks from Dutch freighters; lamps off a British tanker; a pilot's chair from Germany. Claiming all such wreckage, the people tempted fate. In return for their neutrality a curse came upon them. Their island is being depopulated.

Only the king of Inishkeen, Manus Sweeney, is left to hold sway. His subjects are his sons, Philly and Joe, and Philly's wife, Sarah. Manus is appropriately christened. Like his Latin root, he is one-handed, having lost his arm. Philly too is suitably named. Like the Gaelic *file* he finds his voice in storytelling until it is abruptly silenced by self-consciousness when he starts to relate the tragedy behind the three rocks stranded between the island and the mainland. He describes the girl: "So beautiful was she that the fish came up from the sea and the birds down from the trees to watch her walk along the roads."[3] The shocked pause that greets this lyrical recitation from the taciturn Philly makes him question, "Isn't that the way it goes?" A delighted Manus declares that "He has it," only for Joe to ruin it with his pedestrian style of telling the great story. Joe, like his namesake St. Joseph, is dependable, domestic, fitting into the role assigned to him in the Sweeney household. But who is Sarah? To answer that question, the plot must proceed, and that involves the arrival of strangers from the South, Peter and Shane, bringing with them strange ways of loving.

Peter and Shane are not the first homosexuals on the modern Irish stage. Thomas Kilroy scored the opening goal there in *The Death and Resurrection of Mr. Roche* in 1969. But despite the lack of open declaration it is certainly the first appearance of a homosexual couple. These men have a mythical as much as a sociological function in the play. Love between men infects the island. It will be cunningly, ignorantly looked on as a plague to be eradicated. It is, at a terrible cost. Recognition dawns that this is no disease, this is no alien love. It is native to this place and therefore natural. Nature will not be denied and a love that dares to speak its name develops on the Gentle Island.

Love between man and woman transforms itself into hatred to combat love between men. Heterosexuality poisons itself into deepest perversity. The new love between men requires a new language. It is the product of a new nature. That nature must be stamped out; that language must be silenced. This is precisely what wife and patriarch seek to do through the last act of the play. Sarah claims she has seen Philly fuck Shane, doing for him what he cannot do for her, "the barren one" as she describes herself, "good seed's wasted on me . . . a sterile woman" (61).

More than any other play of Brian Friel's up to 1971, *The Gentle Island* was the most threatening, the most perplexing, the most far-sighted of all. Its power lies in revelation, relentless, painful. It hears the beating of a savage heart. Savagery can sometimes be dependent on steadiness and stability. Stability can be the force of habit, and that force may fail; the result is an outburst of passion such as Sarah's accusation, that is fatally in control of its own destiny. This is not a spontaneous people on the Gentle Island. Given to remembrance and grief, their voice is like the sea that surrounds them. It now resembles, indeed it registers itself as, silence until its swell bursts at moments of greatest disturbance. A silent tribe, how and when do they resort to speech? What transforms desire into action? "Give me the gun" (63), their king Manus demands. Excuses immediately begin to eradicate the consequences of such language, the source of their violence. Who hears the gun go off? No one. Who has it maimed? They must be removed immediately. They are not our kind, not like us, foreign as "the niggerman" (65) once accused of stealing five sovereigns and dumped back on the mainland, crawling like a crab, crippled like Shane tended by Peter, the dirty queers who have destroyed the peace and harmony of Inishkeen. Who crippled the stranger? Who knows? See no evil, speak no evil, hear no evil: a neutral solution for a neutral people.

In *The Gentle Island* Friel's theatre is one of concentration, narrowing immense events within a dramatic logic that leaves nothing to chance. He spares his characters nothing, particularly not their history, for all they may want to defy it. King Manus celebrates luck as the root of survival, believing in the four elements as benevolent agents of fortune. This blind acceptance of fate does not stem from his own life. The uncles of Rosie Dubh, his Dark Rosaleen of a wife, have maimed him for dishonoring their niece. That's how he lost his limb. And she started to wander, throwing herself off a cliff, never to be found. Fact is to be feared: it harms a body. Much better to betray experience and play the part of an entertainer. Manus reinvents his life as a series of wonderful stories, the ancestor of Casimir in *Aristocrats* (1979). He therefore delights Peter, who finds in Manus what he will never be: a father. He ignores the deep strain of failure in Manus the patriarch and prefers to envy Sweeney his luck. But luck on the Gentle Island is a lie. And yet do lies eventually lead to truth? Truth on this hard patch is told by a woman. Rejected mother of the tribe, Sarah deals in honesty, exposing male fantasy. It is she who tells how Manus really did lose his arm. But she has lived too long in the land of the blind, darkening herself to her own destruction. She returns at the play's end to the banality of her and Philly's life together, living the truthful lie of their marriage between man and woman. Once she saw Arcadia – a hotel on the Isle of Man where, working her fingers to the bone, she went to fifty-one dances and wore out three pairs of shoes, celebrating with the gods that dance us to our destiny.

But those gods change nature on the Gentle Island, dragging us to their depth, promising no redemption. In this dark world, how can light shine? For how long? As long as it takes to be extinguished. The Dublin strangers learn this. Peter is a musician in a hotel. Shane is an engineer. Complex and sophisticated art and science are devoured by the appetites of the Gentle Island, swallowing any threat to its supremely ordered existence. That same order, that same existence, will be the island's downfall. It depends on isolation, and there is a price to pay for being alone. The price is deprivation, denial of pleasure, the joy of change, the happiness of new voices. Manus tells Peter, "You came at a time when we were hungry for new voices" (55). But that great hunger is denied. Joy is taken from Inishkeen. As Ibsen knew in *Rosmersholm* (1886), as Friel knows in *The Gentle Island*, the taking of joy is the taking of life. Being a people sentenced thus, who, we ask, are judge and jury? That question, of course, begs another question: Where is the Gentle Island? Find an atlas. Open it. Have a good look. When I searched for it, I was given a clue by some experts well versed in the shifts and moods of the ocean, the great Atlantic drive running through Brian Friel's theatre. They said, keep an eye out for its capital city. It is called Ballybeg. But that does not exist, does it?

These plays do. Testimony to the craft, the learning, the loneliness of Friel's imagination. He was not in the business of taming monsters here. Rather he unleashed them, and in doing so let himself go through thirty-five more years of writing plays. Stamina? He had it. He just needed to know. *Crystal and Fox*, *The Mundy Scheme*, *The Gentle Island* – strange proof to himself and to his audience. I firmly maintain that these plays, the various crises of creative challenge they each present, were the making of the master. I've always distrusted that description of Friel the playwright. It implies he knows something. He does, but that knowledge is rooted in these rough, rabid, devious texts. In writing them he learned to go out and take a chance in every play he writes after them.

NOTES

1. Brian Friel, *Crystal and Fox* (Dublin: Gallery Books, 1984), p. 11. All subsequent references are to this edition and will be incorporated in the text.
2. Brian Friel, *Crystal and Fox and The Mundy Scheme* (New York: Farrar, Straus and Giroux, 1970), p. 158. All subsequent references are to this edition and will be incorporated in the text.
3. Brian Friel, *The Gentle Island* (Oldcastle, County Meath: Gallery Press, 1993), p. 32. All future references are to this edition and will be incorporated in the text.

4

STEPHEN WATT

Friel and the Northern Ireland "Troubles" play

"Since the fateful year of 1968, everything [Friel] has written has been imbued, however obliquely or indirectly, with the events of the northern crisis."
Fintan O'Toole, *The Irish Times*, 7 January 1989

Seldom in my experience has a topic such as the one I intend to address here been, at the same time, both so straightforward and so mired in complexity. Even if Fintan O'Toole had qualified the above assertion about the Northern crisis inflecting *everything* Brian Friel has written since the later 1960s to include only the two plays to be discussed here – *The Freedom of the City* (1973) and *Volunteers* (1975) – the matter would be far from settled. Much of the difficulty originates in the phrasing "Friel and the Northern Ireland 'Troubles' play," a title that implies clear relationships between author, contemporary history and dramatic form and, as a result, situates these plays on a horizon of expectations Friel seemed determined to disappoint.

The Freedom of the City concerns the killing of three innocent civil-rights marchers in Derry by British soldiers, a scenario that parallels the events of "Bloody Sunday" on 30 January 1972, when thirteen civilians were shot by British paratroopers.[1] The similarly doomed protagonists of *Volunteers* are five internees for whom the term "volunteer" possesses a double resonance in recalling the nationalist commitment of heroes in Ireland's past and commenting ironically on the prisoners' decision to work on an archaeological excavation in Dublin, an unpopular volunteerism which has motivated fellow detainees to plot their murder when they return to their prison block. Like "Bloody Sunday," internment was in the forefront of political consciousness in the early 1970s after the Special Powers Act was enforced in 1971, leading to the immediate arrests of several hundred men suspected of involvement with the IRA. In part because of this extra-textual reality, this relationship to real historical events, *The Freedom of the City* and *Volunteers* seem to elicit greater critical attention – and, especially at the times of their inaugural productions, sharper detraction – than other plays by Friel, and they are often linked together, as they will be here.

That is to say, even though both works found champions in the 1970s and have attracted more admirers today, it was "still surprising," as Seamus Deane recalls, "to see the ferocity and the blindness with which

30

critics, especially in London and New York, reacted to them."[2] *The Freedom of the City*, for example, after being produced in London and Dublin, closed in New York in 1974 after only nine performances, in part because Clive Barnes, the influential theatre reviewer of the *New York Times*, condemned the play as "luridly fictionalized," "far-fetched" and "impossible." No viewer could believe, he demurred, that the British army would mobilize against just three protestors "22 tanks, two dozen armored cars, four water cannons" and more.[3] Although the support of producer Joseph Papp of the New York Shakespeare Festival and Richard Watts of the *New York Post* countered these charges, its New York production could not be saved. *Volunteers* fared no better after the Abbey Theatre's March 1975 production. Gus Smith of the *Sunday Independent*, who had passed a negative judgment earlier on *The Freedom of the City*, was similarly harsh in his verdict on *Volunteers*, headlined "Friel Must Dig Deeper."[4] Responding in the *Times Literary Supplement* under the headline "Digging Deeper," Seamus Heaney began his rejoinder by juxtaposing Smith's allusion to "the great dramatic subject of internment" with the "pieties and patriotism implicit in another phrase, now heard less and less ... but once almost *de rigueur* when speaking of the Catholic minority in Ulster, who were 'our people in the North.'"[5] In *Volunteers*, Heaney concluded, Friel finds "a form that allows his gifts freer expression," and reviewers like Smith "simply refused to accept the dramatic *kind* that Friel has broken into, a kind that involves an alienation effect but eschews didactic address."[6]

Here, Heaney suggests the vexing issues of dramatic form and generic "kind" that often attend literary representations of a historical moment, especially one so contemporaneous with its composition. In a 1973 interview with Eavan Boland, Friel admits the difficulties of "writing about events which are still happening," regarding *The Freedom of the City* not as a dissertation on this history but rather as a "study of poverty." Boland observes that the play "provides the scenario of a political play," yet "it would be surprising if it was" as its author seems uninterested in polemics or propaganda.[7] Such comments, taken in toto – those critical of *The Freedom of the City* and *Volunteers*, and those more congenial appraisals like Heaney's and Boland's – thus inevitably return to matters of genre and generic expectation. As such, they intimate again the problematic nature of the phrase "Friel and the Northern Ireland 'Troubles' play." How are we to understand it?

To begin with, let's assume we know who Friel is and that we share a common understanding of the word "and." Even so, it is precisely in the connective power of "and," its linking of playwright and genre, that interpretive disagreement begins: if Friel *isn't* a political playwright, but instead one "obsessed with the personal, interior world of self-deception,"[8] why would he intervene in what is a very public conflict? (Perhaps the term "Friel" is more complicated than one might suspect.) More problematic, the phrase "Northern Ireland 'Troubles' play" is saturated with political implication and the vicissitudes of literary – in this instance, genre – theory. In a recent study of contemporary fiction, Elmer Kennedy-Andrews explains the "intensely problematic notion of 'Northern Ireland Troubles.'"[9] For him, the term "Northern Ireland" connotes "some recognition of constitutional-ized partition and is thus an unacceptable designation to Nationalists," and redacting Northern Ireland as "the North" seems too mindlessly geograph-ical to satisfy Unionists. Equally difficult and following David Lloyd's lead, Kennedy-Andrews argues that "Troubles" distorts a nationalist view of resis-tance to British domination by appearing to endorse a view of violence as a "spasmodic" and disruptive "outrage" which at its foundation lacks "a legit-imating teleology."[10] "Troubles" scarcely communicates a sense of Unionist outrage, as it also mismanages the motives behind an organized resistance to social marginalization, discrimination and impoverishment. From either side of the sectarian divide, the term is a failure, though lacking a better alternative I will employ it throughout.

Then, there is the matter of dramatic genre, the idea that a discrete variety of contemporary performance text definable as a "Troubles" play exists. Of course, on one level of abstraction there is no such dramatic form, any more than such a distinct kind of drama as the Elizabethan revenge tragedy exists. But doesn't it also matter in this phrasing what connotations inhere in the word "exists"? The concept of an Elizabethan revenge tragedy *exists* in the academy and in theatre history – and has for quite some time – even if it was unavailable to Shakespeare and his audiences for *Titus Andronicus* and *Hamlet*.

The Northern Ireland Troubles play, and my sense of the term encom-passes a wide variety of works, most often shares a significant exclusionary principle in imaging the Troubles: it is rarely "emplotted" as melodrama.[11] Instead, such plays typically exhibit a formal experimentation seldom seen in recent novels or film and address a wide array of concerns, in part because, as Ronán McDonald has observed, Northern playwrights in particular need "to find suitable means to engage with the civic strife around them" and, at the same time, avoid cliché.[12] A partial list might include Patrick Galvin's *We Do It for Love* (1975), Graham Reid's *The Death of Humpty Dumpty* (1979), Martin Lynch's *The Interrogation of Ambrose Fogarty* (1982), Anne Devlin's *Ourselves Alone* (1986), Christina Reid's *The Belle of Belfast City* (1989), Robin Glendinning's *Donny Boy* (1990), Marie Jones's *A Night in November* (1994), Martin McDonagh's *The Lieutenant of Inishmore* (2001) and Owen McCafferty's *Mojo Mickybo* (2002). Perhaps the most radical in dramatic form, Jones's play is written for one actor, while the seventeen roles in McCafferty's *Mojo Mickybo* are played by two. Reid's play concerns the lives of a working-class Protestant family, while Devlin's *Ourselves Alone* treats the lives of Catholic sisters whose father, brother and lovers are actively involved in the struggle, imprisoned or – in one case – acting as an undercover operative for the British government (another sister is involved with an abusive Socialist activist). McDonagh's "Lieutenant" is a one-man terrorist group who delights in torturing his enemies perhaps even more than the hoodlums do in Quentin Tarantino's *Reservoir Dogs* or Martin Scorsese's *Casino,* obvious influences on McDonagh, while Devlin's women seek more palatable fulfillment: a place to be themselves, a place where they will not be perpetually waiting for their men, and a place far away from the Provos, the UDA, and British soldiers battering in their doors.

Formal experimentation in most of these plays, however much it may subdue the melodramatic, does not finally eliminate emotion – or, in McDonagh's case, a combination of repulsion and detached, nervous laughter as severed limbs litter the stage at the end of *The Lieutenant of Inishmore.* The violence of the summer of 1970 intrudes upon the psyches and friendships of two Belfast kids in *Mojo Mickybo*, leading to a replication of the tragic ending of their favorite film, *Butch Cassidy and the Sundance Kid.* The conclusion of *Ourselves Alone* requires two sisters and their sister-in-law to plot different courses, none of them certain, in an effort to survive the traumas they have experienced. One even admits that she "may have lost the capacity for happiness"; another, preparing to emigrate to England, declares that she would rather "be lonely" there "than suffocate" in Northern Ireland.[13] And in Jones's *A Night in November* Northern Protestant Kenneth McCallister follows the Republic's soccer team to the World Cup in New York, where his growing sense of estrangement from the biases with which he had been raised leads to an exuberant epiphany: "I am free of it, I am a free man . . . I am a Protestant Man, I'm an Irish Man."[14] Whether offering pathos or disgust, tragic catharsis, or comic refulgence as in the case of Jones's "free man," and however different these are from the emotional satisfactions of melodrama, these plays nonetheless originate in a dramaturgy of sentiment in which dramatic action leads to closure; and, again, with the possible exception of the alienating excesses of McDonagh's *Lieutenant of Inishmore*, these plays engage their audiences' emotions.

The forms of *The Freedom of the City* and *Volunteers* work differently, as Heaney implies in his defense of *Volunteers.* That is to say, both produce a distinctly Irish "alienation effect" reminiscent of Brechtian epic theatre, beginning with the clear notion that its protagonists are, in the former case, already dead before any words are spoken and, in the latter, soon to be murdered. Brecht insisted that in the epic theatre, among other reforms of the conventional theatre, each scene is played for itself and regarded as a complete aesthetic unit rather than as a mere component in a larger narrative machine churning toward closure. More recently, Declan Kiberd has argued that in "classic" Irish literature "a person may die and yet go on talking."[15] Referencing Samuel Beckett's *Malone Dies* and *All That Fall*, Kiberd asserts that in such works not only is "every sentence a death sentence, in the sense that every statement is no sooner begun that it is already starting to die on an exhalation of breath," but that discourse itself is reduced to the function of shortening "the wait for the day of judgement, a day that may never come."[16] The first stage picture of *The Freedom of the City* assures the audience that death has indeed come for Michael, Lily and Skinner, its three protagonists, as their corpses "*lie grotesquely across the front of the stage*" illuminated by a "*cold blue*" light.[17] The first scene initiates the judicial hearing that will ultimately lead to "a day of judgement" in determining if their deaths were justified. In the subsequent action of the play, Friel combines various explanations of the deceased marchers' motives and accounts of the fatal events – sociological, nationalistic, journalistic, none of which is accurate – with scenes inside Derry's Guildhall, where the three had taken refuge from the turmoil outside before finally complying with the British military's demand to exit the building with their hands raised over their heads. In these latter scenes, therefore, the dead literally *do* speak, as Leos Janáček does in Friel's recent *Performances* (2003), until the moment of their murders by what, in his testimony near the play's conclusion, a forensic expert estimates were some thirty-four bullet wounds from high-velocity rifles.

Volunteers announces the death of its protagonists somewhat differently. In the closing moments of Act 1, Keeney, one of five internees who has agreed to work on an archaeological excavation that will soon be the site of a luxury hotel, informs his compatriots of what awaits them upon return to prison:

> [. . .] our fellow internees held a meeting the night before last – no, not really a meeting – a sort of kangaroo court. And they discussed again our defection in volunteering for this job. [. . .] And the assembled brethren decided that the only fit punishment would be . . . capital. (52)

While clarifying the prisoners' fates later than *The Freedom of the City* does, *Volunteers* nonetheless communicates the presence of death from the beginning, as the opening stage picture registers. Much of the action of the play takes place in a "*huge crater*," which, as Friel relates in his stage directions, functions as both a "*womb*" and "*prison yard*" (9). Recalling Pozzo's line in *Waiting for Godot*, "They give birth astride of a grave,"[18] this womb also functions as a grave containing bones which, after being organized and assembled, form the skeleton of Leif, who is displayed right of stage center. Offstage left is a smaller excavation, the cesspit, a Beckettian reminder of the material realities of the body for those who await final judgment. Still other judgments are awaited throughout the course of the play, the most significant of which is the contractors' irreversible demand to conclude the archaeological project so that construction on the hotel might begin. Des, a sympathetic graduate student working on the site, attends a board meeting hoping to have the decision reversed, but with no success. Thus, the action of the play – comprised to a great extent of stories, limericks and skits instigated most often by Friel's comic tandem of Keeney and Pyne – captures a project on its last day, its endgame. The play concludes with the volunteers bidding farewell to the project's managers, being led off to a van that will return them to prison, and Keeney re-entering momentarily to provide both comic and contradictorily tragic comments on the volunteers' futures. The low comedy is created by the last of his several limericks:

> On an archaeological site
> Five diggers examined their plight
> But a kangaroo court
> Gave the final report – [. . .]
> They were only a parcel of . . .
>
> (88)

"Shite," the last word of the limerick, metaphorically combines the site's two excavations, tomb and cesspit. After concluding the poem, Keeney quickly adds "[g]ood night. sweet prince," one of several echoes of *Hamlet* in the play, resulting in what might initially appear to be an incongruous and irreverent joining of forms, profane limerick and "classic" tragedy.

As is often the case in Brecht's theatre of alienation, then, both *The Freedom of the City* and *Volunteers* inform the audience of what will happen to their protagonists, leading to an adjustment of its emotional engagement with them. This is not to suggest that either play is devoid of emotion, but rather to argue that Friel's form delimits this engagement as it also incorporates ironic allusions to Shakespeare. *Hamlet*, as I have mentioned, is referenced throughout *Volunteers*; *King Lear*, as quoted by Skinner, informs *The Freedom of the City*. Scholars have recognized the influence of *Hamlet* on *Volunteers*: the presence of a Yorick-like skeleton "*banked slightly*" onstage "*so that it can be seen fully and clearly*" (9), the parallels between the graduate student Des and Laertes, and so on.[19] But, while arguably the centre of dramatic focus, Keeney is hardly a tragic hero; he is a self-described

"Friday night-man" whom Patrick Burke aptly terms an "emblem of celebratory individuality and joyous anarchy," a working man who, after receiving his pay packet, goes home, cleans up, and heads out for a night on the town to exercise his agency. On Friday night, countless numbers of working men like Keeney experience an "almost overwhelming sense of power and control and generosity and liberation" (57),[20] none of which is afforded them as detainees. By contrast, their lives in captivity are surveyed and controlled, which through their powers of invention Keeney and Pyne in particular transform into a "sumptuous destitution" (Kiberd's evocative phrase to describe Irish literature more generally) of bawdy humor, critical insight and ironic commentary. We sympathize with the diminution of their everyday lives, yet enjoy their productive humor and share their concern when it is discovered that Smiler, a simple-minded detainee in no way so mentally competent as the others, has escaped. We worry that, upon the men's return to prison, Keeney, whose wit and inventiveness have entertained us, will be "the one they'll go for first," because he persuaded the others to volunteer (75). But Friel never shows us this potentially gruesome scene, a closing spectacle of mass murder conventional to revenge tragedies like *Hamlet*. All the audience is afforded at the curtain is Keeney's "Good night, sweet prince" and the actions of another character beginning to tidy up the now abandoned site. Engagement, in other words, comes in fits and starts, not in the arc of dramatic action in *Volunteers*.

Functioning much like placards or other explanatory signs in Brecht's theatre, the "*grotesquely*" displayed bodies of Michael, Lily and Skinner in *The Freedom of the City*, as I have suggested, assure the audience of their fates from the beginning. What remains uncertain, however, is how and why their shootings occurred. The first scene initiates a judicial inquiry into such questions by calling soldiers, a brigadier in charge of security forces, a forensic expert and others to testify; to create larger contexts, Friel introduces an American sociologist, a newsman, a balladeer and a priest to explain the deaths of these three citizens in broader terms. Why did they break into the Guildhall in the first place? What larger political motives did the three possess? How should their deaths be remembered? Not surprisingly, with the possible exception of the forensic expert's testimony and his physical examination of the bodies, almost all the other speculation is inaccurate, occasionally offensive. Equally unsurprising, given earlier testimony that soldiers believed as many as forty heavily armed terrorists occupied the building – and that, according to the Brigadier in charge, the three "emerged firing from the Guildhall," thereby offering "no possibility whatever of effecting an arrest" (134) – the Judge's ruling at the play's end exculpates the security forces of any wrongdoing:

> There is no evidence to support the accusation that the security forces acted
> without restraint or that their arrest force behaved punitively.   (168)

Ironically, the physical "evidence," most likely the fact that two of the bodies
exhibited significantly more wounds than the other, leads the judge to conclude that Michael Hegarty and Lily Doherty "used their arms" while the
third, Adrian Casimir Fitzgerald or "Skinner," did not deploy any weapons.
The questions with which the play opened are thus answered: we now know
why these bodies are exhibited so grotesquely.

Although judicial proceedings might generate dramatic conflict and excitement – as in Jim Sheridan's film *In the Name of the Father* (1993), for example – such is not the case in *The Freedom of the City*. The monologues of
Friel's experts are similarly uneventful. Professor Philip Alexander Dodds, an
American sociologist who specializes in the "subculture" of poverty, spec-
ulates on the three victims' motives, most often incorrectly. The poor, he
asserts, are "provincial and locally orientated" with "very little sense of history" (111); their culture aids them in adapting to "their marginal position
in a society which is capitalistic" (110); and, given to feelings of inferiority,
they are "present-time orientated" and seldom plan for the future (133). As
if describing colonized or primitive "Others," he adds that, because they
are less repressed than more successful middle-class citizens, they may also
"have a hell of a lot more fun than we have" (135). Such generalizations
hardly describe the three "terrorists." Lily Doherty endures a life of grinding poverty with an infirm, unemployed husband and eleven children in a
tenement with one tap and one toilet for eight families' use. She does indeed
enjoy the present moment, a glass of sherry or a dance inside the Guildhall,
but hardly lives a life marked by its potential for "a hell of a lot of fun."
Michael Hegarty, unemployed and engaged to be married, cannot be accused
of being solely "present-time orientated." On the contrary, while waiting for
work, he has enrolled in school to study economics, business administration
and computer science. He has participated in every peace march and reports
that the civil-rights movement, now infiltrated by hooligans, was not originally the project only of the underclass, but included "rich and poor, high
and low, doctors, accountants, plumbers, teachers, bricklayers – all shoulder
to shoulder" (129).

Less idealist and committed than Michael, Skinner enjoys drinking and
betting on horse races, but he is neither the victim of feelings of inferiority – another of Dodds' generalizations – nor provincial. His capacity for
fun emerges tellingly moments after Dodds pronounces his hypothesis about
the "culture of poverty" emancipating its victims from repression. Moving
from Dodds' lecture back to the scene inside the Guildhall, the action begins

with Skinner emerging from a sideroom wearing the Lord Mayor's robe, a chain and an *"enormous ceremonial hat jauntily on his head"* (135). As he enters, Skinner quotes Edgar's lines from Act 4 of *King Lear* when Gloucester, thinking he is being led up a mountain to throw himself off, recognizes an inconsistency in his son's impersonation. Edgar responds, "You are much deceived. In nothing am I changed/But in my garments" (4.6.9–10). After Lily reacts to his gaudy appearance with "O Jesus, Mary and Joseph!" Skinner quotes Lear in the same scene: "'Through tattered clothes small vices do appear;/Robes and furred gowns hide all'" (4.6.161–162). As Skinner distributes the mayoral gowns, both lines appropriately accompany the trio's impromptu costume party, but the latter passage continues in Shakespeare's play to foreshadow the judicial inquiry's conclusion that their deaths were justified. As Lear advises Gloucester, when sin is plated with gold, "the strong lance of justice breaks"; in other words, when the powerful control judicial inquiry, justice cannot be rendered. This allusion, more so than all of Dodds' sociological theorizing about the poor, the priest's invocation of Marxist radicalism misleading the three and the Balladeer's inclusion of them in the long line of heroes who have sacrificed their lives for Mother Ireland, illuminates the inevitable course taken by final judgments in *Freedom of the City*. Like Gloucester and Lear, Friel's characters are the victims of history and Time, following Shakespeare's aged monarch into what Polish critic Jan Kott once termed a theatre of cruelty within which "the tragic element has been superseded by the grotesque. Grotesque is more cruel than tragedy."[21] Like flies killed by "wanton boys" in *King Lear* – like Lear himself – Skinner, Michael and Lily never really have a chance.

But must such an inevitability instantiate "polemics" against the British or lead to political "propaganda," two options Eavan Boland considered and excluded from her reading of *The Freedom of the City*? An alternative reading, one consistent with Kiberd's privileging of death sentences and the speech of dead characters in *Irish Classics*, might recognize the proximity of both *The Freedom of the City* and *Volunteers* not to Brecht's epic theatre, but to Kott's Grotesque and Beckett's absurdism. In fact, Skinner admits that "a short time" after he realized they had entered the Mayor's parlor he "knew that a price would be exacted," but elected to respond to the army's seriousness with a "defensive flippancy" (150). This is not to argue that Skinner and Keeney in *Volunteers*, the most flippant and entertaining of Friel's characters, caused their own deaths and those of others, but rather to suggest that awaiting these deaths constitutes the principal action of both plays. This reading is reinforced by Richard Pine's suggestion that "[n]aming, for Friel, as for Beckett is the key to identity."[22] If a proper name in a literary text is truly the "prince of signifiers,"[23] then both plays might be re-read by way of the names Friel creates. Much like pairs of names in Beckett's plays, for example – Hamm and Clov in *Endgame*, Didi and Gogo in *Waiting for Godot* – several names in *Volunteers* might be regarded as marking one half of a meaningful pair. The two detainees Smiler and Butt come to mind, but more important are the comic duo Keeney and Pyne, whose names both resemble those of a comedy team, a clever or "keen" one perhaps, and echo types of mourning or longing: to keen (from the Irish *caoine*, to wail) and to pine. In *The Freedom of the City*, Michael and Lily bear the names of ill-fated characters in James Joyce's short story "The Dead." At 17, Joyce's Michael Furey, whose health had declined from working in the gasworks, died out of love for Gretta Conroy, while at 22, Michael Hegarty, engaged to be married, may find a job in the gasworks; Joyce's Lily views men cynically as only interested in "what they can get out of you," while Friel's Lily in middle age has given all she can to an unemployed and idle husband. More significantly, lilies are traditionally symbols of peace, while Casimir – Skinner's real name is Adrian Casimir Fitzgerald – literally means "to destroy" (*kazic*) "peace" (*mir*). In this subtle way Friel, like Beckett, uses names suggestively to contextualize the "Troubles" within a larger existential dilemma.

The Freedom of the City and *Volunteers*, therefore, effect a kind of rapprochement between one element common to the Irish classics Declan Kiberd discusses and a dramatic genre I have labeled the "Northern Ireland 'Troubles' play." But the union, as I have tried to indicate, is problematic, and fraught with difficulties some audiences and reviewers have been unwilling to accept. As comments on the "Troubles," neither play conforms to audience expectations or lapses into cliché; neither advances a discernible sectarian politics; and neither subscribes to a dramaturgy of excitement or sentiment. As such, their reception has been uneven and at times hostile. But in an ever-increasing canon of literary and filmic representations of a real historical impasse, both stand as unique dramas of real significance. That is, they may bear a mark of genre, but there is quite literally nothing else quite like them – they participate but don't belong.

NOTES

1. In a 1986 interview with Laurence Finnegan, Friel described *The Freedom of the City* as an "ill-considered play because it was written out of the kind of anger at the Bloody Sunday events in Derry." This interview is reprinted in Christopher Murray (ed.), *Brian Friel: Essays, Diaries, Interviews: 1964–1999* (London and New York: Faber and Faber, 1999), pp. 123–134.
2. Seamus Deane, "Introduction," Brian Friel, *Selected Plays* (London: Faber and Faber, 1984), p. 19.

3. Quoted in Fachtna O'Kelly, "Can the Critics Kill a Play?," in Paul Delaney (ed.), *Brian Friel in Conversation* (Ann Arbor: University of Michigan Press, 2000), p. 117.
4. Ibid.
5. Seamus Heaney, "Digging Deeper," *Times Literary Supplement*, January–March 1975, p. 306; reprinted in Seamus Heaney, *Preoccupations: Selected Prose 1968–1978* (London and Boston: Faber and Faber, 1980), pp. 214–220.
6. Ibid.
7. Eavan Boland, "Brian Friel: Derry's Playwright," *Hibernia*, 16 February 1973; reprinted in Delaney, *Brian Friel in Conversation*, p. 114.
8. Ibid.
9. Elmer Kennedy-Andrews, *Fiction and the Northern Irish Troubles Since 1969: (De)-Constructing the North* (Dublin: Four Courts Press, 2003), p. 10.
10. Ibid., p. 11. Here Kennedy-Andrews is quoting from David Lloyd's *Anomalous States: Irish Writing and the Post-Colonial Moment* (Dublin: Lilliput Press, 1993).
11. In *Metahistory: The Historical Imagination in Nineteenth-Century Europe* (Baltimore: Johns Hopkins University Press, 1973), pp. 7–11, Hayden White argues that history comes to us as a narrative of events fashioned into a story. The historian's "mode of emplotment" thus implicitly offers an explanation of those historical events without the historian commenting upon them.
12. Ronán McDonald, "Between Hope and History: The Drama of the Troubles," in Dermot Bolger (ed.), *Druids, Dudes and Beauty Queens: The Changing Face of Irish Theatre* (Dublin: New Island, 2001), pp. 232–233.
13. Anne Devlin, *Ourselves Alone* (London: Faber and Faber, 1986), pp. 89–90.
14. Marie Jones, *A Night in November* (Dublin: New Island Books, 1995), p. 47.
15. Declan Kiberd, *Irish Classics* (Cambridge, MA: Harvard University Press, 2001), p. 574.
16. Ibid., pp. 39, 581.
17. All quotations from *The Freedom of the City* come from Brian Friel, *Plays One* (London and Boston: Faber and Faber, 1996). Here, the reference is to p. 107. All quotations from *Volunteers* come from Brian Friel, *Volunteers* (Oldcastle, County Meath: Gallery Press, 1989), and will be followed by page numbers in the text.
18. Samuel Beckett, *Waiting for Godot* (1954) (New York: Grove Press, 1982), p. 103.
19. See, for example, Patrick Burke, "'Them Class of People's a Very Poor Judge of Character': Friel and the South," *Irish University Review* 29:1 (Spring/Summer 1999), p. 47.
20. Ibid.
21. Jan Kott, *Shakespeare Our Contemporary*, trans. Bolesław Taborski (New York: Norton, 1964), p. 130.
22. Richard Pine, *Brian Friel and Ireland's Drama* (London and New York: Routledge, 1990), p. 15.
23. Roland Barthes, as quoted in Jeremy Parrott, *Change All the Names: A Samuel Beckett Onomasticon* (Szeged, Hungary: The Kakapo Press, 2004), p. 9.

5

ANTHONY ROCHE

Family affairs: Friel's plays of the late 1970s

In *The Freedom of the City* (1975) and *Volunteers* (1977) Brian Friel closely engaged with key political developments in Northern Ireland in the early 1970s (Bloody Sunday, internment). The two plays I wish to examine in this chapter – 1977's *Living Quarters* and 1979's *Aristocrats* – show a complex repositioning. On the one hand, there is a distancing and a greater mediation in terms of direct representation of the politics of Ireland north and south. This is primarily achieved through a more studied deployment of the language of world culture – such as the music of Chopin, which is so central to the dramaturgy of *Aristocrats* – and in particular an engagement with a number of classic playwrights from the world repertoire.

Living Quarters is acknowledged as being "after Hippolytus,"[1] and in dramatizing an Irish version of Phaedra it also brings Racine to mind. The play has eight characters in search of an author-director in ways which recall Pirandello, as well. None of this is new in Friel. The music of Wagner provided an important emotional and structural resource in *The Loves of Cass McGuire* (1966) and Pirandello was also crucial to its self-conscious theatricality. What is new is the increased dramatic and emotional sophistication of how these materials are handled. This may in part derive from the presence of Chekhov, who is going to feature so prominently in Friel's career from here on. Friel was working at the time on a translation of *Three Sisters*, which was to be staged in 1981 by Field Day. The presence of three sisters in the households of *Living Quarters* and *Aristocrats* marks them as no less versions of Chekhov's plays, fully transplanted from a Russian historical setting to a (then) contemporary Ireland.[2] But if these plays see a more international Friel emerging in his drama, they are no less a return to origins, a going home. For they forsake the cities of the recent plays – the Dublin of *The Mundy Scheme* (1969) and *Volunteers* (1975), the Derry of *The Freedom of the City* (1973) – and mark a return to Donegal and Ballybeg. They also mark a return to the family, a family which is now expanded and complicated (especially in terms of gender) and which becomes the obsessive focus of its characters.

The two families represented, the Butlers and the O'Donnells, are a distinct progression up the social scale from the humble background of the father, son and housekeeper of *Philadelphia, Here I Come!* (1964). Friel had already shown (and satirized) the aspirant Irish bourgeoisie in earlier plays. The difference here is that the two families, or more precisely the fathers of the two families, occupy important roles in the society's power structures. Commandant Frank Butler of *Living Quarters* is in the Irish Army and returns from service with the United Nations in the Middle East to a hero's welcome in Ballybeg attended by both the Taoiseach (Prime Minister) and the President. District Justice O'Donnell of *Aristocrats* comes from a long line of highly placed members of the judiciary and lives in a "Big House" environment more traditionally associated with Protestants than with Catholics. Both families, therefore, live at a considerable social remove from the immediate environs of Ballybeg. Frank has lusted all his life to receive a transfer from the remoteness of Donegal to the city of Dublin, and has rejected all intermediate postings that have come his way. The O'Donnell family have been educated away from the locality and all three of the "girls" sent to a finishing school on the Continent. *Aristocrats* particularly confronts the issues of class surrounding the relationship of Ballybeg Hall to the town from which it takes its name and which it surveys from a height. Eamon and Willie are the two local "lads" who have sought a relationship to the House through romancing the daughters; it is questionable to what extent either has succeeded. Eamon's grandmother has worked in service all her life at the Hall and reacts with heart-scalding shock and disapproval when she learns her grandson is to marry "Miss Alice."[3]

The distancing of the two families from their immediate surroundings has a further, political resonance. Both plays are set in Donegal, as the texts repeatedly remind us. But the place names of the locality extend (and do not have to extend very far) to reach into Northern Ireland. When Eamon and Willie reminisce about a local dance they attended in their youth, it takes place in Derry: "Remember dancing to that in the Corinthian in Derry?" (287). When people come and go to Ballybeg in *Living Quarters*, they do so via Derry or Omagh. These were names that acquired a worldwide fame in the 1970s through the repeated media coverage of events in Northern Ireland. Yet those events are never mentioned at all in *Living Quarters* and only rarely in *Aristocrats*. It is in the interests of both fathers to have it so. Commandant Butler has spent a lifetime in the Irish Army. The first experience for Irish soldiers of engaging in a conflict would have occurred since 1960 and Ireland's involvement in peacekeeping UN activities in Africa and the Middle East, since the country remained neutral in the Second World War. Commandant Butler is being celebrated for having carried nine of his wounded men to safety when under guerrilla fire. This is an incident that would have shrunk into its true proportions if its army were engaged in more continuous military activity. Instead, the encounter is magnified by its rarity into a heroic event to be celebrated by the attendance of the country's leaders. Another war is going on somewhat closer to home, but it is one in which the Irish Army is not involved and which must on no account be mentioned, especially in Donegal, where the physical proximity is so great.[4] Northern Ireland is never mentioned in Ballybeg Hall and would have remained unspoken, were it not for the presence of the American academic Tom Hoffnung. He questions Alice on her father's view of the civil-rights campaign in the North. She answers: "He opposed it. No, that's not accurate. He was indifferent: that was across the Border – away in the North" (272). Tom's quiet reply is to point out that the distance was a mere "twenty miles away." This is one of the very few explicit references to the border in the whole of Friel's drama.

Commandant Frank Butler at no point expresses any personal or idealistic commitment as to why he has sought to serve in an army representing itself as national; his own social advancement would appear to have been the sole motivation. So it is that he presents himself in Act 2 as "Lieutenant-Colonel Frank Butler," since he assumes his promotion is "in the bag" (232–233). In *Aristocrats* Eamon describes the O'Donnell family (or more precisely its patriarch) to Tom Hoffnung as "a family without passion, without loyalty, without commitments; administering the law for anyone who happened to be in power" (294). It is in this political context that the re-emergence of the theme of father–son relationships in Friel's drama needs to be evaluated. In an important essay "Fathers and Sons: Irish-Style," Declan Kiberd has written of the position of fathers in a society where a colonial regime, while on the wane, still operates. The "unsuccessful" father occupies an abject role in the household, unemployed and alcoholic. The "successful" father scarcely has it any better, living "out his life in a posture of provincial dependency, as a policeman or bureaucrat or petty official in an oppressive or despised colonial administration."[5] Kiberd's comments, though deriving primarily from *Philadelphia, Here I Come!*, apply with even greater force to the socially more prominent fathers of *Living Quarters* and *Aristocrats*.

A sense of huge emotional distance is conveyed in the theatrical space by the fact that, in the course of the drama, fathers and sons rarely if ever meet face to face. Frank in his moment of triumph surrounds himself with the women in his life, his three daughters and his beautiful new trophy wife, Anna, who is young enough to number among them. Ben has left home, physically if not emotionally, to live in a portable caravan on the outskirts of Ballybeg. The son makes a delayed entrance into the play, and only has two brief encounters with his father. In the first re-encounter between the estranged pair, he manages to overcome the stammer his father's presence induces to congratulate him; and Frank is sufficiently relaxed and offguard to embrace him. But this state of play cannot persist; and when Ben makes several attempts to confess to his father the relationship with his stepmother, he is brusquely silenced by the father who does not know what is coming and can only view the son as trying to usurp his parade. In the closest he comes to self-criticism in the play, Frank Butler holds that the necessary distinction between public and private spaces has broken down in his case, and that he has inappropriately acted as a military officer in relation to his rearing of the family:

> I was thinking: what has a lifetime in the army done to me? Wondering have I carried over into this life the too rigid military discipline that – that the domestic life must have been bruised, damaged, by the stern attitudes that are necessary over – I suppose what I'm saying is that I'm not unaware of certain shortcomings in my relationships with your mother and with Ben [. . .] (194)

In *Aristocrats*, it is the father who is pushed into the dramatic background and the son who occupies center-stage. Here, the displacement and distortion of the relationship are even more grotesque. District Justice O'Donnell is bedridden, dying, and so remains upstairs for almost all of the action, being obsessively ministered to by the eldest daughter, Judith. In the play's opening action, local handyman Willie Diver installs a baby alarm on the downstairs wall so that Judith or any member of the family can respond to their father's requests. The device serves more as a loudspeaker to issue their father's commands, to broadcast publicly the most intimate exchanges in which his soiled body is cleaned, and – most surrealistically of all – to have him address people who are present as if they were not there and to speak from his family bed as if from his judge's stand, condemning the members of his family for what he sees as their various betrayals. The non-communication is expressed in a Beckettian mechanical device. In his father's absence, his one son Casimir is at large to roam the garden, to encourage his sister Claire in her piano playing and to tell anecdotes about the O'Donnell family's association with great historical and cultural figures over the decades. The nervous, fussy Casimir seems less free than driven by inner demons, and nowhere is this more graphically or dramatically presented than in the closing moments of Act 1, when he is bringing a carefully prepared lunch onto the lawn and the baby alarm suddenly erupts into life: "Casimir!" (282). At the sound of his father's command, Casimir jumps to attention, "*rigid, terrified*," and sinks to the ground with the tray. He ends "*in a kneeling position*," weeping and comforted by Judith. This negative transformation wrought by the appearance of the father is on a grander, more operatic scale than that which befalls Gar in *Philadelphia* or Ben in *Living Quarters*. The father's command is that Casimir bring him his homework; if the father is undergoing a second childhood, where Judith has to wash, change, and chastise him, he is also refusing to relinquish patriarchal control and continuing to treat his son as a child. Casimir may be in his mid-thirties, with a wife and two children in Hamburg, but his atrophied emotional life continues to center itself in Ballybeg Hall.

What most seriously complicates and challenges the father–son relationship, in both theatrical and gender terms, is the presence in both plays of three sisters. The opening scenes of *Living Quarters* foreground the overlapping dialogue between the three reunited Butler sisters – Helen, Miriam, and Tina – as they simultaneously engage with their present-day lives and collectively remember and re-enact their past. As they do so, they evoke "the whole atmosphere – three sisters, relaxed, happy, chatting in their father's garden on a sunny afternoon. [But] there was unease [. . .], there were shadows" (188). That current of sisterly energy establishes the prevailing atmosphere of the play and is something both father and son are going to have to enter and engage with.

The reference to "three sisters" also foregrounds the Chekhovian reference and resonance. In theatrical terms, it indicates a shift from the direct opposition between father and son in *Philadelphia*, however mediated and complicated by the splitting of Gar into two separate identities. The progression is into a dramatic ensemble, with anywhere from three to five characters sharing and having to negotiate the stage space. In *Aristocrats* the three sisters are more dispersed in terms of the stage, but no less present in their different ways. Judith, the eldest, runs Ballybeg Hall, having the care both of her ailing father and a sister who suffers from manic depression. For much of the first act she remains offstage; but her voice is also broadcast over the baby alarm as she copes not only with her father's physical needs but with his non-recognition and his accusations. Her entrance at the end of the act is timed to witness Casimir's breakdown and to "*rock him in her arms as if he were a baby*" (283). The image of thwarted maternity has a context. For Judith's "great betrayal" has consisted of going over the border to engage on the Catholic nationalist side in the Battle of the Bogside and in having a child through an affair with a Dutch reporter. That political and sexual act cannot be acknowledged, and so Judith has put her child up for adoption. The youngest sister, Claire, is offstage for much of the first act. But her presence registers strongly through her offstage piano playing to which both the characters onstage and we become an audience. Casimir suggests that their father has strongly opposed Claire's wish to become a concert performer, and so she has been forced to keep her performing to the private family stage rather than the public platform. The absent and long-dead mother is her double, also suffering from a nervous condition and having been transferred from her profession as actress to a mother and wife in the private sphere. Alice is the sister most continuously onstage throughout the three acts. She stalks the limits of the stage, freed up from the physical restraint inhibiting all her siblings by her drinking and also freed up vocally to tell some home truths concerning the O'Donnell family.

This complication and expansion of the family accompanies a further development of the conflicted identity of the two brothers/sons. The absent mother in *Philadelphia* could be idealized by her son in a relationship fraught with Oedipal overtones. To develop this scenario *Living Quarters* evokes another classical precedent, that of Phaedra and Hippolytus, in which a hero returns from the wars to discover that his beautiful second wife has been having an affair with his son. As Richard Allen Cave has noted, Friel does not seem particularly drawn to following his classical source in examining "the guilty passion of stepmother for stepson."[6] The theme of quasi-incest is refracted through more than one relationship in the play; it is achieved not just through Ben's relationship with his stepmother Anna (though this plays its part), but through his relationship with his sisters. It is the middle sister Miriam who, from the complacent position of the one sister married with children, makes biting remarks about her brother: "let there be no romantic aul' chat about brother Ben. He's a wastrel – a spoiled mother's boy" (187). There is confirmation of the latter, the displacement of husband by son in the family romance, from the eldest sister, Helen. She describes the interview in which her mother expressed ferocious opposition to Helen's proposed marriage with her father's batman, Private Gerald Kelly: "And you [her brother Ben] stood there at Mother's side – and held her hand – and held her hand as if you were her husband" (215). Helen persisted in marrying "her Gerry" and is now a divorcee living in London. But the closest family relationship is still that between Ben and his eldest sister. They share confidences and a greater degree of emotional and physical intimacy than anything we see represented between Ben and Anna. Helen has also become the living visual and acoustic image of their mother. As Ben remarks when she orders a cup of coffee from the youngest sister, Tina: "Mother's voice – exactly!"

In *Aristocrats* Casimir admits that he has always known he was "peculiar" (310). As his father has declared to him at one stage, had Casimir been born and lived in Ballybeg itself, he would have had to occupy the role of "the village idiot. Fortunately for you, you were born here and we can absorb you." Although Casimir claims he has a job in Germany, he contradicts this by revealing that, while his wife Helga works in the bowling alley, he minds their two children, a role for which they dub him the "children's maid [or] nanny" (278). The presence of three sisters in both plays allows for the suggestion of incest to be extended through the brother–sister relationship. Casimir dotes on Claire, encouraging her in her music and enacting through it a quasi-romantic flirtation. His outrageous, funny and heartbreaking campness encourages the possibility that the greatest denial in this house of secrets is of his own possible gayness. In revealing to Eamon the "great truth" he discovered about himself when he was nine, he strenuously – overstrenuously – denies the most obvious possibility: "When I say I was different I don't mean [I was] as they say nowadays 'homo-sexual'" (310). Casimir carries out such an elaborate pantomime of heterosexual married life throughout the play, with his endless phone calls to Hamburg and his loud protestations of love to wife and children, that Eamon (and the audience along with him) is led to see this as yet another of his elaborate fictions. All of the exiled characters in the two plays are depicted leading lonely lives; this is one reason the emotional lure of old family ties is still so strong. But there is equally the strong possibility that Casimir has left Ireland and gone to Hamburg to avail himself of a greater sexual freedom than would have been condoned by the Ireland of the time – or than could have been discussed in its microcosmic equivalent, the family. Likewise, Miriam has moved to a society where she has legal entitlement to a divorce and where her brief return makes her a source of voyeuristic attraction to the local males; but someone whose return will be as short as possible, who comes back in the guise of temporary visitor or tourist. The exiled characters may well be leading lonely lives because their emotional involvement in the family has *been* so absolute as to rule out other, more individuated sexual relationships. When Ben thinks of how difficult it must have been for Anna to break into the Butler family, "with our bloody boring reminiscences and our bloody awareness and our bloody quivering sensibilities" (229), he utters a protest that is as political as it is personal and which can be applied to both plays (and much beyond): "There must be another way of ordering close relationships, mustn't there? (*Shouts.*) Mustn't there?"

Friel brings to *Living Quarters* an unprecedented degree of theatrical experiment by presenting what we are seeing as a consciously constructed performance rather than unmediated realism. The tragedy of the Butler family is not being realized in the dramatic present. Not for the first or last time there is a Frielian narrator who recounts the lives of the people we are about to witness. This narrator is a Pirandellian creation, a figure known as "Sir" who appears to combine the roles of playwright and director. He summons up the cast of the play – Frank and Anna, the three sisters, Ben, Miriam's husband Charlie, and a priest who is a longtime family friend, Father Tom – and gives them their allotted roles as they prepare to play out the familiar scenario one more time. Father Tom protests that on this occasion at least may he not be portrayed as a drunken buffoon; but that is precisely what occurs as the drama unfolds. When Frank turns to his oldest friend and spiritual advisor in his hour of need, Father Tom is too out of it with drink to respond. The progress and outcome of the drama therefore seems set and Sir is extremely authoritarian in the way he gives orders and deals with tardy actors. Repeatedly he insists that the "ledger," in which everything is written down, be absolutely adhered to. The fact that Ben addresses his father as "Sir" makes for a conscious parallel between the worlds within and without the drama. And Friel's oft-repeated view that his theatrical texts ought not be deviated from surely finds an echo here.

But the situation is more complicated than that, as any practitioner in the field of live theatre has to concede. The authority structures of *Living Quarters* are called into question and challenged at every level. Sir, in his opening speech, reveals that he only exists because the characters have created both the ledger and him:

> in their imagination, out of some deep psychic necessity, they have conceived me – the ultimate arbiter. [. . .] And yet no sooner do they conceive me with my authority and my knowledge than they begin flirting with the idea of circumventing me, of foxing me, of outwitting me. (177–178)

The character who most resists and challenges Sir's authority is Anna. The Butler family are happy to re-enact the family rituals with which they are all so familiar, to revisit Eden before the Fall. Helen is the one member of the family who expresses dissatisfaction with the representation, as omitting the uneasiness which should accompany it. But it is Anna who most reacts against and protests the refusal and inability of the family to admit or talk about what has occurred during their father's absence: her affair with Ben, about which they all know. She insists on speaking out from the margins to which she has been confined, by the family because she is not one of them, and by Sir who has allotted Anna her role and (like her husband) will not let her speak: "No, I won't go back to my room and cry. I'll tell them now" (202). She proceeds to do this, but nobody in the play-within-the-play can "hear" her. At the end Anna and Sir are left alone onstage. She has returned to ask what remains about her in the ledger. The few facts he recounts about her current life in America prompt her to ask, "That's all?" (246). Nowhere is the inadequacy of the ledger more manifest than in these closing moments, challenged and questioned as it is by the living presence of the character

Anna and in particular of the actress playing her. We may say that Brian Friel has scripted it all – the play without as well as the play within. But the whole of *Living Quarters* works to challenge the absoluteness of that statement.

In these plays of the late 1970s Friel is consciously developing his drama to the achievement of a greater expressivity. The requirements of design are particularly important and challenging in this respect. Where *Philadelphia* split the central character into two, *Living Quarters* and *Aristocrats* (with no single character dominating) divide their stage space in two, wishing to present simultaneously an interior and an exterior. The living room of the Butler household is fronted by a garden running the length of the stage. Ballybeg Hall has its study upstage right; but two-thirds to three-quarters of the set (depending) is the outside garden. In both cases, the wall is missing, so that we can see directly into the interior and characters can step straight from one setting into the other. In the production of *Aristocrats* at London's Royal National Theatre in 2005, Tom Cairns combined the roles of director and designer. He used the Lyttelton's revolving stage to brilliant effect to adjust the relationship between the inside and the outside in each act. In the first the study was the most exposed, revealing Tom Hoffnung at his cataloging activities and suggesting how enclosed within the claustrophobia of the house and its past the family still remained. In Act 2, with Claire outside the house and away from the piano, a wall now screened off most of the inside and the emphasis was thrown on the exterior – thus increasing the logic by which even the father struggles to emerge from the house's Gothic interior at the act's close. In Act 3 the settings were at their most evenly balanced, but with the actors all placed very much to the fore as they faced into the future. The size of the garden space on the Lyttelton stage seemed for once equal to Friel's demands – with the gazebo to which Alice retreats very far downstage indeed. The exposed interiors and the various groupings around the garden conveyed well the challenge of all of Friel's plays: to enter the public space of a theatre without sacrificing the integrity of these private individuals and the worlds they imaginatively inhabit.

This is particularly the case with Casimir and the stories he tells. For each of the objects in the household he has a story to tell, one which is designed to evoke a famous figure from the past and their social interaction with the world of the O'Donnells. At first these have a certain plausibility and seem little more than socially conscious name-dropping, with Casimir giving Tom the "facts." As the academic puts it, "this is where Gerard Manley Hopkins used to sit – is that correct?" (264). But as the play goes on, the list becomes increasingly absurd, culminating with a surrealistic birthday party for Balzac and Tom's empirical proof that Casimir could not personally recollect Yeats since the famous Irish poet died a full three months before Casimir was born. Tom glosses over the disparity by saying that it was natural Casimir should translate a story he had heard as a child into a personal narrative. This half-truth is as far as Tom's "kind of scrutiny" (310) can carry him. What *Aristocrats* goes to considerable lengths to demonstrate is that memory in Friel's drama is best understood in cultural rather than purely personal terms, that it operates as something constructed, made. The O'Donnells of Ballybeg Hall have sought to shore up their uncertain sense of self, their lack of political and cultural importance, by developing a mythology, a pantheon of the great and the good who have been personal friends of the family. In one sense, they have done so because in the Irish Big House context they are unusual in being Catholics rather than Protestants. The O'Donnells suffer a double isolation: cut off from the rest of Ballybeg by their aristocratic status; cut off from other Big Houses by virtue of not being Protestant.

But as Tom Hoffnung accurately remarks, there historically existed in Ireland a "Roman Catholic big house – by no means as thick on the ground [as the Protestant] but still there" (281). That people think otherwise has to do with mythology, specifically the mythologizing of W. B. Yeats as cultural propagandist for the Irish Literary Revival. The start of the Theatre Movement involved three landlords from the west of Ireland – Lady Gregory, Edward Martyn, George Moore – and the suburban middle-class Yeats. Martyn and Moore were both from Catholic landowning families. Within a few years they were gone, and Yeats embarked on his mythologizing of the Big House setting as the locale of an invented Protestant Ascendancy: Lady Gregory's Coole Park, the Gore-Booth sisters at Lissadell. Yeats's myth of the Protestant Big House is challenged by Casimir's counter-mythologizing, where the great figures tend to be Catholic with papal associations. Yeats is, of course, mentioned; as is George Moore, though Casimir cannot remember how he fits in (perhaps because Moore converted to Protestantism). Most of the figures Casimir mentions – Cardinal Newman, Hopkins, G. K. Chesterton – were apotheosized in Catholic homes and schools in the North: figures who had achieved prominence in the cultural sphere and had not renounced their faith. One example will serve: Count John McCormack. In 1986, Brian Friel edited and introduced the transcribed oral history of a Donegal weaver, Charles McGlinchey, in *The Last of the Name*. McGlinchey had left his home in Donegal in the course of a very long life on only two occasions; one was to attend the Eucharistic Congress in Dublin in 1932 when John McCormack sang "Panis Angelicus" to an audience of over one million in Croke Park.[7] Casimir's pantheon is empirically and historically false; these figures did not crowd into Ballybeg Hall to meet the O'Donnell family. But they were nonetheless beloved presences in the homes of Irish Catholic families, giving a greater sense of cultural self-worth to people for whom economic and political opportunities were few.

The other connection to the greater world is through the music of Chopin. The importance of music to the dramatic and emotional structure of *Aristocrats* is enunciated by Casimir at the very start: "When I think of Ballybeg Hall it's always like this; the sun shining; the doors and windows all open; the place filled with music" (256). The prominence of music serves to connect the play with the two breakthrough family plays, *Philadelphia, Here I Come!* and *The Loves of Cass McGuire* (1966). In the face of the cultural and emotional deprivation he faces, Gar retreats to his bedroom and mixes Mendelssohn with céilí. Cass MGuire's alternative to her family's rejection is the refuge of Eden House and the music of Wagner. There has not been much music in the plays between but it returns full force in *Aristocrats* and is to remain fundamental to his drama ever since. Like Beckett, Friel is all too aware of the limitations of language; deprived of one tongue, the Irish have rendered themselves fluent in another. And neither language, at this point, is adequate to the historical situation. For all of their loquacity, characters in Friel find it difficult to access their emotions. Friel himself has particularly looked in his plays at how only music is adequate "to explode theatrically the stifling rituals and discretions of family life" and provide "another way of talking, a language without words."[8] (There is a conscious echo here of the famous concluding lines of *Lughnasa*, where that supralinguistic expression derives from the combining of music with dance.) One dramatic extreme of Friel's interest in music is reached in the late play, *Performances* (2003), which centers on the composer Leos Janáček and his creation of *String Quartet No. 2*; musicians mingle with actors onstage and in its final movement the play surrenders to music as the string quartet plays out the last two movements of the piece. There is a balance preserved in *Aristocrats* with the Chopin pieces featuring throughout, always as an essential component of, rather than at the expense of, the drama. The music keeps at bay and presents a romantic alternative to Claire's present prospect: her marriage to the local greengrocer, a man old enough to be her father. As Harry White puts it, "The music of Chopin as an image of the elusive past in the subsequently disturbing present is a resource vital to the dramatic and theatrical efficacy of *Aristocrats*."[9]

The music of Chopin, the drama of Chekhov and Pirandello – Friel is here making conscious and astute use of a range of internationally renowned artists. But he is at the same time digging deeper into the local territory which is to remain from here on out his preserve, extending his intimate articulation of the lives of a few Ballybeg families. As his concerns grow more wide-ranging, his focus on the local grows more intense.

NOTES

1. Brian Friel, *Living Quarters*, in *Plays One* (London and Boston: Faber and Faber, 1996), p. 171. All future references to the play are to this edition and will be incorporated in the text.
2. Thomas Kilroy, in his 1981 version of Chekhov's *The Seagull*, transposed characters and setting from Russia to late nineteenth-century Ireland.
3. Brian Friel, *Aristocrats*, in *Plays One*, p. 277. All future references to the play are to this edition and will be incorporated in the text.
4. On the implications of the absence of the conflict in the North from *Living Quarters*, see Conor McCarthy, "Brian Friel: Politics, Authority and Geography," in *Modernisation: Crisis and Culture in Ireland 1962–1992* (Dublin: Four Courts Press, 2000), pp. 61–66.
5. Declan Kiberd, "Fathers and Sons: Irish-Style," in Michael Kenneally (ed.), *Irish Literature and Culture* (Gerrards Cross: Colin Smythe, 1992), p. 132.
6. Richard Allen Cave, "'After Hippolytus': Irish Versions of Phaedra's Story," in Marianne McDonald and J. Michael Walton (eds.), *Amid Our Troubles: Irish Versions of Greek Tragedy* (London: Methuen, 2002), p. 104.
7. Charles McGlinchey, *The Last of the Name*, ed. and introduced Brian Friel (Belfast and Dover, NH: The Blackstaff Press, 1986), p. 2.
8. Brian Friel, "Music," in Christopher Murray (ed.), *Brian Friel: Essays, Diaries, Interviews: 1964–1999* (London and New York: Faber and Faber, 1999), p. 177.
9. Harry White, "Brian Friel, Thomas Murphy and the Use of Music in Contemporary Irish Drama," *Modern Drama* 33:4 (1990), p. 557.

6

NICHOLAS GRENE

Five ways of looking at *Faith Healer*

One of the measures of a great work of the imagination is not just its openness to several different interpretations, but the unexplained residuum that it leaves after any and every interpretation. *Faith Healer* is a dramatic enactment of the fictions of memory; it is a portrait of the artist as charlatan/miracle worker; it is a parable of Irish exile and return; it is a secular theatrical recreation of religious rites: all true, or at least valid, illuminating readings. Yet watch or read the play once again, and something within the experience continues to elude any of these constructions of its meaning. The formal closure of Frank Hardy's final monologue, as he moves to leave the stage and face the death that has already taken place, does not yield itself to such explanation. Instead it enforces belief in what can be acted out but not fully understood.

Contested narratives

One story, three storytellers, each with their own way of recalling the past they have shared. On the surface *Faith Healer* looks like the sort of fiction where different narratives of the same events reveal the unreliability of the narrators: Faulkner's *The Sound and the Fury* has been suggested as one model; Kurosawa's film *Rashomon*, another.[1] Certainly, the four monologues that make up the play – first by Frank the traveling faith healer, then by his partner Grace, followed by his manager Teddy, and then by Frank again – do highlight the divergences between their accounts. There are significant discrepancies in the retelling of some of the principal events of their life together: the time when Grace and Frank were living in a converted byre in Norfolk, the miraculous cure of ten disabled people in Llanbethian in Wales, the baby stillborn in Kinlochbervie, Scotland, and the terminal encounter with the wedding guests in Ballybeg, County Donegal. The play puts up to an audience the puzzle of who is telling the truth, or what the individual distortions of the story may reveal about the characters.

There are simple cases that are evidently undecidable, like the choice of Jerome Kern's song "The Way You Look Tonight" as the music to introduce Frank's "performance." Frank maintains it was Teddy who insisted on it: "I fought with him about it dozens of times and finally gave in to him"; Grace says it was Frank: "I begged Frank to get something else, anything else. But he wouldn't"; and Teddy confides in us that "it was Gracie insisted on that for our theme music."[2] These are the sort of details where it is easy to believe that each person is misremembering in his or her own way. Again it is impossible to judge between the rival accounts of the crisis in Frank and Grace's relationship in Norfolk (an incident Teddy apparently did not witness). For Grace it was the occasion when she summoned the resolution to leave Frank, going back home to her father the judge in Ireland, only to be so repelled by his unforgiving attitude that she returned defiantly to her "mountebank" husband (346–349). In Frank's version this long and plausible description by Grace of leaving him never happened; instead what is recalled is a threat of suicide if *he* ever left *her*. There is no way of knowing who is telling the truth, though Frank's version is tragically fulfilled when Grace does kill herself after he has left her by dying. On the night in Llanbethian, a story Grace does not relate, there is not much difference between Frank and Teddy's versions. This, moreover, is the only event for which there is documentary evidence, the "clipping from the *West Glamorgan Chronicle*," which Frank carries round with him for so many years (370). Significantly, though, Frank only remembers his celebrations with Grace afterwards; he does not recall, as Teddy does, that they left the luckless manager behind while they went on a four-day spree in which they spent all the money they had been given as a reward for Frank's miracle-working.

The real drama of the play begins with Grace's account of Kinlochbervie: "Kinlochbervie's where the baby's buried" (344). In Frank's first monologue, he told us, "we were in the north of Scotland when I got word that my mother had had a heart attack. In a village called Kinlochbervie, in Sutherland, about as far north as you can go in Scotland." At the time there is no reason for an audience to doubt him; it is a circumstantial account of a set of events which he recalls with authenticating topographical detail: "a picturesque little place, very quiet, very beautiful, looking across to the Isle of Lewis in the Outer Hebrides" (337). When Grace remembers what is evidently the same place on the same occasion, but tells it as the story of her stillborn baby, we realize one of them must be lying. What is dramatic here, in a play that early reviewers criticized for its lack of drama, is the presence on stage of conflicting witnesses, each of whom gives testimony alone in the witness box unaware of the others' evidence. An audience is confronted with each one telling his or her version with apparently complete sincerity and conviction, and must struggle to discriminate between truth and false-hood. This is no juridical process of collating the several variant views and deducing likelihoods. We must judge not just the stories but the storytellers and the way they address us: Frank with his professional charm, his engag-ing performer's authority; Grace who has the compulsive confessionalism of a person in breakdown; and Teddy, the confidential buttonholer in the pub, full of digressive anecdote and personal reminiscence. While each one is onstage, he or she creates an immediate reality, which is then completely effaced by the appearance of the next monologuist. The drama builds in the clash of these irreconcilable impressions.

On Kinlochbervie, we do have to apply one of the basic principles of evidence, the superiority of two witnesses against one. Both Grace and Teddy describe the birth of the baby; what is more, Teddy says that Frank willfully absented himself from the delivery and pretended it had not happened, and Grace says that "he never talked about it afterwards" (345). We are bound to reach the conclusion that Grace and Teddy are telling the truth, and that Frank (for whatever reason) has deliberately suppressed the fact of his child's birth and death at Kinlochbervie. Yet even here, Grace and Teddy do not tell the same truth. For Grace the aftermath of the birth was a moment of shared grief between herself and Frank, when he "made a wooden cross to mark the grave and painted it white and wrote across it *Infant Child of Francis and Grace Hardy*" (344). But Teddy makes himself the protagonist in Frank's absence; it was he who had to support Grace through the birth, he who had to make the grave for the dead baby and put up the cross. It is characteristic of their different temperaments that Teddy is hopeful the cross is still there, Grace convinced that it must be "gone by now" (344). Each recasts the sad story as they want to remember it: for Grace it is an exceptionally dignified memory of togetherness with Frank; in Teddy's account, it provides an occasion for him to take Frank's place with Grace as the person on whom she has to depend emotionally.

For each of us, the magnetic field of the self makes for reconfigurations of memory. But Frank's falsifications are of a different order. We see this most strikingly in the case of Grace's name, origin, and marital status. It is Frank who first introduces her: "And there was Grace, my mistress. A Yorkshire woman. [. . .] Grace Dodsmith from Scarborough – or was it Knaresborough?" (335). Even the uncertainty about which of the two Yorkshire towns she comes from makes this sound the more convincing. Grace's monologue comprehensively undoes this set of apparent facts:

One of his mean tricks was to humiliate me by always changing my surname. It became Dodsmith or Elliott or O'Connell or McPherson [. . .] and I came from Yorkshire or Kerry or London or Scarborough or Belfast [. . .] and we weren't married – I was his mistress [. . .]   (345)

In this case there will once again be Teddy's evidence to support Grace against Frank: they *were* married; she *was* Irish, not English. But what is significant here is that Frank's introduction of Grace as his mistress from Yorkshire is revealed as typical of a generic habit of changing her identity, not just a one-off lie. And this makes us realize that Frank is not like the other two, or like any of the rest of us for that matter – someone inclined to misremember the past; he is a compulsive, even a professional maker of fictions.

Artist or performer

Like many writers, Friel resists endorsing interpretations of his work. But in press interviews he did accept the widely canvassed view that the faith healer is a version of the artist: "It was some kind of a metaphor for the art, the craft of writing [. . .]. And the great confusion we all have about it, those of us who are involved in it. How honourable and how dishonourable it can be. And it's also a pursuit that, of necessity, has to be very introspective, and as a consequence it leads to great selfishness."[3] *Faith Healer* dramatizes both the psychology of the writer and the emotional consequences for those around him. Grace gropes to try to account for why Frank should have so constantly and cruelly denied her real identity: "it was some compulsion he had to adjust, to refashion, to re-create everything around him." The people he cured, too, she suggests, were "real enough but not real as persons, real as fictions, his fictions, extensions of himself that came into being only because of him." It was as if, she concludes, "he kept remaking people according to some private standard of excellence of his own [. . .]. But I'm sure it was always an excellence, a perfection, that was the cause of his restlessness and the focus of it" (345–346).

There is corroboration for this in Frank's first monologue, when he speaks of the effect on himself of the rare occasions when miracles did take place and he succeeded in healing the sick: "I knew that for those few hours I had become whole in myself, and perfect in myself" (333). For both creator and created, the process of imagination is conceived as an ideal refashioning of what is otherwise incomplete and imperfect, Sidney's neoclassical concept that Nature's "world is brazen, the poets only deliver a golden."[4] The emphasis for much of the play, however, is on a more Romantic concept of the artist, doomed always to doubt his own gift. What constantly undermines the faith healer and drives him to torment and destroy himself and those nearest to him is the uncertainty as to what he is and what he does: "*Am I endowed with a unique and awesome gift?*" or, on the other hand, "*Am I a con man?*" (333). The artist, as Friel conceives him in the figure of Frank Hardy, lives always on this sickening seesaw between messianic arrogance and self-abasing cynicism.

What sort of an artist is a faith healer? Though it is easy to see the connection between Frank's mythomania and the writer's compulsive creativity, in other respects the analogy is a blurred one. Is he intended to be seen as a creative artist or a performer? Teddy's comically comprehensive definition of "great artists," taking in Fred Astaire, Laurence Olivier, and Rob Roy the Whistling Whippet, only compounds the confusion. Teddy is talking about show-business *artistes* whose success, according to his formula, depends on a combination of talent, ambition, and a complete lack of brains. What fatally handicapped Frank Hardy, Teddy maintains, was his brain power: "what did they do for him, I ask you, all those bloody brains? They bloody castrated him" (357). This sort of capacity for self-reflective self-doubt destroys the confidence of the performer. But is it equally disabling for the writer or a necessary part of his creativity? "The faith healer is both artist and failed artist," wrote Richard Eder in his *New York Times* review of the play; "Mr Friel makes the two inseparable."[5] The artist must always lie open to the fear of failure. Arguably, in fact, Teddy's diagnosis of what is wrong with Frank as a performer, his self-destructive introspection, is exactly what makes him a figure for the creative writer.

The alternative interpretations available for *Faith Healer* work rather like the several monologues within the play itself. Each one seems convincing until you hear the next, and then there appear irreconcilable inconsistencies between them. The play may look at first like a dramatization of the distortions of memory, each unreliable narrator reshaping the past to suit his or her emotional needs. But then the misrepresentations of Frank are of such a different order they demand another sort of explanation. The faith healer is, by Friel's own admission, some sort of version of the writer, exploring the artist's need to reshape the world, his restless anxiety, and the painful consequences for himself and his loved ones. That still leaves unanswered questions about the other participants in faith healing, those who suffer and are or are not healed. Are they the creatures of the writer's imagination, or his audience? Is writing therapeutic for the writer only, or can it work to cure its readership of their ills? And then there is the matter of Frank's Irishness. We hear again and again of all the Welsh and Scottish villages where Frank,

Grace, and Teddy toured in their van, the little halls where the faith healer "performed." The action builds to the final confrontation in which Frank is to die in Ballybeg. The pattern of exile and return is crucial to the dramatic structure and has to be accounted for in any analysis of the play's meaning.

Exile and return

On the last day of August we crossed from Stranraer to Larne and drove through the night to County Donegal. And there we got lodgings in a pub, a lounge bar, really, outside a village called Ballybeg, not far from Donegal Town. (338)

This description of the journey to Ballybeg is repeated in identical words by all three monologuists. The exact repetition is a measure of the importance of the event around which all the narratives circle. They, of course, agree about nothing else in their evocations of the night in the Ballybeg pub that followed, nor yet on whose decision it was to go. It's the usual case of pass the blame: Frank makes out it was Teddy's proposal to which he reluctantly agreed; Grace says it was Frank; Teddy says nothing either way. Equally, Grace and Frank give different versions of how they got involved with the group of wedding guests. In Frank's memory, the man called Donal suddenly challenged him to cure his crooked finger. Grace places the initiative with Frank, in approaching the young men in the first place, in theatrically asserting his capacity to heal the finger. Frank presents himself as a victim of events he could not control, Grace sees him as acting recklessly and provocatively. Teddy, by all accounts, including his own, is out of it, happily unaware of what is about to take place.

For Frank, and we have to assume for Grace, in spite of Frank's denials that she is Irish, Ballybeg is a fatal homecoming. For years they had confined their tours to Wales and Scotland. "Seldom England," Frank tells us in his first monologue, "because Teddy and Gracie were English and they believed, God help them, that the Celtic temperament was more receptive to us. And never Ireland because of me—" (332). Frank breaks off without explaining why Ireland was out for him, but the audience is conditioned to expect that returning there will be disastrous. The theme of the tragic homecoming goes back a long way in Friel and evidently haunts his imagination. In one of his first staged plays, *The Blind Mice* (1963), an Irish priest escaped from Communist imprisonment is treated to a hero's welcome home until it is discovered that he has renounced his faith.[6] It is a motif that was to be effectively reused with Father Jack in *Dancing at Lughnasa*. The pattern of action in *Living Quarters* is again analogous, the triumphant return to

Ballybeg of the military hero Frank Butler which ends in his suicide. In exile there is safety; return to Ireland brings danger or death.

The ending of *Faith Healer* must be seen in relation to this imaginative preoccupation. Seamus Deane puts it with characteristic clarity: the play "shows a man creating his own death by coming home out of exile."[7] But what does this signify? For Ulf Dantanus, Frank "becomes the exiled Irish artist who, when he loses touch with his gift, returns home in search of restoration. What he finds, however, is only an occasion for self-sacrifice."[8] The idea of the Irish writer who must go into exile in order to write success-fully has been a commonplace since the time of Joyce and George Moore; Ireland, claimed Moore, in *Hail and Farewell*, was "a country to which it was fatal to return."[9] Associated with this trope in Joyce and in Yeats is the figure of Parnell, the Irish leader rejected and persecuted by the people to whom he devoted his life. On the subject Yeats was fond of quoting Goethe: "The Irish always seem to me like a pack of hounds dragging down some noble stag."[10] Frank Hardy, beaten to death by the friends of the paralyzed McGarvey whom he has failed to cure in the Ballybeg pub, becomes the type of the despised and rejected Irish artist crucified by his own people.

Maybe. But there is surely something rather paranoid and hysterical about such a reading. Whatever Yeats and Joyce's problems with Irish readers and publishers, whatever the problems of mid-twentieth-century Irish writers with a repressive censorship, there is nothing in Friel's personal experience to connect him with this pattern of alienation. In terms of residence, few Irish writers have been more loyal to their own country. Apart from his famous three months in 1963 as an observer at Tyrone Guthrie's theatre in Minneapolis, Friel never seems to have spent any extended period outside Ireland. Allowing for the occasional ups and downs of any career, his work has been consistently admired and respected both in the North of Ireland and in the Republic. Indeed, in a number of cases plays of his that have failed abroad have succeeded at home, the most obvious example being *Faith Healer* itself. A disaster when first produced on Broadway in 1979, in spite of what was apparently a fine performance by James Mason in the central role, it was a triumph for actor Donal McCann and director Joe Dowling in the Abbey Theatre the following year. Of course it is naive to think it necessary thus literally to disassociate the dramatic character Frank Hardy from his creator Brian Friel. No one imagines that, in the Ballybeg death of the faith healer, Friel is dramatizing his reception at the hands of Irish audiences and critics. But it is another case of the mismatch of two ways of reading *Faith Healer*. Yes, the play does explore the psychology of the artist, to some extent that of the writer himself; yes, the pattern of exile and disastrous return to Ireland is fundamental to the drama. Put that hermeneutic two and two together, however, and the result is an impossible five. The faith healer's self-destructive, self-sacrificial death has to be read another way.

Rituals

> The kirks or meeting-houses or schools – all identical, all derelict. Maybe in a corner a withered sheaf of wheat from a harvest thanksgiving of years ago or a fragment of a Christmas decoration across a window – relicts of abandoned rituals. (332)

This evocation of the kind of venue where Frank conducted his faith healing, coming as it does very near the start of the play, might not have been noticed by the first audiences of *Faith Healer*. Equally, the description of the drinking session of Frank and his new friends the wedding guests, partying after the departure of the newly married couple, might not have seemed more than mood-building:

> Toasts to the departed groom and his prowess. To the bride and her fertility. To the rich harvest – the corn, the wheat, the barley. Toasts to all Septembers and all harvests and to all things ripe and eager for the reaper. A Dionysian night. A Bacchanalian night. A frenzied, excessive Irish night when ritual was consciously and relentlessly debauched. (340)

But retrospectively, after *Dancing at Lughnasa* and *Wonderful Tennessee*, these two passages in *Faith Healer* appear heavy with meaning. The references to harvest are illuminated by Michael's exposition in *Dancing at Lughnasa*: "in the old days August the First was *Lá Lughnasa*, the feast day of the pagan god, Lugh; and the days and weeks of harvesting that followed were called the Festival of Lughnasa."[11] It may even be that the date of the faith-healing party's arrival in Ballybeg is significant: they cross from Larne to Stranraer on "the last day of August." In *Dancing at Lughnasa*, there are dark rumors of what goes on in "the back hills" at the time of the Festival of Lughnasa, what the pious Kate denounces as the "pagan practices" that have endangered the life of the Sweeney boy. In *Wonderful Tennessee* we hear the story of a young man ritually killed in this same Donegal hinterland at the time of the 1932 Eucharistic Congress in Dublin. The comparative religionist connections Friel makes in the two later plays between pagan and Christian rites, the seasonal festivities of harvest and the archetypal pattern of the god who must die in autumn to be reborn in the spring, alert us to a similar thematic substructure in *Faith Healer*.

In relation to ritual George Hughes traces the influence of Friel's mentor Tyrone Guthrie. Summarizing an essay of Guthrie's called "Theatre as

Ritual," Hughes comments that "Friel like Guthrie has assumed that a plum-pudding of available rites, ancient and modern, can be mixed into a new drama."[12] Margaret Strain, drawing on Celtic and Christian traditions of spirituality, has a much more positive interpretation of Frank's last line: "rather than a declaration of resignation, 'renouncing chance' becomes an affirmation of the sacred and the salvific."[13] Friel, like Synge before him, sees in Irish Christian culture a pagan underlay of practice and belief. The question for the interpretation of *Faith Healer* is how he sees the survival of "relicts of abandoned rituals" in the modern period.

The word "debauched" may be some sort of clue. Frank and his fellow Ballybeg drinkers may be mimicking Dionysian fertility rites, but if so it can only be as a latter-day travesty. The epithets – "A Dionysian night. A Bacchanalian night" – are used in ironic hyperbole. There is a similar sense of the grotesque in the stage description of the sisters' famous dance in the first act of *Dancing at Lughnasa*: "*With this too loud music, this pounding beat, this shouting – calling – singing, this parodic reel, there is a sense of order being consciously subverted, of the women consciously and crudely caricaturing themselves, indeed of near-hysteria being induced*" (37). These are Euripides' *Bacchae* as the order-loving King Pentheus might have seen them. But Friel makes it clear from the contrast with Father Jack's positively rhapsodic vision of African festive dancing that it is only within a modern Christian ethos that the survivals of this sort of pagan rite degenerate into caricature. When the boy Michael's kites are finally seen in the play's last tableau, "*[o]n each kite is painted a crude, cruel, grinning face, primitively drawn, garishly painted*" (106).

In fact, it could be argued that *Faith Healer* represents a modern time that is all but post-Christian. Belief lives on, if at all, in the Celtic fringes, remote villages in Scotland and Wales. It is not, as conceived by the leaders of the Literary Revival, an idealized Celtic Twilight but a grubby half-world of faith healing, a last refuge of the irrational among disbelievers. Those who came to Frank Hardy, he tells us, "were a despairing people" (336–337). For such a people who no longer have any assured structures of belief, evidence of the supernatural can only come as a terror: "Because occasionally, just occasionally, the miracle would happen. And then – panic – panic – panic! Their ripping apart! The explosion of their careful calculations! The sudden flooding of dreadful, hopeless hope!" (337). It is, we may conjecture, because Frank arouses in the wedding guests this "dreadful, hopeless hope" that they feel driven to tear him apart when he fails to satisfy it. The return of repressed ritual in a modern context brings a savage destructiveness in revenge for lost belief.

And yet Friel insists that "Ritual is part of all drama. Drama without ritual is poetry without rhythm – hence not poetry, not drama. This is not to say that ritual is an 'attribute' of drama: it is the essence of drama. Drama is a RITE, and always religious in the purest sense."[14] If this is the case, then *Faith Healer* is not about ritual, whether Christian or pagan; it is not a dramatization of the violent consequences of suppressed belief in a secular society. It is rather itself a theatrical ritual enacted for its audience. What can we say of the experience of such a ritual that is other than a summary of the several interpretations that may be made of it?

Tragic closure

Friel is in many ways a very austere dramatist, suspicious of the showier and more spectacular effects of theatre. At the time of its composition *Faith Healer* was his most extreme experiment in dramatic minimalism: an almost completely bare stage; four monologues from three characters who never communicate with one another – two of whom, it transpires, are already dead. The play's form forces an audience to concentrate on language, on listening to Frank, Grace, and Teddy, watching them struggle to express themselves, interpreting not only what they say but the whole way each one of them addresses us. But it also moves language towards music, for Friel the very purest form of communication. It is with a playwright's envy that Friel has the composer Janáček declare in *Performances*: "The people who huckster in words merely report on feeling. We *speak* feeling."[15] In *Faith Healer*, he tries to go beyond a report on feeling in the musical form and structure of the play.

This is most obvious in the use of the recited place names, the mantra that Frank Hardy uses to prepare himself for a performance, and which act as incantatory overture to the play itself, heard out of the darkness: "Aberarder, Aberayron,/Llangranog, Llangurig [. . .]" (331–332). The unfamiliar names, the symmetrical rhythmic cadences, the alternation of pairs of "Llan-" and "Aber-" prefixes, make this a mesmeric spell in sound. When Grace begins her monologue, it is with an identical recitation, only varied by one line: "Penllech, Pencader" (341). The principle of repetition and variation is established here. Grace and Frank alone speak these names; it is a way of expressing the relationship between them across their separated monologues. In both of their litanies, the key name of Kinlochbervie comes to return insistently, breaking the set pattern. And it is Grace's last repetition, symptomatic of her imminent collapse, that Frank replicates exactly word for word at the opening of his final monologue:

Aberarder, Kinlochbervie,
Aberayron, Kinlochbervie,
Invergordon, Kinlochbervie . . . in Sutherland, in the north of Scotland . . .

(353, 370)

The drama of *Faith Healer* is enacted not through direct communication but by the counterpointing of repeated and varied phrases between the characters. It is not coincidental that Friel uses the analogy between drama and poetry: "Drama without ritual is poetry without rhythm – hence not poetry, not drama." At the structural level also, the four speeches are like the four movements of a string quartet, with Teddy's comic allegro a deliberate contrast to the more somber tempi of Frank and Grace. The play involves little of the forward linear movement of plot: we know from as early as Grace's monologue that Frank is dead, killed by the wedding guests in Ballybeg; it hardly comes as a surprise to learn from Teddy that Grace has killed herself. What Frank's final monologue offers is not so much the sense of narrative ending but the spatial closure we look for in the completion of a piece of music. It is also the formal closure of tragedy.

Less means more in this minimalist theatre. What we see onstage in Frank's first speech are three rows of empty chairs and a tatty old banner, synecdochal signs of all those past performances. In the final monologue, even this is stripped away and there is just one chair "*across which lies Frank's coat exactly as he left it in Part One*" (370). The taking off of the coat in Part One was a casual gesture, part of his informal self-introductory getting-to-know-you relationship with the audience. Just the one remaining chair with the coat upon it in Part Four is theatrically spotlit with significance. At a key moment in his climactic narration of the meeting with the wedding guests, "*He puts on the hat and overcoat and buttons it slowly*" (374). This is drama as ritual, the moment at which the tragic hero knowingly, willingly, accepts his destiny.

The final sequence of Frank's speech, as he describes and enacts for us his movement towards the four men who are going to kill him out in the yard, is one of the most mysterious passages in Friel's drama:

And as I walked I became possessed of a strange and trembling intimation: that the whole corporeal world – the cobbles, the trees, the sky, those four malign implements – somehow they had shed their physical reality and had become mere imaginings, and that in all existence there was only myself and the wedding guests. And that intimation in turn gave way to a stronger sense: that even we had ceased to be physical and existed only in spirit, only in the need we had for each other.

(He takes off his hat as if he were entering a church and holds it at his chest. He is both awed and elated. As he speaks the remaining lines he moves very slowly down stage.)

And as I moved across that yard towards them and offered myself to them, then for the first time I had a simple and genuine sense of home-coming. Then for the first time there was no atrophying terror; and the maddening questions were silent.

At long last I was renouncing chance. (375–376)

This is open to multiple interpretation. What makes it so deeply satisfying in the theatre, however, is the way it incorporates and brings to resolution the many themes that the play has enunciated: the anxiety of the faith healer about his gift; the relationship between healer and healed, exile and home-coming. This fictional re-creation of a remembered event creates its own sovereignty as theatrical truth.

NOTES

1. See Declan Kiberd, "Brian Friel's *Faith Healer*," in William Kerwin (ed.), *Brian Friel: A Casebook* (New York and London: Garland Press, 1997), pp. 211–225, for the connections with Faulkner; parallels with *Rashomon* were detected in a review of the first production by T. E. Kalem, *Time*, 16 April 1979, p. 94, quoted in Paul N. Robinson, "Brian Friel's *Faith Healer*: An Irishman Comes Back Home," in Wolfgang Zach and Heinz Kosok (eds.), *Literary Interrelations: Ireland, England and the World vol. III, National Images and Stereotypes* (Tübingen: Gunter Narr Verlag, 1987), pp. 223–227.

2. Brian Friel, *Faith Healer*, in *Plays One* (London and Boston: Faber and Faber, 1996), pp. 336, 350, 354. All quotations from the play are taken from this edition and will be incorporated in the text.

3. Brian Friel, "In Interview with Fintan O'Toole (1982)," in Christopher Murray (ed.), *Brian Friel: Essays, Diaries, Interviews: 1964–1999* (London and New York: Faber and Faber, 1999), p. 111.

4. Philip Sidney, *An Apology for Poetry*, in D. J. Enright and Ernst de Chickera (eds.), *English Critical Texts* (Oxford: Oxford University Press, 1962), p. 8.

5. Richard Eder, "Drama: Friel's 'Faith Healer,'" *New York Times*, 6 April 1979, Section 3,1, quoted in Robinson, "Brian Friel's *Faith Healer*," p. 224.

6. See George O'Brien, *Brian Friel* (Dublin: Gill and Macmillan, 1989), pp. 39–41.

7. Seamus Deane, "Brian Friel: The Double Stage," in *Celtic Revivals* (London and Boston: Faber and Faber, 1985), p. 173.

8. Ulf Dantanus, *Brian Friel: A Study* (London and Boston: Faber and Faber, 1988), p. 174.

9. George Moore, *Hail and Farewell: Vale* (London: Heinemann, 1914), p. 191.

10. W. B. Yeats, *Autobiographies* (London: Macmillan, 1955), p. 483.

11. Brian Friel, *Dancing at Lughnasa*, in *Plays Two* (London: Faber and Faber, 1999), p. 7. All further quotations are taken from this edition and will be incorporated in the text.

12. George Hughes, "Ghosts and Ritual in Brian Friel's *Faith Healer*," *Irish University Review* 24:2 (1994), p. 181.
13. Margaret M. Strain, "'Renouncing Chance': Salvation and the Sacred in Brian Friel's *Faith Healer*," *Renascence* 57:1 (2004), p. 81.
14. Quoted in Dantanus, *Brian Friel*, p. 87.
15. Brian Friel, *Performances* (London: Faber and Faber, 2005), p. 25.

7

MARTINE PELLETIER

Translations, the Field Day debate and the re-imagining of Irish identity

Translations occupies a place apart, both among Brian Friel's dramatic works and in the history of theatre in Ireland. It is Friel's best-known play – a title it may now have to share with *Dancing at Lughnasa*. If it is true that the fate of every play is its first production, then the specific circumstances surrounding the opening night of *Translations* on 23 September 1980 deserve some discussion. Brian Friel had agreed to team up with Belfast-born actor Stephen Rea in order to set up a new Derry-based theatre company, christened Field Day (a phonetic pun on the two names, but also a phrase with both military and festive connotations), with the aim of touring Ireland, North and South. Some funding had been secured from both the Northern Irish and the Irish arts councils, eager to support community theatre and a touring company. The civic authorities in Derry had allowed the Guildhall, long a symbol of Unionist domination in a city notorious for its gerrymandering, to be turned into a theatre since this was seen as a great occasion, a source of pride for the local population and their representatives. The first night proved a great success and *Translations* went on to triumph at the Dublin Theatre Festival, toured a number of venues in Ireland, and transferred to London. Since then, *Translations* has been widely hailed as a masterpiece, a watershed in Irish theatre, has enjoyed countless revivals, has toured extensively – in 2001, for example, the Abbey took *Translations* to the US but also to France and Germany as well as Barcelona, Prague, and Budapest – and has been translated into several languages. Beyond its stage success, *Translations* has proved of abiding interest to academics and intellectuals in Ireland and abroad.

What kind of play could arouse such sustained critical interest and retain its popular appeal? What deep chord did and does *Translations* strike? The play is set in a Donegal Irish-speaking community in 1833, the specific location being a hedge-school in Baile Beag, the Irish "ancestor" of Ballybeg, Friel's favored fictional small town. Hedge-schools were the informal institutions that many rural Catholics attended, after the Penal Laws deprived them of the right to an education. This situation was about to change in the 1830s as the British government sought to replace such schools with National Schools, which would use English rather than Irish as the medium of instruction. Thus the play's hedge-school is a threatened space as confirmed indirectly by the schoolmaster's insistence on teaching his students Latin and Greek, encouraging a cross-cultural conversation exclusively with dead civilizations. The Irish language is also under a different attack as the British Army is engaged in mapping the country. This process involves the translation of every Irish place name into an English equivalent, either through direct translation or through transliteration, retaining either the meaning of the name or trying to approximate its phonetics within a different linguistic system.

Hugh O'Donnell, the hedge-school master, his son Manus and their pupils – Maire, Sarah, Doalty and Bridget, Jimmy Jack – meet the two English officers, Lancey and Yolland, in charge of the Survey for the Baile Beag area. The two Englishmen are accompanied by a civilian interpreter, who turns out to be none other than Hugh's younger son Owen, who had gone to Dublin to seek his fortune. Behind the initial, fragile goodwill of this first encounter between the soldiers and the representatives of the local community lurk a number of dark shadows: Manus is instantly suspicious of his brother's admittedly somewhat loose translation of Lancey's speech on the Survey; he does not conceal his indignation that Owen should be known to his English companions as "Roland," an abdication of his Irish identity that strikes Manus as ominous, almost a betrayal. Captain Lancey's condescending, patronizing attitude is a clear indication that the British Empire whom he serves faithfully has little interest in the local Gaelic culture. By contrast, Yolland's naive enthusiasm for all things Irish, his desire to learn the language, his hope that their presence will not be "too crude an intrusion" on the lives of the locals, testify to his romantic temperament and his great sensitivity.[1]

As the play unfolds, the military nature of the operation, the symbolic and cultural consequences attendant upon the eradication of the Irish place names – "an eviction of sorts" (420) – dawn upon Yolland first, then upon Owen. Yolland falls in love with Maire – the local girl whom Manus was hoping to marry – and finds his feelings reciprocated; but this love is doomed to fail as Yolland mysteriously disappears, no doubt abducted and killed. Owen, who had mistakenly thought he could mediate between the two communities, is forced to translate Lancey's threats of violent retaliation unless Yolland is found. This time, his translation no longer seeks to conceal the brutal violence that lies behind the official jargon as the previously metaphorical eviction becomes literal. Sarah, one of the pupils who had been coaxed by Manus into speaking her name, reverts to silence upon being questioned by Lancey, a scene that suggests a possible symbolic reading of this character as Ireland, struck dumb through fear and the imposition of English. Maire, distracted by grief, pleads with Hugh to be taught English as emigration to America now beckons. Hugh picks up the Name-Book in which the work of Owen and Yolland has been recorded and admonishes his son that they must now learn to accept these new names, make them their new home. Owen remains deaf to his father's advice, however, and opts to join the forces of resistance against the English, exiting to find the Donnelly twins, those offstage characters the audience has understood to be responsible for Yolland's disappearance. As the curtain falls, Maire is trying to draw the map of Norfolk Yolland had drawn for her, while Hugh vainly seeks to remember and recite the opening lines of Virgil's *Aeneid*, the epic tale of Carthage's destruction and Rome's triumph.

For his first foray into the genre of the history play, Friel drew on a wide range of sources and contemporary documents – in particular, John Andrews' *A Paper Landscape* (1975), Thomas Colby's memoir (1837), John O'Donovan's letters, Patrick Dowling's *The Hedge-Schools of Ireland* (1935), as well as George Steiner's *After Babel* (1975). Friel had been reading Steiner's influential book on the history and theory of translation while working on a version of Chekhov's *Three Sisters* in an idiom that would be recognizably Irish and would give a new relevance to this Russian classic. Out of such disparate materials Friel constructed his elegant, multilayered play. The playwright's stroke of genius is the theatrical conceit he invented in order to solve the linguistic conundrum at the heart of the play. Baile Beag in 1833 would have been an Irish-speaking community, though some characters would also have been fluent in English. Yet the language the audience hears onstage throughout is English, except of course when it comes to the place names or some Latin and Greek words and quotations. Since the focus of the play is very much on language, its role in shaping and expressing personal and collective identity, the very fact that English onstage represents two separate languages – the Irish we are asked to imagine and the English which is now the "natural vehicle" for a play on an Irish stage – is immensely ironic and hugely significant.

Translations dramatizes this key transitional moment when Irish gave way to English, when a culture was forced to translate itself into a different linguistic landscape. The Ordnance Survey map acts as a powerful metaphor of the transformation of this linguistic and cultural environment. Irish loses the ability to describe what is, and becomes, like Latin and Greek, a language that is only capable of saying what used to be. This shift from one language to another is presented in the play as the inevitable result of a number of pressures, some external, others internal. It was indeed London and the colonial authorities that set up National Schools and commissioned the Ordnance Survey, but it was Daniel O'Connell, the champion of Catholic Emancipation, who said that "the old language is a barrier to modern progress" (400), as Maire points out in her attempt to convince Hugh that it is English they now need. English had already become the language of trade, of politics, of modernity. Soon, the Great Famine of the 1840s would wipe out a large proportion of Irish speakers and force countless others to emigrate to English-speaking areas. Yet adopting English does not mean that the language spoken in Ireland will carry the same wealth of association, the same connotations, the same emotional resonances as in England. Again, *Translations* demonstrates, through the conceit of English standing in for Irish, that "once Anglicization is achieved, the Irish and English, instead of speaking a truly identical tongue, will be divided most treacherously by a common language."[2] Contemporary Irish audiences must also confront their own lack of proficiency in Irish, their historical responsibility in having accepted English as the everyday language of the Republic as well as the extent to which they have succeeded in making Irish-English their own distinctive tongue.

Translations problematizes the relationship between language and identity, drawing on Steiner's insights into the nature of translation while remaining alert to the central irony that the supposed first official language, Irish, is only present residually. All through *Translations* there are hesitations between a positivist view of language – embodied by Lancey, and partly by Owen, for whom translation, mediation between one linguistic system and another, is quite possible and almost straightforward – and a more poetic or ontological view, derived in part from Martin Heidegger. The latter view posits a deep and complex connection between language and identity, doubting the possibility of any true translation as each language possesses its own history, its own way of inhabiting and perceiving the world.[3] When Yolland objects to the translation of Irish place names into English on the ground that something he cannot quite pinpoint is being eroded, Owen rebukes him at first and Hugh warns the young Englishman, in terms borrowed from Steiner's *After Babel*, that "words are signals, counters. They are not immortal. And it can happen – to use an image you'll understand – it can happen that a civilization can be imprisoned in a linguistic contour which no longer matches the landscape of . . . fact" (419). Hugh, for all his attachment to the past and avowed contempt for the modern, material world of trade and commerce, seems increasingly aware of the disjunction between the rich language and culture of Gaelic Ireland, and the sad reality of his impoverished community, surviving on a diet of milk, soda bread and potatoes. From the

vantage point of the twentieth century, the playwright also points to a possible reading: Gaelic Ireland has become imprisoned in a distorted linguistic
landscape as a result of the subsequent mythologizing of nationalist history.
As Hugh further admonishes, "it is not the literal past, the 'facts' of history,
that shape us, but images of the past embodied in language. [. . .] We must
never cease renewing those images; because once we do, we fossilize" (445).
Brian Friel acknowledges the power of language in shaping our perception
and understanding of the past, and the potency of such images or myths,
once they have achieved cultural acceptance. But life is change, not stasis,
so myths need to be subjected to critical and imaginative scrutiny. This is
what *Translations* attempts: it offers us a sophisticated exploration of a set
of highly emotional images – the hedge-school, that beloved locus of nationalist history and folk memory; the Irish language; the military presence of
the British Empire; the impending Famine – to problematize the simple story
of linguistic dispossession with the benefit of hindsight and contemporary
linguistic theory.

In the diary he kept while writing *Translations*, Friel made several observations that betray his own ambivalence towards received images of Gaelic
Ireland: "One aspect that keeps eluding me: the wholeness, the integrity of
that Gaelic past. Maybe because I don't believe in it."[4] In Ballybeg, at the
point when the play begins, the cultural climate is a dying climate – no longer
quickened by its past, about to be plunged almost overnight into an alien
future. The strong sense of alienation attendant upon Ireland's brutal entry
into the modern world caused various critics to read the play entirely as a
lament for a lost Ireland. But averting to this traumatic transition need not
imply that the playwright wished his audiences to see it in wholly idealized,
nostalgic terms. Friel was in fact largely working against such images whilst
acknowledging their hold on the collective imagination, including his own.
Many early reviewers concentrated on the "brutal suppression of a perfect,
self-sustaining native culture" motif. For the playwright, such readings were
simplifications that missed the point, or were deliberately seeking to make a
largely political point:

> Several people commented that the opening scenes of the play were a portrait
> of some sort of idyllic, Forest of Arden life. But this is a complete illusion,
> since you have on stage the representatives of a certain community – one is
> dumb, one is lame and one is alcoholic, a physical maiming which is a public
> representation of their spiritual deprivation.[5]

Hugh's final, almost stoical, recognition that the new English place names
now make up the linguistic and cultural landscape is accompanied by an
exhortation to appropriate these new unfamiliar names, to endow them with

meaning, to make English identifiably Ireland's language. Such a challenge has been taken up as subsequent generations of Irish writers have given expression to that very discontinuity, turning the new vernacular into an adequate vehicle for creative expression, including Friel himself.

Friel felt it necessary to write his next play as an antidote to the pieties offered to *Translations*. *The Communication Cord*, performed by Field Day as their 1982 production, is also set in a cottage in Ballybeg, but the vantage point is that of the present, the early 1980s in the Republic. The characters are no longer Irish-speaking country folk but middle-class English-speaking Dubliners. Many parallels can be drawn, however, as the playwright visibly conceives the characters in *The Communication Cord* as symbolic heirs to the nineteenth-century protagonists. The restored cottage is not a home but a holiday or weekend hideaway: it belongs to the McNeillises and Jack, the son of the family and a successful barrister, uses it chiefly to carry out his numerous romantic liaisons. Jack feels no emotional commitment to the cottage and mocks the familiar and familial discourse that would suggest he must have reverence for such a place as the repository of Irish identity. Jack's friend, Tim Gallagher, a lecturer in linguistics, is eager to impress Senator Donovan, whose patronage he needs to secure a tenured post at the university, and whose daughter Susan is in love with him, though he is less sure of his feelings for her. Jack has devised a plan to enable Tim to impress Donovan, who fancies himself as an amateur antiquarian: the Donovans have been invited to stop at the cottage on their way to a dinner party and Tim will pretend to be the proud owner of this little Irish gem. This deception worries Tim, who nonetheless allows Jack to talk him into playing this seemingly harmless ploy. As the dramatic mode is comic, even farcical, everything that *could* go wrong will go wrong . . .

The emphasis is again on language but within a context in which signifier and signified run riot as the play exaggerates the arbitrary connection between word and thing. Tim's thesis on "Discourse Analysis with Particular Reference to Response Cries" foregrounds communication as dependent on a shared context, an agreed code without which chaos would ensue, echoing somewhat mischievously Steiner's key concerns with the possibility of interpersonal communication and intra-linguistic translation. Tim's theory, expounded enthusiastically for the benefit of a skeptical Jack and an indifferent Donovan, is put to a severe test in the play. In *The Communication Cord*, no identity is stable as characters pretend to be, or are mistaken for, who they are not. Each is forced to play roles while Tim and Jack turn into frantic theatre directors trying to keep one step ahead of each new twist in the plot. *Quid pro quos* and misunderstandings proliferate, chaos reigns and inanimate objects, like the door and the fireplace, seem to have a will of their own. Any tendency to mythologize language in *Translations* is ruthlessly derided as language becomes a means of concealing, lying, playing, but proves decidedly inadequate when it comes to expressing genuine feeling or emotion. The obvious butt of Friel's satire is Senator Donovan, a committed revivalist, a proponent of what Sean O'Faolain derisively called "fanciful celtophilism."[6] The Senator waxes lyrical and accumulates clichés when it comes to expressing his admiration for the cottage, this symbol of Ireland's past: "This is the touchstone. [. . .] This is the apotheosis. [. . .] I suppose all I'm really saying is that for me this is the absolute verity."[7] Seemingly unaware of the glaring inauthenticity of the cottage, the Senator insists on miming the traditional rural scene of milking and finds himself chained to one of the wooden posts, tethered irrevocably to his beloved Irish past. In his compromised situation the Senator's discourse alters radically: "This determined our first priorities! This is our native simplicity! Don't give me that shit!" (75). His previous extravagant nostalgic fervor proves to be mere rhetoric devoid of any significance. This is terrain Friel had already covered in his bleak satire *The Mundy Scheme* (1969), in which he lampooned a morally corrupt Irish political establishment all too ready to turn the west of Ireland into a graveyard in return for financial advantage. Thirteen years later, Friel's view of Irish politicians does not seem to have changed for the better.

Instead of Latin and Greek we now have German and French, through the presence of Barney the Banks, the German tourist eager to buy a genuine Irish cottage, and Evette Giroux, who works at the French Embassy in Dublin. Ireland's frame of reference, linguistic, cultural, economic and political, is no longer the classical world, nor is it imperial or post-imperial Britain, but the European Economic Community that Ireland joined in 1973 and whose funds have contributed in no small measure to Ireland's modernization of its economy and infrastructures. The restored cottage is an object of great interest, a valuable property for the German tourist, a supposedly reliable means of accessing Ireland's sacred soul for Donovan, a convenient nest for amorous encounters for Jack and Tim's unlikely meal ticket for a university post and material security – in each case, a commodity with material, not spiritual or communal value. At the play's close, Tim finally throws in the towel and stops pretending; this enables a more genuine form of communication to be established in a scene that parodies the moving love scene between Yolland and Maire in *Translations*. Tim realizes that he is still in love with his ex-girlfriend, Claire, whose presence in the cottage contributed in a major way to the confusion and mayhem. As the pair are about to kiss, leaning dangerously against the upright beam supporting the loft, they conclude that language may actually matter less than communication, that "maybe silence is the perfect discourse" (92). The play ends on the collapse of the cottage as the beam gives way, and Jack utters one of those emotional "response cries" which are the topic of Tim's thesis on linguistics: "O my God."

Though *The Communication Cord* remains a slight piece in a minor key as compared to *Translations*, it is a pity that Stephen Rea's idea to revive the two plays and do them on the same set was not taken up. Both plays offer imaginative and partly conflicting explorations of the sociocultural role of language in the historical evolution of Ireland. Instead, the corrective vision of *The Communication Cord* was soon forgotten or dismissed as disingenuous or irrelevant. Criticizing the Republic's hypocritical idealization of its rural past struck many commentators as a less dangerous exercise than confronting what Nationalists and Republicans did in the name of that ideal in the North. Meanwhile, *Translations* kept on being performed, was translated into different languages for the benefit of audiences who recognized in the play the situation of many a minority culture faced with the trauma of assimilation or integration into a majority, dominant culture.

The context provided by Field Day itself had changed since 1980. In the wake of the play's initial success, Friel and Rea had decided to set up a formal board of directors for the company, inviting four fellow Northerners – musician David Hammond, poets and academics Seamus Deane, Seamus Heaney and Tom Paulin – to join them. By 1986 the ad hoc theatre company had become a formidable intellectual enterprise, adding a series of critical pamphlets to its theatrical activities. *Translations* was therefore understood to be the foundation stone, the defining text that had set the agenda for later developments in the debate initiated by Field Day, since there was an obvious coincidence between the topics addressed in the pamphlets and the issues, linguistic, literary and cultural/historical, addressed in the play. There was a growing anxiety that these Northern intellectuals were promoting a revamped nationalism in a climate characterized by political instability in Northern Ireland. Thus, while early critical attention had been directed towards the politics of language in *Translations*, after 1985 a new and more aggressively political line of criticism developed: Friel's anachronistic portrayal of 1830s Ireland was denounced as a deliberate distortion of historical truth in a play that sought to equate nineteenth-century Donegal and 1970s Derry. A reviewer of the 1986 Belfast production of *Translations* warned prospective audiences that the play was dangerous, seductive and dishonest.[8] Literary critic Edna Longley accused it of repeating myths of dispossession and oppression instead of submitting them to critical scrutiny.

Historian Sean Connolly concluded that Friel had remained the prisoner of a particular image of the Irish past grounded in a Manichean opposition between "a wildly idealized Gaelic culture and an improbably debased and philistine English alternative."[9] While a close reading of the play makes it difficult to substantiate such views, it cannot be doubted that these hostile reactions owed much to the new context provided by the development of Field Day.

After *The Comunication Cord* and three years of unstinting commitment to the new company, Brian Friel left the stage floor to other Field Day members, whom he encouraged to write plays or to commission texts from playwrights outside the Field Day ambit. Between 1983 and 1987, Tom Paulin and Derek Mahon, Stewart Parker and Thomas Kilroy – the latter being subsequently offered a place on the board of directors – penned Field Day plays. From the outset, Field Day's commitment to touring Ireland North and South had rightly been understood as a highly political gesture. Affirming an Ireland culture beyond partition clearly marked Field Day off as a nationalist project in the eyes of many commentators. In 1985 the company published their first six pamphlets in book form. Increasingly there was a sense that the critical activity represented by the publication of the pamphlets and Seamus Deane's controversial project of producing a massive, three-volume *Field Day Anthology of Irish Writing* now occupied centerstage. By using both the page and the stage Field Day acknowledged their responsibility in shaping perceptions and generating debate, initiating a dialogue or rather a dialectic between the two mutually supportive sides of their activities. Throughout the latter part of the 1980s it could be said that Field Day set the critical agenda in Irish studies. Two related features dominate their critical writings of the period: increasing attacks against historical revisionism and the promotion of modes of analysis that view the Northern crisis as part of the legacy of a colonial situation. Postcolonial readings of Ireland's literature are now commonplace but one needs to remember that this was not always the case, as early studies of postcolonial literatures deliberately excluded Ireland from their inquiries and, in Ireland, the model offered seemed – and still seems – irrelevant or dangerous to those many historians and intellectuals who favor the revisionist mode of interpretation that has gradually superseded nationalist history. In a 1986 article entitled "We Are All Revisionists Now,"[10] historian Roy Foster expressed his satisfaction that Ireland was finally ready to cast away the dangerous nostalgia of nationalist history. Among his most vocal and articulate opponents was Field Day's Seamus Deane, who objected in particular to the preference given by many revisionist historians to the "Archipelago model," analyzing the relationship between Ireland and England in terms of a peripheral region becoming integrated into a centralizing state system, thus playing down or rejecting the colonial dimension of the Irish experience, and of the Ulster crisis. Field Day, through Deane, championed the postcolonial model, as demonstrated by the fifth series of pamphlets with the "Yeats and Decolonization" essay by Edward Said.

In that same year, 1988, *Making History* by Brian Friel opened in Derry, with Stephen Rea in the very demanding lead role. Did Friel know already that this would be his last Field Day play? *Making History* dramatizes the life of the sixteenth-century Earl of Tyrone, Hugh O'Neill, a central figure in this key period in Irish history with the fall of the Gaelic aristocracy and the subsequent accelerated plantation of Ulster. The playwright starts from Sean O'Faolain's famous 1942 biography, itself considered a revisionist text as it portrays O'Neill as a great European statesman, whose true stature has never been fully understood because of an early and continuing emphasis on the man as pious patriot and on Irish nationalism as the only relevant context.[11] O'Faolain regards the early biographical account, hagiographic in tone, by Archbishop Peter Lombard as responsible for the development of such a limiting myth. *Making History* rewrites O'Neill's history, focusing on his hybrid identity as hereditary Gaelic chief and as Earl of Tyrone, by the Grace of Her Majesty, Queen Elizabeth of England. Friel's O'Neill admits the influence of the formative years he spent in England: "I was only a raw boy at the time but I was conscious not only that new ideas and concepts were being explored and fashioned but that I was being explored and fashioned at the same time."[12] His recent marriage to Mabel Bagenal, a Protestant and the sister of the Queen's Marshal, suggests a further, very intimate, English influence. But O'Neill also knows his responsibility as a leader of his people: "I have spent my life attempting [. . .] to hold together a harassed and a confused people by trying to keep them in touch with the life they knew before they were overrun. [. . .] And at the same time I have tried to open these people to the strange new ways of Europe, to ease them into the new assessment of things" (299). This dual identity is represented linguistically and theatrically by his shift from a Tyrone to an English accent.

While part of the play dramatizes Hugh's dilemma, his reluctant decision, the defeat at Kinsale and the subsequent exile known as the Flight of the Earls, another plot line concentrates on the task Archbishop Lombard has set himself, the writing of Hugh's life for the benefit and enlightenment of future generations. The hero and the biographer, the man of action and the man of words, are in disagreement from the start, as Lombard evinces great skepticism about the value of truth in the writing of history: "If you're asking me will my story be as accurate as possible – of course it will. But are truth and falsity the proper criteria? I don't know. Maybe when the time comes my first responsibility will be to tell the best possible narrative. Isn't that what history is, a kind of story-telling?" (257). At the end of the play, exiled in Rome and mourning Mabel's death in childbirth, Hugh pleads with Lombard to tell the whole truth, to no avail since the Archbishop has his own agenda: "Think of this [book] as an act of *pietas*. Ireland is reduced as it has never been reduced before – we are talking about a colonized people on the brink of extinction. [. . .] So I am offering Gaelic Ireland [. . .] this narrative that has the elements of myth. And I'm offering them Hugh O'Neill as a national hero" (334–335). Friel's Lombard certainly does not fall into the category of the deluded historian who believes he can remain objective. He is actively constructing a narrative that, in his view, serves a superior purpose which justifies his tampering with "the truth," and the type of history-writing that dominated the post-independence period and that revisionist historians were actively challenging. It is obvious that Friel orchestrates this confrontation between O'Neill and Lombard the better to show us the relativity of all narrative records, whether historical or fictional. Against Lombard's account, Friel offers his own subjective myth of O'Neill, centered on his doomed love for the beautiful and intelligent Mabel. One could argue that the play is less a critique of revisionist historians and more a calling into question of all historical inquiry. The text he wrote for the program to the play is deliberately provocative: "When there was tension between historical 'fact' and the imperative of the fiction, I'm glad to say I kept faith with the narrative. . . . But then I remind myself that history and fiction are related and comparable forms of discourse and that an historical text is a kind of literary artifact."[13] This postmodern assertion of the constructedness of all narratives enables him to settle accounts with those historians who still believe in "objectivity," while the claim for the primacy of fiction also offers the prospect of liberation from the demands of history.

The central position of Mabel, both in the play and in O'Neill's understanding of his life, may also suggest an interpretation that would make O'Neill's objection to her exclusion from Lombard's official account almost a prophetic warning. When the *Field Day Anthology of Irish Writing* came out in 1991, the relegation of women to the margins of Irish literary history caused great outrage and led to the commissioning by Deane of a further volume to be devoted to women's writings, eventually published as two volumes in 2002. Friel took his distance from the company around 1990 and has no association with the ongoing, somewhat sporadic Field Day publications supervised by Seamus Deane. Taken together, Friel's three original Field Day plays can be seen to offer thought-provoking explorations of Irish cultural identity, a journey in three stages, starting in the nineteenth century, moving forward to the twentieth, and taking us back to 1603, charting the fortunes of an elusive, fractured identity in need of new, imaginatively sympathetic and critically challenging articulations.

NOTES

1. Brian Friel, *Translations*, in *Plays One* (London and Boston: Faber and Faber, 1996), p. 407. Subsequent references are to this edition and will be incorporated in the text.
2. Declan Kiberd, *Inventing Ireland* (London: Jonathan Cape, 1995), p. 622.
3. This reading of the linguistic dimension of *Translations* is partly based on "The Language Plays of Brian Friel," in Richard Kearney, *Transitions: Narratives in Modern Irish Culture* (Manchester: Manchester University Press, 1988); Kearney's chapter is reprinted as "Language Play: Brian Friel and Ireland's Verbal Theatre," in Willam Kerwin (ed.), *Brian Friel: A Casebook* (New York and London: Garland Press, 1997), pp. 77–116.
4. Brian Friel, "Extracts from a Sporadic Diary (1979)," in Christopher Murray (ed.), *Brian Friel: Essays, Diaries, Interviews: 1964–1999* (London and New York: Faber and Faber, 1999), p. 74.
5. Paddy Agnew, "Talking to Ourselves, An Interview with Brian Friel," *Magill*, December 1980, p. 61. Reprinted in Murray, *Brian Friel*, p. 87.
6. Sean O'Faolain, "The Stuffed Shirts," *The Bell* (June 1943), quoted in "Provincialism and Censorship 1930–65," in Seamus Deane (ed.), *The Field Day Anthology of Irish Writing*, 3 vols. (Derry: Field Day Publications, 1991), vol. III, p. 105.
7. Brian Friel, *The Communication Cord* (Oldcastle, County Meath: Gallery Press, 1989), pp. 32–33. Subsequent references will appear parenthetically in the text.
8. Lynda Henderson, "A Dangerous Translation," *Fortnight* 235 (10 March 1986), p. 24.
9. Sean Connolly, "Translating History: Brian Friel and the Irish Past," in Alan Peacock (ed.), *The Achievement of Brian Friel* (Gerrards Cross: Colin Smythe, 1993), p. 158.
10. Roy Foster, "We Are All Revisionists Now," *Irish Review* 1 (1986), p. 1.
11. Sean O'Faolain, *The Great O'Neill: A Biography of Hugh O'Neill Earl of Tyrone, 1550–1616* (Cork: Mercier Press, 1942, reprinted 1970), p. 277.
12. Brian Friel, *Making History*, in *Plays Two* (London: Faber and Faber, 1999), p. 292. Subsequent references are to this edition and will be incorporated in the text.
13. Brian Friel, Programme Note, *Making History* (1988), p. 7.

8

HELEN LOJEK

Dancing at Lughnasa and the unfinished revolution

When *Dancing at Lughnasa* premiered at Dublin's Abbey Theatre in 1990 it was the first time in ten years that Brian Friel had presented work unconnected to Derry's Field Day Theatre Company or the Troubles of Northern Ireland. This play is firmly situated within the 1930s Irish Republic and focuses on difficulties facing women struggling to realize themselves in a society whose revolution produced not greater opportunities for women but a codification of secular and religious paternalism. What *Dancing at Lughnasa* shares with previous Friel plays like *Translations* (1980) and *Making History* (1988) is an awareness of the past as connected to the present. The play takes the pulse of the 1930s, but also of the 1980s by recognizing the unfinished revolution in the lives of Irish women.

Since before independence, the defining characteristics of Irish identity have been embedded in the island's rural west, often portrayed as the picturesque embodiment of the purest, because most Celtic, Irish culture. In the independent state that emerged in the 1920s the image of suffering Mother Ireland joined the ideal of the "sainted" Irish mother to become a hallmark of national patriarchal assumptions. The Republic's 1937 Constitution famously incorporated not only the tenets of conservative Catholicism, but also a romantic vision of Irish woman, a term that clearly meant "wife and mother": her "life" (not her work) within the home "gives to the State a support without which the common good cannot be achieved." Such legislative paternalism restricted women's roles outside the home and granted them less than equal citizenry. It was widely criticized at the time (usually by women) for its failure to preserve the promise of equality offered in both the 1916 Declaration and the 1922 Constitution. And it forms the background for *Dancing at Lughnasa*.

The play occupies familiar Friel territory: the fictional town of Ballybeg in the real county of Donegal – rural, western, and poor. Donegal is the part of southern Ireland that you must travel north to reach. Partition split it from the rest of its traditional province of Ulster, and in other plays Friel uses the territory to explore Northern Irish issues. Here he is concerned with the Irish Republic. The year is 1936. In 1935 the Public Dance Halls Act had been passed, largely in response to complaints by the clergy that unregulated dancing was lewd and immoral. In 1937 came the new constitution. The Irish political revolution seemed complete. A conservative social revolution was well under way. The industrial revolution was just beginning. Geographic and cultural isolation from Dublin did not insulate Donegal from policies enacted in the capital, and the alliance between church and state produced legislation and cultural expectations particularly oppressive to women.

Earlier Friel plays frequently center on father–son relationships. The focus here on women was inspired (ironically) when Friel and fellow Irish playwright Thomas Kilroy were in London for the 1987 production of Friel's dramatization of Turgenev's *Fathers and Sons*. As Kilroy remembers it:

> It was Thatcher's London. As we came down to the Embankment [. . .] the homeless were settling down for the night and Irish accents came out of the darkness. [Friel] turned and said to me that he had had two aunts who ended up like that. [. . .] [H]e told me the story of himself as a young man setting off for London to search for the two aunts who had left Donegal years before. What he found was destitution. I made the obvious, if cold, remark that he would simply have to write a play about them.[1]

In what is generally regarded as his most autobiographical play, Friel *did* write about five Donegal sisters, two of whom end up homeless in London. The play is dedicated to "those five brave Glenties women," and Mel Gussow reported that "each of the characters bears the first name of the real-life model on whom she is based."[2] Friel's mother's maiden name was McLoone; Loone is related to the Irish word for Monday; hence, the five Mundy sisters in *Dancing at Lughnasa*. Friel's father, like Kate, taught school in the 1930s.[3] The play, however, is neither autobiography nor documentary, but a drama that explores complex issues in the lives of invented characters.

Friel had created compelling women characters before, in plays like *The Loves of Cass McGuire* (1966), *The Freedom of the City* (1973) and *Faith Healer* (1979), but he had never before written about women in quite this way. The Mundy sisters are seen in the kitchen of their rural western home – the stereotypical locale of Irish plays throughout the 1950s – and the grinding challenges of their lives are clear. Endowed with wisdom and crankiness and often with grace, these women neither know nor keep their "place," but must exist within a patriarchal, claustrophobic society. This is Friel's first ensemble piece for women. Relationships to men and to patriarchy are subsumed to the primary theme – the relationship among the sisters – and even their disagreements reveal a powerful mutual bond. Each of Friel's previous women characters was isolated in a world of men. The Mundy women face Ballybeg's patriarchal world together.[4]

The complicity of the oldest sister, Kate, in upholding patriarchal precepts emphasizes the complexity of gender issues. Kate may uphold those precepts partly out of concern for her job as a teacher, but she assumes authority on the basis of her income and dismisses the value of unpaid household work, just as the 1937 Constitution was to do. Agnes's bitter retort sounds contemporary:

> I wash every stitch of clothes you wear. I polish your shoes. I make your bed.
> We both do – Rose and I. Paint the house. Sweep the chimney. Cut the grass.
> Save the turf. What you have here, Kate, are two unpaid servants.[5]

When Kate notes that "control is slipping away; [. . .] It's all about to collapse" (56), she is lamenting the decline of 'good order'" (35), unable to withstand the paternalism with which she is herself allied.

Like Tennessee Williams's *The Glass Menagerie* (1944) and Frank McGuinness's *Observe the Sons of Ulster Marching Towards the Somme* (1985), *Dancing at Lughnasa* is a memory play. References to memory toll throughout, but the controlling memory is the retrospective gaze of Chris's son Michael, whom all the sisters have helped to raise. Michael's closing memory, lit by "*a very soft, golden light*" (106), is sentimental, and (he is careful to specify) "owes nothing to fact" (107). Michael's retrospection embodies what Seamus Heaney has described as Friel's concern with "the laws of love and all their complicated relations to the operations of memory."[6] Friel has often focused on memory before (in *Philadelphia, Here I Come!* and *Faith Healer*, for example), demonstrating an almost postmodernist conviction that personal and cultural memories both require revisitation and perhaps transfiguration. Remembering, like storytelling and writing history, depends upon point of view in relation to time as well as space.

Arguably Michael's retrospective gaze perpetuates the typical male gaze that has historically defined images of women, but the issue goes beyond narrative voice. As a man Friel cannot escape the reality that his plays will have a male gaze. Here he foregrounds the fact of a male gaze rather than obscuring it. Michael's biographical similarity to Friel diminishes suspicion that the playwright has unfairly appropriated either women's subject matter or the subject matter of Ireland in the 1930s. And because it is the adult Michael who speaks the lines of the child he once was, the narrative perspective is kept before audiences in ways it would not be were he a child onstage.

Friel's previous play, *Making History* (1988), addressed the issue of gendered narrative directly. When Hugh O'Neill protests that his wife Mabel is being excluded from written history, sixteenth-century historian Lombard delivers a familiar-sounding response: "In the big canvas of national events," he notes, women have no importance, but "[a]t some future time and in a mode we can't imagine now I have no doubt that story will be told fully and sympathetically. It will be a domestic story."[7] *Dancing at Lughnasa* presents a sympathetic domestic story of women, emphasizing its significance for both private and public life.

Dancing at Lughnasa links contrary theatrical modes. Irish plays often rely heavily on storytelling of the sort Friel explored in *The Loves of Cass McGuire*, *Faith Healer* and *The Freedom of the City*. In those plays, characters deliver narrative monologues directly to the audience, just as Michael does in this play. Among other things, Michael's opening monologue identifies Lughnasa, the harvest festival in honor of the pagan god Lugh. Though Michael does not dwell on festival details, Lughnasa typically involved bonfires, dances (often competitive dances associated with courtship), and the picking of bilberries (which are dark blue or black, like the berries Agnes and her sister Rose pick). The fact that this Celtic festival needs to be identified for a 1990s Irish audience is part of the point. In the 1930s, residents of Donegal would not have needed the explanation. Friel, who has noted the irony of his need to write *Translations* in English, despite the fact the characters are understood to be speaking Irish, establishes a similar irony here.[8] Michael also narrates the ends of various story threads. The sad concluding details – Chris's grinding factory work, Agnes and Rose's destitution in London, Father Jack's death, Michael's reaction to the news his father has a second family – are summarized, and the storyteller's voice dominates.

Michael is not the only storyteller in *Dancing at Lughnasa*. The voice of the raconteur (familiar in Irish plays from J. M. Synge's 1907 *Playboy of the Western World* to Conor McPherson's 1997 *The Weir*) is also evident as characters speak not to the audience but to each other. Kate describes the impressive return of Bernie O'Donnell. Maggie remembers slipping out at night for a dance contest. Father Jack details a Ryangan ritual. Characters narrate conflicting versions of the Lughnasa celebration that burned young Sweeney. In a different play – or in a film – these events would be *shown*. Here they are narrated.

Friel balances narration with a second theatrical mode. A stage is a space to be filled, and the play's narration is accompanied by significant non-verbal moments. The opening tableau, for example, provides a visual emphasis on gender differences: the sisters' "drab" clothing contrasts with the "magnificent" uniform of Father Jack and with the "splendid" plumage of Gerry's hat. To a degree clothing distinguishes the genders throughout the play, and the faintly ridiculous note of male plumage in this opening tableau persists.

Visually the women are fully recognizable in the naturalistic kitchen setting. The men are visitors from some other, exotic world. Michael's monologue, delivered during the tableau, emphasizes things "changing too quickly" and transformation (8), but leaves the audience to connect monologue and tableau. The sisters' manic dance, the play's best-known episode, is another striking non-verbal moment. Typically, Friel (who regards scripts as musical scores that ought not to be varied by directors) attempts in his stage directions to choreograph the dance carefully. Ultimately, though, the dance depends upon an ensemble cast of women to portray a moment during which unity is accompanied by individuality and sexual frustration finds an almost frightening release. Audiences *see* that, without an intervening male narration, so Friel's script allows for an unmediated gaze at a band of women. The brevity of this explosive moment – like the "one quick glimpse" Maggie says is all one gets of a wonderful (imaginary) bird (26) – heightens its powerful contrast with the ongoing dullness of life. Its dangerous freedom is a direct contrast to Michael's closing memory, in which "everybody seems to be floating on those sweet sounds, [. . .] those assuaging notes and those hushed rhythms" (107–108).

In 1936 the Mundy sisters have just acquired a wireless. Michael's description of the wonderful machine focuses attention not just on music and dance but on other major themes. Maggie, "the joker of the family," wants to name the machine Lugh, after the Celtic god. Kate protests that "it would be sinful to christen an inanimate object" (7). The wireless is a modern intrusion into an otherwise machineless world. *Lugh* versus *Marconi* – the pagan Celtic god versus the European inventor of the wireless. Beginning in 1898, Guglielmo Marconi, whose mother and wife were Irish, established broadcast test points along Ireland's western coast. The continued significance of the wireless in Irish history includes tales of the brave "Marconi operators" who radioed from the sinking *Titanic* (built in Belfast, departing from Queenstown/Cobh for its fateful 1912 journey) and the seizure of Dublin broadcast facilities by the 1916 rebels. Government-run radio began broadcasting in 1926 and was a powerful instrument in unifying a fragmented post-independence society. Its power and availability increased after the 1933 opening of the Athlone transmitter. Radio also brought outside voices and ideas into previously isolated rural areas. (Seamus Heaney's Nobel prize acceptance speech pays tribute to the powerful impact of radio a decade later in rural Northern Ireland.) Michael specifies that the wireless beams music "all the way from Athlone" (8). Donegal residents in the 1930s would have been just as likely to pick up Northern Irish broadcasts, but Michael's specification of Athlone keeps the setting firmly within the Republic and emphasizes the distance of Dublin from Ballybeg.

Marconi's arrival coincides with the return of Father Jack, Ballybeg's "own leper priest," whose twenty-five years working in an African leper colony were broken only by time as a First World War British Army chaplain, serving the very colonial force that was simultaneously subduing rebellion in Ireland. In his memory, Michael says, the two arrivals are linked. Though he does not specify the implications of that linkage, the machine arrives just as Ireland severs ties with Britain and just as Jack's career in the Catholic church (an equally powerful colonial force) ends in disgrace.

Seismic changes in Ireland are signaled by Marconi's intermittent music: American show tunes by Cole Porter, "The Isle of Capri" (to which Maggie does a deliberately parodic tango and suggests a foxtrot), and (improbably) "The British Grenadiers," a regimental slow march. Maggie compares herself negatively to Ginger Rogers. Stage directions compare Gerry to Fred Astaire. Kate rejects such music and dance as pagan, echoing church and civic guardians of public morality, who saw dancing in "foreign" styles as a danger to Irish religion and nationalism. Jazz, often described as the music of Jews and Negroes, was regarded as particularly dangerous, and the Public Dance Halls Act was seen as a method of protecting Irish youth from foreign contamination. In 1943 Radio Éireann actually proscribed broadcasts of jazz.

In 1991 Friel noted that "it's music from a different culture that liberates [the Mundys]. They haven't absorbed it into their life and into their culture and tamed it. It's still slightly exotic."[9] This description fits most of Marconi's broadcasts, but not the music that prompts the sisters to explode in dance, pushing back at the narrow confines of their kitchen lives. That music is "The Mason's Apron," an instrumental Irish reel played by a céilí band. Writing in 1999, Friel emphasized this aspect of the music:

> in *Philadelphia, Here I Come!* I used a piece of céilí music – or what one of the characters calls a "piece of aul thumpety-thump". And a similar piece – only more anguished and manic – in *Dancing at Lughnasa*. And in both plays the purpose was to explode theatrically the stifling rituals and discretions of family life. And since words didn't seem to be up to the job it was necessary to supply the characters with a new language. Because at that specific point in both plays when the céilí music is used, words offer neither an adequate means of expression nor a valve for emotional release. Because at that specific point emotion has staggered into inarticulacy beyond the boundaries of language. And that is what music can provide in the theatre: another way of talking, a language without words. And because it is wordless it can hit straight and unmediated into the vein of deep emotion.[10]

Friel's description reiterates the distrust of language he revealed in *Translations* and emphasizes this play's balance of storytelling and spectacle: "words didn't seem to be up to the job," so music's purpose was "to explode theatrically." It also echoes Michael's concluding memory: "Dancing as if language had surrendered to movement – as if this ritual, this wordless ceremony, was now the way to speak" (107).

Michael's linking of memory to "the music of the thirties" makes sense in the case of his parents, because their partnership is sealed with dance compatible with 1930s music, and because his father has been teaching ballroom dancing. But Michael's 1930s music nostalgia matches neither the sisters' dance nor Father Jack's dance. Father Jack is inspired not by céilí music or Cole Porter, but by more primitive notes. With sticks from Michael's kite, Father Jack creates *"a structured beat whose rhythm gives him pleasure."* His dance is a *"shuffle."* His singing is *"incomprehensible and almost inaudible"* (65). This dance does not typically receive the attention given to the sisters' earlier céilí, perhaps because it is shorter and less fully choreographed by Friel, perhaps because it is individual rather than ensemble. It affords tremendous possibilities, however. Father Jack's description of the Irish climate as "so cold" (31) refers to more than the weather, and his dance (presumably based on African rituals) acknowledges the appeal of the pagan and represents a breaking away from Donegal's repressive environment. A prominent element of the sisters' dance is the thump of their boots. The thump of the kite sticks could be equally riveting. If Jack's dance is staged (as Friel demands the sisters' dance be staged) not merely as caricature, but as *"ominous of some deep and true emotion"* (36), then it can reveal the same primal elements associated with the sisters' dance. Kate ends Father Jack's dance by taking away the sticks: "They aren't ours. They belong to the child" (66). Her ordered adult world has no room for the pagan.

As a young man Friel briefly intended to study for the priesthood. Asked in 1991 whether he could imagine being a priest, Friel responded, "It would somehow have been in conflict with my belief in paganism."[11] Paganism is powerful and potentially dangerous in *Dancing at Lughnasa*. Like Father Jack's African ritual, the Lughnasa ceremony involves dancing, a bonfire and the sacrifice of a goat. Rose finds the dance particularly alluring, perhaps because she is "simple" and has fewer rational restraints, but also because it is Danny Bradley who tells her about it. Rose's sisters recognize Danny's sexual motives (as, on some level, does Rose), and those motives have a clear link with the "back hills" beyond the control of priests and police. The rigid Irish Catholic notion of moral rectitude, voiced by Kate, is assailed by foreign elements brought to Ballybeg by Marconi and Father Jack. It is also assailed by pagan elements that are part of a Celtic tradition often regarded as indigenous. Irish Catholic moral imperatives, forcefully concerned with emotion and sexuality, have a major impact on women's lives. The church–state focus on sexual behavior and religious orthodoxy also distracted attention from failure to address issues like the poverty that constricts the Mundys. The pagan rituals of Lughnasa and Uganda, then, are dangerous not primarily because of drink and fire, but because they release intoxicating, fiery emotions.

The unrestrained emotions of crossroads (outside) dances, which inevitably involved drink, were viewed by the Catholic clergy as a powerful lure toward "improper" behavior and often credited with the increase in illegitimate births. The Public Dance Halls Act required licensing of dance venues, and dances moved inside, under the watchful eye of the clergy, who attempted to eliminate set dancing (regarded as a foreign import) in favor of céilí dancing (regarded as indigenous). Later, as dance halls replaced live music with gramophones or radio, céilí music adapted contemporary rhythms and often yielded entirely to imported music. The Act reflected the Church's increasing influence on Irish statutes and unintentionally diminished participation in Celtic music and dance, rendering ironic De Valera's 1940s vision of Ireland as a rural idyll with comely maidens dancing at the crossroads. It also signaled that the new nation would be distinguished not by its Celticism but by its Catholicism.

The continuing appeal of harvest dances inspires the sisters to plan (briefly) to relive their youth by attending what must be an indoor dance, since there is an admission charge. Dances in the hills, with their simultaneous appeal and threat, are kept before the audience through various accounts of the Sweeney boy's injuries. The 1930s dance music represents changes that accompany the arrival of machines in Donegal. Gerry arrives by motor car and sells gramophones. Rose loves motion pictures. The opening of a mechanized glove factory will end cottage production and displace Agnes and Rose, who are feminine stumbling blocks in the way of progress.

Employment possibilities for women in 1930s Ireland were limited. Women teachers like Kate were a majority in the profession but were paid less than men, and retirement on marriage was compulsory (as it was generally for women in the Irish civil service). Furthermore, control of the national schools was left in patriarchal, denominational (almost always Catholic) hands, so the parish priest can dismiss Kate when Father Jack's orthodoxy lapses. Chris's job in the glove factory will involve work of repetitive monotony for which women were paid less than men. Communication, transportation, employment and education are radically changing, and the impact on the Mundy women is profound.

There are no reliable men in this world. Unfaithful husbands, unsympathetic or renegade priests and men eager to marry younger women surround them. Even Michael, who remembers the sisters with love and admiration, is (like Tennessee Williams's Tom before him) happy to escape the women in his life. The only "solution" is to emigrate to London like Danny Bradley's wife or Bernie O'Donnell, but the fate of Rose and Agnes identifies London as a problematic solution.

Though the Mundy sisters are old enough to have outgrown high expectations, no one would confuse them with the stereotype of passive, sentimental, chaste Irish womanhood. For one thing, except for Kate they are frequently a bawdy lot. More importantly, though their lives are shaped by things they *cannot* do, they are most notable for things they *do not* do. They do not abandon Rose to an institution. They do not relinquish Michael to an orphanage. They do not condemn Chris's unwed motherhood, though Kate is alert to prevent repetition. Chris chooses not to marry Gerry, despite her love for him and despite cultural expectations that unwed mothers will seek to marry. Kate eventually comes to terms with Father Jack's unorthodoxy, deciding that her brother is making "his own distinctive spiritual search" (92). These inactions are no doubt easier because the sisters are isolated even from the small town of Ballybeg, but like their dance of "defiance" they are signs of subversive resistance to patriarchal expectations.

Kate's earlier involvement in the War of Independence, a contrast to her brother's service with the British Army, illuminates the Mundys' experiences by placing them against broader conflicts. They were born at the turn of the century, just as the movement for Irish independence (with the First World War as a backdrop) began to jolt toward eventual success. Forces of colonialism, nationalism, paternalism, Catholicism, war and independence converged in their world. References to Abyssinia and the International Brigade are reminders that Europe as well as Ireland was undergoing transformation. The Anne M. P. Smithson novel Kate brings home, *The Marriage of Nurse Harding*, suggests the complexity of women's lives: its title balances career against marriage, and Smithson herself – romance novelist, nurse and midwife – was once arrested for opposing the 1921 Anglo-Irish Treaty.

Maggie's irreverent parody "Will you vote for De Valera, will you vote?/If you don't, we'll be like Gandhi with his goat" (11), links Ireland and India and highlights postcolonial issues that Field Day had been discussing for a decade. It is also a reminder that De Valera, elected in 1932, will run again in 1938. The constitution that constrained women and seemed an abandonment of revolutionary principles, is widely known as "De Valera's Constitution." Will he get the votes of these women – the first twentieth-century generation of Irish women?

When the play premiered in 1990, the last twentieth-century generation of Irish women were challenging constitutional and cultural restrictions on *their* lives. The all-male Field Day Board was feeling the sting of charges that it was, as Edna Longley put it, one of Ireland's "Ancient Orders of Hibernian Male-Bonding,"[12] though the full storm would not break until the 1991 publication of the compendious *Field Day Anthology of Irish Writing*, which seemed edited by, for and about men.[13] Debate about historical portrayals of women was expanding. Women were suddenly highly visible in Irish politics, especially when Mary Robinson was elected President in 1990 shortly after the play's premiere. Debate about legal and constitutional restrictions on women, to which *Dancing at Lughnasa* contributed, was part of the climate for her election. Similar debates about women in the world of theatre, where Friel's daughter Judy worked, were unavoidable. *Dancing at Lughnasa* provides wonderful roles for women who are not ingénues. Friel's use of a narrator foregrounds the unavoidable male perspective but also invites audiences to follow Michael in casting their minds back and connecting the past to the present.

Several specific late twentieth-century issues particularly illuminate the text. The 1990s, for example, saw increasing challenges to the assumption that unwed mothers need to be punished. In the 1984 "Kerry babies" case, two (unrelated) murdered babies were found in close proximity in rural Kerry. The same year a Longford teen died under a statue of the Virgin, in labor from a concealed pregnancy. Such cases were widely publicized and imaged in popular film and literature.[14] *Dancing at Lughnasa* poses an alternative to the culture of cruelty toward unwed mothers and illegitimate children. Chris (19 when Michael was born) and her son are neither sent away nor rejected, but surrounded by women's love. Father Jack notes that "[i]n Ryanga women are eager to have love-children. The more love-children you have, the more fortunate your household is thought to be" (64). Notably, the Ryangans believe in Obi, the Great Goddess of the Earth, to whom they sacrifice "so that the crops will flourish. Or maybe to get in touch with our departed fathers for their advice and wisdom" (73). The references to a culture ruled by a goddess and to "departed fathers" resonate, but Friel's use of African culture here is undeniably a variety of neo-orientalism, creating an imaginary "other" culture as an alternative to the restrictions of Ballybeg.

Other issues in the play also parallel concerns of its 1990 audience. Friel has often been stern, if elliptical, about what he has termed Ireland's "unique" Catholicism, for example. Though Ballybeg's priest never appears onstage, he is evidently authoritarian and cruel. Chris's donning of Father Jack's surplice suggests not only a desire for the fancier plumage associated with men, but also a lack of reverence for what the surplice represents, and she hints at priestly femininity. Only the artificial stature the Mundys gained when Father Jack was a Ballybeg hero evidences a positive influence of the Church on their lives. In the 1980s scandals rocked Irish Catholicism and decreased the authority of its priests. Similarly, Donegal's long pattern of emigration, for jobs or freedom, spans the decades between the 1930s and the 1980s, and the play makes connections that suggest Thatcher's England does not bear sole responsibility for the plight of London's homeless Irish. Distrust of foreign cultural intrusions and debates about balancing Irish identity with multinationalism re-emerged as Ireland prepared to take over the presidency of the Council of the European Communities in 1990. (In 1992 the Council became the European Union.)

In 1957 Friel suggested that an Irish writer aiming at a non-Irish audience might continue to find his subject matter in Ireland but would need to remember the writing was "for export only":

> there are certain aspects of Irish life that you ignore lest you upset the traditional concept of Irish life which Americans have. You conveniently forget [. . .] that Cork boys and girls can jitterbug as expertly as boys and girls from Chicago. You conveniently forget that our politicians are just like any other politicians and you remember them only as young men who once fought for an ideal [. . . but there] are still plenty of whitewashed, thatched cottages [and] there are still dances held at crossroads and lame fiddlers to play at them.[15]

Writing in 1963, Friel produced an essay clearly for export only: a charming, whimsical, not very interesting account of the Glenties monthly fair. At least since 1980, however, Friel has repeatedly insisted that his plays are aimed at Irish audiences: "If we are overheard – as we often are – then that's fine."[16] In *Dancing at Lughnasa* Friel wrote about his Glenties aunts not for export but for an Irish audience, presenting a past with recognizable connections to the present. The eagerness of non-Irish audiences to overhear indicates that Ireland and the world share many concerns. Since 1990 it has been produced around the world, on national, regional, university and amateur stages. In 1998 a film version appeared, scripted by Friel's fellow Donegal playwright Frank McGuinness and starring Meryl Streep.[17] The Abbey mounted a second production in 1999, as part of the Friel Festival celebrating the playwright's seventieth birthday.

The play's exploration of the unkept promises of a revolution is a major source of its power and appeal. The Mundy sisters' suppressed sexual and political energies break out in frenzied dance that engages audiences. They live out their lives in mean circumstances. But their humor, mutual support and refusal to break allow this play to fulfill what Friel had early identified as the function of a dramatist: to make us "recognize that even in confusion and disillusion, strength and courage can exist, and that out of them can come a redemption of the human spirit."[18] Such redemption is a significant revolution – one that may prompt Irish politicians to remember the ideals for which their predecessors fought as young men (and women).

NOTES

1. Thomas Kilroy, "Friendship," *Irish University Review* 29:1 (1999), p. 88. Friel himself told a similar version in 1991 interviews with Mel Gussow and John Lahr. Both interviews are reprinted in Paul Delaney (ed.), *Brian Friel in Conversation* (Ann Arbor: University of Michigan Press, 2000), pp. 202–217. The Gussow interview is reprinted in Christopher Murray (ed.), *Brian Friel: Essays, Diaries, Interviews: 1964–1999* (London and New York: Faber and Faber, 1999), pp. 139–149.
2. Glenties is the Donegal town where Friel spent summers with his mother and her sisters, at his grandparents' home.
3. Friel himself was a school teacher in the 1950s. He wrote about his aunts in such early stories as "Aunt Maggie, the Strong One" and "A Man's World."
4. A number of contemporaneous Irish plays are similar ensemble pieces for women: Frank McGuinness's *The Factory Girls* (1982), Anne Devlin's *Ourselves Alone* (1985), Tom Murphy's *Bailegangaire* (1985) and Charabanc Theatre Company's *Lay Up Your Ends* (1983) and *Somewhere Over the Balcony* (1988).
5. Brian Friel, *Dancing at Lughnasa*, in *Plays Two* (London: Faber and Faber, 1999), p. 39. Subsequent references are to this edition and are incorporated in the text.
6. Seamus Heaney, "For Liberation: Brian Friel and the Use of Memory," in Alan Peacock (ed.), *The Achievement of Brian Friel* (Gerrards Cross: Colin Smythe, 1993), p. 231.
7. Brian Friel, *Making History*, in *Plays Two*, p. 337.
8. Whether the Mundys (who speak and read English) speak Irish is not clear. Friel has said that his grandparents spoke Irish, but Irish versus English is not an issue in this play.
9. "In *Dancing at Lughnasa*, Due on Broadway this Month, Brian Friel Celebrates Life's Pagan Joys." Reprinted in Delaney, *Brian Friel in Conversation*, p. 215.
10. Brian Friel, "Music," in the programme for the Friel Festival (April–August 1999), pp. 14–15. Reprinted in Murray, *Brian Friel*, p. 177.
11. Mel Gussow, "From Ballybeg to Broadway." Reprinted in Delaney, *Brian Friel in Conversation*, p. 207.
12. Edna Longley, *From Cathleen to Anorexia: The Breakdown of Irelands* (Dublin: Attic Press, 1990), p. 16.
13. Subsequently, vols. IV and V of *The Field Day Anthology of Irish Writing* adjusted the balance.
14. Compare Seamus Heaney's 1972 poem "Bye Child," Frank McGuinness's 1989 television play *The Hen House*, Margo Harkin's 1989 film *Hush-a-Bye Baby* and Patricia Burke Brogan's 1992 play *Eclipsed* (given a public reading in 1988).
15. Brian Friel, "For Export Only," *Commonweal* (15 February 1957), p. 510.
16. "Mapping Cultural Imperialism," interview with Stephen Dixon (1980). Reprinted in Delaney, *Brian Friel in Conversation*, p. 135. 1980 interviews with Ciaran Carty and Paddy Agnew, also reprinted in Delaney, contain almost identical phrasing.

17. See Frank McGuinness, *Brian Friel's "Dancing at Lughnasa"* (London: Faber and Faber, 1998), and Joan FitzPatrick Dean, *Dancing at Lughnasa: Ireland into Film* (Cork: Cork University Press, 2003).

18. Brian Friel, "The Theatre of Hope and Despair" (1967). Reprinted in Murray, *Brian Friel*, pp. 15–24.

9

GEORGE O'BRIEN

The late plays

The truism that the Friel canon has two fundamental characteristics, thematic continuity and formal diversity, naturally facilitates links between the late plays – *Wonderful Tennessee* (1993), *Molly Sweeney* (1994), *Give Me Your Answer, Do!* (1997) and *The Home Place* (2005) – and their predecessors.[1] Moreover, the post-*Lughnasa* works sustain the enduring presence of Ballybeg as a *lieu théâtrale*, extend Friel's repertoire of pivotal roles for women, continue probing the politics of private life – that is, of the distribution of power and authority within the domestic sphere – and reveal an increasingly refined formal interest in parable. But Friel's late quartet is also discontinuous with his earlier works, not least because the plays in question have discontinuity as a theme. Friel's work overall is noteworthy for the consistency with which nothing goes according to plan, as well as for its concern with the quality of those frameworks (including language itself) whereby plans seem viable. The result is a conflicted recognition that the value of plans is not commensurate with the results of their being carried out. Terry's excursion in *Wonderful Tennessee*, Molly Sweeney's operation, the sale of Tom Connolly's archive in *Give Me Your Answer, Do!* and Richard Gore's anthropometric initiatives in *The Home Place* give such incommensurateness a more conscious focus.

Another distinction of the late plays is a heightened sense of place and of theatrical space, most readily evident in Ballybeg's altered standing. Previously, Ballybeg was a site of community. The late plays are largely postcommunal, however, making Ballybeg much more liminal. Thus, thematic concerns such as holding one's ground, awareness of terminus and dead ends, and problems of agency and of forward movement, are significantly more in evidence. Now Ballybeg is as much a condition as a location, a site at which inner and outer worlds collide, a name which instead of designating a place signifies a framework within which outcomes fall through, and the ground upon which Friel's late plays almost, but not quite, articulate a theatre of stasis.[2]

Although these works affirm a known, commonplace world, breaking with it constitutes the scene and pretext of the drama, with the present participle – particularly "waiting" and "seeing" – generating the grammar of events. Further, partnership supplants community, with marriage especially an interrogation of loyalty, fidelity and other modes of continuity. Union is a state in which the late plays do not have much faith, as is repeatedly shown by partners' complicity in undermining what they ostensibly wish to maintain. Enacting such questioning in a place of hiatus and isolation named Ballybeg is also symptomatic of their essential homelessness.[3] In response to homelessness, however, these characters are clearly interested in brave new worlds. Indeed, the possibility of alternatives is what has brought them to the critical point of recognition around which these dramatic tableaux cohere. The great world offstage exerts its attraction as a zone of desire, a realm which is both "too much with us," in Wordsworth's phrase, and of which the characters cannot get enough. The generative dramatic force of memory in Friel's work up to *Dancing at Lughnasa* is, in the late plays, produced by desire. Its stimulus offers the characters a prospect of a future, a destination and a release from the limitations of the current location. It is as though their desire arises from a sense of their having been imagined, by the alluring discovery that they have been given roles in some external agent's plan. Imagination, then, is not merely interpretive or representational, nor is its significance exclusively expressed through the improvisations, games, story-telling, singing and dancing so prominent in the late plays. On the contrary, imagination is a form of power, requiring an apparent emptiness or deficiency on the part of its would-be beneficiaries. It gives those who are imaginatively deficient – who are at the mercy of their amorphous and unrealized desires – a vision of how those desires might assume less transient form.

The opening and closing of *Wonderful Tennessee* emphasize the primary importance of space in the play. The pier at which the outing ends is in an abandoned area. But its *"silence and complete stillness"*[4] declare that this is no waste land, and George's first musical offering, the hymn "Immaculate," confirms this distinctiveness. But the pier is initially overlooked, being merely a starting point for Oileán Draoíchta where, according to Terry's plan, they ought to be. Failure to reach the island and confinement to the pier is one of the ways in which the play suggests that in the characters' end is possibly their beginning.

The approach to this possibility is indirect, since what constitutes action in the play is the characters' uncertainty and circumstantial reversals. Carlin fails to supply the boat to the island; Oileán Draoíchta itself is an uncertain shape – "it keeps shimmering" (368). Anomalies of tone and hackneyed idioms express the characters' uncertainty. "Wonderful" and "lost" become shopworn with repetition. Terry's opening, "Believe me – this is it" (348), is neither informative nor reliable. Turning to storytelling reveals dead ends, wrong turnings and the sad state of the three marriages. Yet their temporary location provides a safe place for such revelations (the hope and promise of such a place being what 'Tennessee' promises in the song "Down by the Cane Brake"). And it is also a site where desire can be acknowledged, up to and including "*a hint of the maenadic*" (354). Thus Oileán Draoíchta's significance is not that it is a place of pilgrimage; the local context is an expression of more universal spiritual emptiness. The play's references to ancient Greek rites, rituals and symbols suggest that civilization's failure as a religious source.[5] It is making the approach that matters; to be, as Berna says, "reminded. [. . .] To be in touch again – to attest" (372), or perhaps to gain a sense of, in Frank's words, "[w]hatever it is we desire but can't express"(398). Berna's leap of faith into the ocean expresses that "offence to reason" (403) needed to take her out of herself, and Frank's "Ballybeg epiphany" (421) is a valuable momentary counterpoint to his large-scale temporal preoccupations. Acknowledgment of an alternative perspective evokes a saving grace.

But there is also another reason why failure to complete the trip to Oileán Draoíchta is significant, which is that the outing is another of Terry's many generous gifts. In return, the recipients allow Terry to imagine what they need. Terry's disposition derives from his occupation of bookie and its narrow economy of wins and losses. He brings his friends to the threshold of wonder, but the significance of doing so is lost on him. The claim "Bookie Buys Island Sight Unseen" (380) is not factually accurate, but still has the ring of truth. Terry's power to translate desires is one more element in *Wonderful Tennessee* which has reached its limits, leaving those who have depended upon him to their own devices.

Relying on the *disjecta* on the pier, they find a means of inhabiting where they are. Angela's game and the decoration of the lopsided, cruciform lifebuoy stand register their presence. This inevitably temporary mark is the product of impoverished resources and unexpected resilience, making the improvisations of Act 2 the opposite of Terry's plan. Indeed, he has to be coerced to adapt to them, though this coercion is in the group's general spirit of play, as its musical accompaniment indicates. Stripping Terry is fundamental to the group's reassertion of agency. The weak flesh has yielded to the willing spirit. Returning next year "not out of need – out of desire!" (442) matters as much as repeating Terry's birthday celebrations. Quite what constitutes need and desire remains a mystery. Faith in the orthodox sense has not been rekindled. No healing has taken place. The six are going back where they came from. Terry's promise of resurrection refers to his finances. The ending inhibits even as it underlines balance and a sense of proportion. Yet, even if all that's vouchsafed is continuity, the six are not simply returning. They are also beginning again. Having been temporarily off their own beaten track has opened their eyes, as is suggested by the contrast between their chorus of particularized farewells – to "whin bush," "oak trees," "dancing dolphin," and so on (443) – and the generalized "'Bye, lovely world! [. . .] 'Bye civilization" (353). Everyone joins in that final chorus, just as everyone sings together exiting, articulating the verbal equivalent of those games and rituals which have both revealed and accommodated their stranded condition.

The concern which *Wonderful Tennessee* has with such themes as vision, healing, belief and beginning anew is treated with a much sharper focus in *Molly Sweeney*. In *Wonderful Tennessee* such matters give rise to a reanimated, even if also transient and transparent, collectivity. The reverse takes place in *Molly Sweeney* and, as in the actual case upon which the play is based, this outcome compromises the presumed values of vision, healing, faith and renewal.[6] That things fall apart is all the more dramatic in view of the collaborative and restorative energies which give the action its pretext and which provide the action's creators, Frank and Mr. Rice, with their change-making impetus. But these are the energies which the play holds up to critical inspection. Once again, the critique is inaugurated by the quality and motivation of outside intervention. Frank's nature is that of the man with the plan. His past projects reveal erratic enthusiasms, and have the contradictory consistency of causing dislocation by attempting to do good. Like Terry in *Wonderful Tennessee*, Frank is a self-appointed provider of alternative brave new worlds. But for Molly it is precisely this "whole new world of her own"[7] that's the problem. Frank's faith is a substitute for healing, disablingly deficient in a sense of proportion, and his imagination of a transformed Molly distorts and denatures.

If Frank is the unreflecting exponent of imagination, Mr. Rice is the narcissistic agent of desire. Whether he claims that Molly "has nothing to lose" (459) by the operation or more soberly acknowledges that "that courageous woman had everything, everything to lose" (481), he intends the surgery to capitalize on "a phantom desire" which rapidly blossoms into "the chance of a lifetime" (460). Rice is Frank's equal and opposite, a healer without faith. And, as with Frank, Rice's deficiency costs him his sense of proportion. If Rice believes that "[w]e aren't given that world [. . .] we make it ourselves" (463), the world he seeks is typified by desire, represented not only by his wife Maria but by "above all the hunger to accomplish, the greed for achievement" (474). In this world, Rice was a member of an elite. Operating on

Molly restores him to this version of himself. He regains "a sense of playfulness" (490) and is able to start over, which enables him, like Frank, to leave Molly as he has remade her. But, unlike Frank, he does not ignore what he has brought about. His valedictory visit to Molly evinces a moment's criticism of his own motives and a heavily qualified admission that "[o]f course I had failed her" (506). Now he sees a Molly who exists beyond himself, someone whom the designs of desire and imagination cannot harm further.

Prior to the operation, Molly seems similarly hampered, having placed her trust in the world and the men in it. This began with the father who ratifies her blindness by asserting that "'you aren't missing a lot; not a lot at all. Trust me.' Of course I trusted him; completely" (457). In a sense, Molly has no need to trust anybody, in view of her self-sufficiency, "her calm and her independence" (458), which Rice admires in her, and her belief that hers is not "a deprived world" (466). Lacking any sense of discrepancy between who she is and what she wants, Molly is the antithesis of Frank's restlessness. And compared to Frank and Rice she appears to be in a state of grace, her integrity and independence enabling her to keep faith with herself. But, human, she falls. She allows herself to be seen through others' eyes. Her trust in the world obliges her to. Although she senses that she is being used and experiences "the dread of exile" (473) before her operation, she nevertheless feels that the plans and prospects have more authority than she does. But the worldly orthodoxy of her treatment results in her previous spatial and sensory relations being no longer trustworthy. Now she has to function in a much more self-conscious way, not only by learning to see, but by adapting to such formidable questions as "How much do I want this world?" (495). Yet, despite all her losses, Molly is still prepared to inhabit her "borderline country" (509) of blindsight. This locale is where undisciplined imagination and the craven egotism of desire collide. Yet in claiming it as where she belongs, Molly attests to internal resources which the peripatetic worldliness of Frank and Rice can never possess.

The very staging of the play maintains the impossibility of the three coexisting in a common space by effacing an awareness of their coexistence. Similarities to *Faith Healer* are clear, but the closer juxtaposition of the speakers in *Molly Sweeney* makes their statements and interrelations a chilling mixture of intimacy and alienation. Each exists in his or her own space, as though blind – or perhaps blindsighted, their perceived reality a tissue of missing connections, their collective experience attaining finality through its breakdowns.

The asylum space where Molly ends up exists also as a kind of shadow cast on the sunlit set of *Give Me Your Answer, Do!* The asylum's basement "hell-hole"[8] is both marginal and central, as is the iconic presence in it of the suffering Bridget Connolly. And the significance of both location and character is revealed by the ease with which, in virtually the play's conclusion, they supplant the garden-party world.

Bridget's condition is a yardstick by which the measure of the other characters may be taken. And she also supplies a thematic focus, since her state of abeyance is in stark contrast to the expectancy of the other characters waiting to hear the price to be paid for the archive of Bridget's novelist father, Tom. Only David Knight, agent of a Texas university, can supply this information – here again, an outsider to Ballybeg possesses decisive power. And acceptance of David's scale of values will certainly change the Connollys' current circumstances. There is nothing undesirable about this Knight's intervention. Yet David has no credibility. Understandably, Tom has difficulty believing in such a "Mister God" (15), since he is unsure whether this type of value can be attached to his life and to the work which is inextricable but necessarily distinct from it.[9] But David seems conspicuously out of place, his antennae attuned not to literature and music but to his bosses' orders to "Deliver Ireland" (75). So, while in one sense David can give Tom an answer – "My entire goddamn life for Christ's sake! Touch it, feel it, sniff it, *weigh* it! And then, Mister God, please tell me it's not altogether worthless" (23) – this is not an answer for which Tom, ultimately, has any regard. But he can hardly dissociate himself from David's criteria, and his addition to the archive of the two pornographic novels he wrote in response to Bridget's initial institutionalization allows bulk to trump value. Yet when David expects him to respond to his impending offer, Tom resists the other's power to be so final: "I don't have to give you an answer this very second, do I?" (75).

Although the archive is obviously the centerpiece of Tom's individual life as an artist, it is not his whole life. The mixed company of Daisy and her parents, Jack and Maggie Donovan, as well as fellow writer Garret Fitzmaurice and his wife Gráinne, sees to that. And the ways in which these characters frame Tom's uncertainty also disclose those problems of measurement and proportion of which that uncertainty is emblematic. Looking through the eyes of Garret and Gráinne, Tom can see himself merely as a library exhibit. Garret's recent sale of his own archive to David has not altered his embattled marriage. Garret and Gráinne remain an "uneasy couple" (73), in Jack's understatement. Jack's marriage, however, has its own problems of desire and fulfillment. Maggie's fidelity suggests that the relationship is the opposite of the Fitzmaurices'. Yet Maggie's loyalty is also costly. She admits the humiliations and disruptions caused by Jack's petty thefts, but she ultimately declines to give them their due weight and measure, opting instead to believe in the amnesia which accompanies Jack's bouts of kleptomania. Not surprisingly, we learn from Jack that Maggie has also chosen to deceive herself about the severity of her arthritis, seeing a doctor in whom "she has no faith" (30). In contrast, Jack's playing the piano obliges him to "keep it bubbly, act out the fake affectations" (74). The price of partnership is self-deception, which is reason enough for Tom not to accept David Knight's proposal.

If Tom is torn between the versions of himself projected by David and embodied by Garret, Daisy is comparably trapped between her parents. Having withdrawn from being either a parent or a musician, she is both the gathering's most passive character and the one with telling insights on the writer's temperament and way of life. And although she initially considered David's offer in a remedial light, she gives the culminating speech about not selling out, affirming the "necessary uncertainty" (79) as the *sine qua non* of being in the world.

Yet the play does not offer Daisy any security in rhetoric. Speaking for Tom the writer is not speaking for the whole Tom. It's not alone his work or his archive that he's faithful to, it is also Bridget, who in her inability to respond to his imagination calls its value into question. Tom is the "one of us [who] has to face up to it" (22), and perhaps it defines him as an artist that he is willing not to turn his back on what he doesn't understand. Or perhaps the value of the imagination is in how Tom applies it during his visits to Bridget – playfully, hopefully, colorfully, engagingly – as though it's the intention that matters, not the result. In his attention to Bridget, he answers to the promptings of his imagination. That is the best he can do. It's not an answer, of course – "No change. There'll be no change" (54) – and it does not enable him to respond to the heartfelt plea with which Daisy closes the play. But it is a conscious engagement with a space he will never inhabit, one which exists in opposition not only to the construction which David Knight would put on his life but which is also beyond desire. Tom's visits to Bridget's home may not amount to much; indeed, they are a sympathetic critique of the imagination, since by visiting Bridget Tom reaches the limits of his consciousness, too. His uncertainty inhibits faith. His gift cannot heal. Yet he attests. By doing so he expresses himself as he is, enacting his condition rather than evading it, like the other characters in the play.

Spatial considerations are inevitably a part of a play entitled *The Home Place*, which is concerned with the tenability of a local habitation and a name and which, to even a greater degree than *Give Me Your Answer, Do!*, addresses those concerns through the flexible and continual use of exits, entrances, arrivals, departures, absences and presences. As in *Give Me Your Answer, Do!* – and in contrast to both *Wonderful Tennessee* and *Molly*

Sweeney, where all the characters are onstage virtually all the time – such comings and goings suggest realistic representation. The pretext of entertainment which in both plays brings all the characters together provides a patina of convention and coherence which only leads to a more inescapable sense than ever of the structural fissures underlying the place of hosting and celebration. Thus, while the unities of time, place and action act as important organizing principles in both *Give Me Your Answer, Do!* and *The Home Place*, they are technical resources only, having no application whatsoever to the characters' relations with each other. In both plays, a pattern of order coexists with, and contributes to, the elucidation of a state of disorder and breakdown.

In *The Home Place* two spatial referents at the outset suggest a critical framework in which the subsequent action may be viewed. The first of these is the *"wondrous"*[10] sound of the local school choir singing the Thomas Moore melody "Oft in the Stilly Night," a performance which, in seeming to transport Margaret, "chatelaine" (15) of the Lodge, also isolates her within that house's social standing. Her initial position between her father's choir and her duties as an employee in the house where she now lives is an overture to the ensuing disharmonies of home.

The second spatial referent is also something in the air, the marauding falcon, whose return Margaret thinks might well be taken care of by the local police sergeant. This thought suggests not only the quality of Margaret's sense of domestic responsibility but reveals the absence of a falconer to return the bird to the sphere of domestic harmony. Echoes of W. B. Yeats's "The Second Coming" are inescapable, and already a "blood-dimmed tide" has appeared in the offing, with the murder of Lord Leitrim. An omen of violence counterpoints a ceremony of innocence. These two things of the air are analogues of the Lodge's coexisting but incompatible identities, predatory and vulnerable, and together raise the question of whether, to use another spatial idiom, the Lodge can be a center which will hold; that is, a home, in a sustaining and permanent sense.

The fact that the music remains offstage and that the audience promised for a repeat performance of it disperses without hearing it, indicates that it exists in a *"different world"* (4) to which it has drawn Margaret and with which she alone, of all the members of the household, identifies. As her home place, it is an alternative to the Lodge, and to the disintegrative energies which invade the Lodge. And it is a more acceptable alternative than the Scotland and Kenya proposed by David Gore as visions of the life they might have together, options as untenable as a new "life somewhere else – Africa, South America, India – anywhere where roles aren't imposed on us" (67), which a desperate and defeated Christopher puts to her. Expressions of desire though both proposals are, they merely reproduce what the Lodge is: a home which cannot be a home. And both proposals' unacknowledged notion of the colonies as places where desire may be fulfilled allies Gore father and son with fellow Gore family member Richard. The imperium of his desires – his intellectual *droit de seigneur* – is what brings the racial and political chickens home to roost.

But the song's realm has its own problems, as is indicated by her father Clement's view that Thomas Moore is the authenticator of national character. An additional aspect of Moore's significance is his friendship with, his acceptance by, English poets. Thus Moore is given two homes, that of Irish song and that of English literary fashion. Such a perspective is tenable only in Clement's imagination. But it also reinforces the play's conception of a two-homes syndrome, being one more instance of unity imposed upon division, the division in all instances being Anglo-Irish. Clement's position is the inverse of Richard Gore's. Margaret dismisses Richard as "[j]ust so caught up in his own world" (13). But so is her father. Indeed, all concerned are in a state of detachment and unrelatedness, including Margaret. It's as though everybody suffers from political and cultural blindsight.

Clement envisages the application to reality of Moore's imaginative translations from an irrecoverable past. Richard, on the other hand, projects the application to reality of extrapolations from future anthropometrical research. Both these fabrications fail as measures of national character. But, whereas Clement's ineffectual yardstick is calibrated by works of imagination, Richard's derives its authority from the unrestrained energies of imperial desire, the exploitative nature of which are underlined by his sexist perceptions of Margaret. Richard's scientific mandate expresses itself in bullying and humiliation. The antidote to his performance does not derive from the imagination, however, further emphasizing the limitations of imaginative power. On the contrary, instead of sweetness and light, Richard is obliged to take a dose of his own medicine by Con and his henchmen. In declaring himself the voice of a "we," Con reveals that his outlook too is prefabricated. His cousin Margaret, for example, forcefully dissociates herself from whatever sociopolitical structure Con believes himself to represent.

Yet if Margaret seems to be the character most capable of facing current conditions and their implosive, uprooting consequences, her outlook too has questionable aspects. Pointing out to David that "[t]his is your home" (21) is a necessary corrective to his ill-conceived notions of escape. But telling Christopher "this is your home" (64) does not have the same effect, not merely because of the difference in Margaret's attachment to the two men. In Christopher's case, she seems to tune out the rose-tinted evocation he has just provided of "the home place"; that is, the original family seat in

Kent. In electing to listen to Con instead of Richard, thereby overriding the obligations of host as well as the claims of kinship, Christopher seemingly rejects Kent. But the result is a view of himself which he cannot sustain. He becomes the thing that has fallen apart – "I'm shattered" (78) – and David's accidental and facetious whitewashing of his father as a tree fit for cutting is an ominous echo of the Lord Leitrim episode.

Roots are required so that trees may rise above. Christopher seems able to "rise above" (12) Lord Leitrim's end. Events on the home front are what sap him. It seems too much to expect him to meet the requirement that "[t]he planter has to be resilient" (71), even if the conditions of the planter's life – "No home, no country, a life of isolation and resentment" – make resilience imperative. Christopher belatedly realizes that, as Wittgenstein has it, "the world is everything which is the case." His realization produces neither an apprehension nor appreciation of the two entities which by their intrinsic presence rise above him – the choir and the falcon – whose second coming at the close of *The Home Place* delimits the dramatic potential of that eponymous conflicted space.

The date of the action of *The Home Place* is 1878, the inaugurating year of the Land War, which brought permanent change to rural Ireland. The date, as well as contemporary references both to anthropometry and to Lord Leitrim's murder, obviously enhance the play's historical dimension and sharpen the point and focus of its various discourses on power. But such contextual particularity also draws attention to the absence in the play's three predecessors of an overt Irish dimension. In Friel's late plays, the Irish element gives way to a preoccupation with states of mind. Instead of engaging with the world of historical conditions, these works engage with the world of belief, perception, decision-making, ideology. The dramatic contexts from which these interests emerge are supplied by the characters' ostensibly more mature and settled emotional states and commitments (in contrast to Friel's more familiar focus on young, unformed characters). And they present, without presuming to resolve, the conflict between what the characters need and what the world provides. This lack of resolution may indeed confirm that "[i]n the course of his career as a dramatist, Friel's work has moved ever closer to a theatre of chaos."[11] But moving closer is not succumbing. There is a great deal of brinksmanship in the late plays. Yet, though they may be pushed to the limit, manipulated and distracted, their characters still manage to achieve some facsimile of holding their ground. From this point of view, the late plays can be read as parables of superfluity and tenacity.

One of the means by which they retain their grip is through their subliminal, unexamined but consistent indications that they "pine for ceremony,/customary rhythms."[12] Their ceremonies are improvised, secular, in many ways amateurish, informal field days without leadership or unanimity. The very deficiencies of these occasions, however, allow their meaning and function to emerge as attempts to find a rhythm with which to stay the press of outside events. Typically, these occasions do not allow very much room for maneuver, but they do clear a space where a spirit of improvisation, counter-positioning and adaptability can assert itself. And this, also typically, is a spirit which the characters cannot put into words. To do so would be to abstract them from the absorbing but inevitably fleeting moment. Instead, they introduce music to register the spirit, which music does through its inimitable combination of formal patterning and sensory immediacy. And the collective aspect of these events, their creation of a temporary community, is also noteworthy, even if by being assembled the communities in question discover how vulnerable they are. The exception is *Molly Sweeney*, where there is no shared experience and, perhaps as a consequence, there is no music.

One purpose in delimiting the space in question is to entertain the possibility of change. But, as these plays show, change has a dual identity. It has the name of improvement, the name of releasing and potentially ratifying desires. And it disrupts those to whom it appeals by tempting them to imagine how these desires might be ratified. Thus it is not merely that change speaks, as it were, with a certain type of allure and authority and intentionality. It is also a question of how change may be accommodated. Quite possibly, "*Molly Sweeney* could be read as an unconscious defense of maintaining certain nationalist values."[13] But its enactment of radical change is more broadly applicable to conditions in Northern Ireland, deriving as it does from such humanistic concerns as freedom of choice, independence, autonomy and related presuppositions of self-control. And yet, for all change's apparent empowerment, Friel's late plays regard it pessimistically. It is always somebody else's big idea – usually some outsider's. In acceding to change, sight is lost of the primacy of the inner landscape. The world's wealth supplants the self's essences. And change's inevitable and definitive rhythms leave those it affects divided, disconcerted and giving the impression that, for them, the timing is wrong, it will always be already too late.[14]

The externalization of internal conditions which the late plays undertake is obviously relevant to a representation of Northern Ireland reality, where the acknowledgment of inner realms is so troubled. At the same time, by universalizing the late plays' conflicts – that is, by not grounding his perspectives in a specific community, much less in a particular ideology – Friel aligns the divided world of his native province with divisions typical of modern conditions generally. Such an alignment suggests that the late plays exemplify a late style. Yet they do not conform to what Edward Said terms "[t]he accepted notion . . . that age confers a spirit of reconciliation and serenity on late works."[15] Friel knows that this loss is in the nature of things. But his knowledge irradiates rather than compromises the sympathetic detachment he brings to these works' inscription of *"les géographies solonnelles des limites humaines."*[16]

NOTES

1. See José Lanters, "Violence and Sacrifice in Brian Friel's *The Gentle Island* and *Wonderful Tennessee*," *Irish University Review* 26:1 (1996), pp. 163–176; Christopher Murray, *Twentieth-Century Irish Drama: Mirror up to Nation* (Manchester: Manchester University Press, 1997), p. 228; Maria Germanou, "Brian Friel and the Scene of Writing: Reading *Give Me Your Answer, Do!*," *Modern Drama* 46:3 (2003), p. 470; Fintan O'Toole, Review of *The Home Place*, *The Irish Times*, 2 March 2005.

2. Beckettian echoes in the late plays have been noted by Anthony Roche, *Contemporary Irish Drama* (New York: St. Martin's Press, 1995), p. 5, and by John Hildebidle, "Simultaneously Actual and Illusory," in Richard Harp and Robert C. Evans (eds.), *A Companion to Brian Friel* (West Cornwall, CT: Locust Hill, 2002), p. 10.

3. Csilla Bertha and Maria Kurdi, "Hungarian Perspectives on Brian Friel's Theatre after *Dancing at Lughnasa*," in Dermot Bolger (ed.), *Druids, Dudes and Beauty Queens: The Changing Face of Irish Theatre* (Dublin: New Island, 2001), pp. 173–195; Murray, *Twentieth-Century Irish Drama*, p. 170.

4. Brian Friel, *Wonderful Tennessee*, in *Plays Two* (London: Faber and Faber, 1999), p. 347. All future references are to this edition and will be incorporated in the text.

5. Csilla Bertha, "Six Characters in Search of a Faith: The Mythic and the Mundane in *Wonderful Tennessee*," *Irish University Review* 29:1 (1999), pp. 119–135.

6. See Oliver Sacks, "To See and Not See," *New Yorker*, 10 May 1993, pp. 59–73, reprinted in his *An Anthropologist on Mars: Seven Paradoxical Tales* (New York: Knopf, 1995), pp. 102–144; also Christopher Murray, "Brian Friel's *Molly Sweeney* and its Sources: A Postmodern Case History," *Études Irlandaises* 23:2 (1998), pp. 81–97, and Julia Temple, "The Gift of Sight in *Molly Sweeney*," in Harp and Evans (eds.), *A Brian Friel Companion*, pp. 133–149.

7. Brian Friel, *Molly Sweeney*, in *Plays Two*, p. 464. All future references are to this edition and will be incorporated in the text.

8. Brian Friel, *Give Me Your Answer, Do!* (Oldcastle, County Meath: Gallery Press, 1997), p. 22. All future references are to this edition and will be incorporated in the text.

9. Richard Pine, *The Diviner: The Art of Brian Friel* (Dublin: University College Dublin Press, 1999), p. 305.

10. Brian Friel, *The Home Place* (London: Faber and Faber, 2005), p. 3. All future references are to this edition and will be incorporated in the text.

11. José Lanters, "Brian Friel's Uncertainty Principle," *Irish University Review* 29:1 (1999), p. 175.

12. Seamus Heaney, "Funeral Rites," in *North* (London: Faber, 1975), p. 16.

13. F. C. McGrath, *Brian Friel's (Post)Colonial Drama: Language, Illusion, and Politics* (Syracuse, NY: Syracuse University Press, 1999), p. 279.
14. Belatedness is a substantial theme in the other late plays: in *The Yalta Game* (2001) and *Afterplay* (2002) – in Brian Friel, *Three Plays After* (London: Faber and Faber, 2002) – and in Brian Friel, *Performances* (London: Faber and Faber, 2005).
15. Edward Said, "Thoughts on Late Style," *London Review of Books* 26:15 (5 August 2004), p. 3.
16. "The solemn geographies of human limits"; Paul Eluard, *Les Yeux fertiles*, quoted in Gaston Bachelard, *The Poetics of Space*, trans. Maria Jolas (Boston: Beacon, 1969), p. 211.

10

RICHARD PINE

Friel's Irish Russia

Graham Greene once wrote that "[t]here are writers – Tolstoy and Henry James to name two – whom we hold in awe, writers – Turgenev and Chekhov – for whom we feel a personal affection, other writers whom we respect. . . . [R. K.] Narayan more than any of them wakes in me a spring of gratitude, for he has offered me a second home."[1] Brian Friel's plays offer a "second home" to those of his audience for whom he holds up a mirror to their secret and perhaps unknown places. This is also the place where he meets Turgenev and Chekhov, where the "personal affection" and "gratitude" that emanate from his audiences are enhanced by his astute and intimate association with the Russians over a period of forty years.

In 1999 Friel wrote of his affinity with nineteenth-century Russia:

> Maybe because the characters in the plays behave as if their old certainties were as sustaining as ever – even though they know in their hearts that their society is in melt-down and the future has neither a welcome nor even an accommodation for them. Maybe a bit like people of my own generation in Ireland today. Or maybe I find those Russians sympathetic because they have no expectations whatever from love but still invest everything in it. Or maybe they attract me because they seem to expect that their problems will disappear if they talk about them – endlessly.[2]

Friel has written of Turgenev that "[he] fashioned a new kind of dramatic situation and a new kind of dramatic character where for the first time psychological and poetic elements create a theatre of moods and where the action resides in internal emotion and secret turmoil and not in external events."[3] Turgenev, Friel tells us, paved the way for Chekhov and the kind of theatre that today is called "Chekhovian": "And between them they changed the face of European drama."[4]

This chapter explores the themes and topics which inhere in two of Friel's most "Chekhovian" plays – *Living Quarters* (1977) and *Aristocrats* (1979) – in his "translations" or "versions" of work by Turgenev (a dramatization of the novel *Fathers and Sons* [1987] and *A Month in the Country* [1992]) and by Chekhov. His *Three Sisters* (1981) is described as "a translation"; *Uncle Vanya* (1998), as "after Chekhov." The *Three Plays After* comprehend *The Yalta Game* (2001), a dramatization and expansion of the story "Lady with Lapdog"; the vaudeville *The Bear* (2002); and *Afterplay* (2002), the work in which he took the greatest liberty with characters from preceding plays, where Sonya Serebriakova from *Uncle Vanya* meets Andrey Prozorov from *Three Sisters* in a Moscow café in the early 1920s.

All three playwrights challenged the dramatic conventions of their time. For example, Chekhov said of *The Seagull*: "I began it *forte* and finished it *pianissimo* – against every rule of dramatic art. It's turned out more like a novella."[5] Turgenev called *A Month in the Country* "a novel in dramatic form."[6] Friel, who responded warmly to the absence of plot and dramatic climax in *Three Sisters*,[7] would in his turn write plays whose core is conversation rather than action (such as *Faith Healer*) and which end without resolution, retaining Friel's characteristic "necessary uncertainty"[8] (such as *Give Me Your Answer, Do!*). The inconsequentiality of many Friel plays (*Crystal and Fox* is perhaps the most painful, *The Home Place* the most puzzling and *Molly Sweeney* the most uplifting) tallies closely with that of *Three Sisters* and *Uncle Vanya*, and gives Friel the license to indulge in the afterlife of *Afterplay*. The monologues of Turgenev's *A Month in the Country* become the raison d'être of *Faith Healer* and *Molly Sweeney* and have met with criticism, particularly in America, for telling stories rather than presenting drama[9]; but the monologual has all the power of the confessional, which is a cardinal topos of both Russian and Irish drama.

As Turgenev wrote when planning *Fathers and Sons*, "the writer must be a psychologist, but a secret one."[10] The skill at divination, of finding the "real" people within the fabric of everyday life, is an attribute for which Friel has become noted. Turgenev, Chekhov and Friel, who have all been writers of short stories, see in the drama a means of bringing to life on the stage the controlling contours of the Russian/Irish mindscape. Trigorin in *The Seagull*, for example, wants to describe people's sufferings and their future, and in his version of *Fathers and Sons* Friel acknowledges that "you have got to plough the land – deep."[11] Turgenev's estate at Spasskoye, Chekhov's at Melikhovo and Friel's home village of Glenties provide microcosms (or "Ballybegs") in which the processes and processions of Russia/Ireland can be observed spatially, physically, metaphysically, psychologically and emotionally; as Mel Gussow has suggested, they underline "the importance of a provincial place as an adjunct of character."[12]

Apart from his finished works of "translation," Friel has toyed with several other notional "Russian" projects, including a whimsical play featuring a joint production by Turgenev and Dostoyevsky of Gogol's *The Inspector-General*, with Gogol in the cast (not a million *versts* from *Afterplay*). Over the years he has "circled around Gorky and Gogol and Ostrovsky but for some reason [I] haven't attempted them."[13] In 2004 Friel was regretting that Chekhov's story "The Kiss," which he characterized as "spare, elusive, quicksilverish, haunted," was "too insubstantial for the stage."[14]

Friel, like Chekhov, is "a private and guarded person who [keeps] people at arm's length."[15] There is a striking range of personal similarities in their circumstances. They both sang in a choir conducted by their respective fathers – Chekhov's in church, Friel's in school. When Friel speaks of his texts as "written to be sung,"[16] the concepts of music and ritual take on a special dramatic quality that suggests the cadences and rhythms of his characters' speeches and silences. The ritualistic nature of Friel's drama, with the dramatist speaking through one of his characters as a shaman, is underscored by his association with Chekhov. For Chekhov, theatre was at the heart of the Russian Orthodox ritual which saturated his boyhood and against which, as Rosamund Bartlett argues, he rebelled in his last four plays where "unvoiced emotions, silences, and muted climaxes" are the antithesis of the Orthodox Easter services.[17] Friel, too, was alienated from the conventional forms of religion early in life by his unspoken experiences at the national seminary in Maynooth. Nevertheless, he has affirmed that "[r]itual is part of all drama. [. . .] Drama is a RITE, and always religious in the purest sense."[18] For every antithesis there must be a precedent thesis, and both Friel and Chekhov acknowledge, however implicitly or subliminally, the presence of religious or quasi-religious authority (including, of course, that of the author) and the notion of a supervening fate, as in "Sir," the master of ceremonies of *Living Quarters*, and his "ledger" in which the characters' past lives are written and with which they remonstrate in their attempt to escape fate.

Another echo of Chekhov's life which finds an uncanny resonance in Friel's drama is the fact that Chekhov's father, as a grocer, "sold a variety of goods, including oil, fish, flour, tobacco, buttons, coffee, knives, confectionery, candles, spades, shoe polish, and herrings,"[19] and that Chekhov spent "hours of misery [. . .] serving behind the counter."[20] The grocer's shop setting and the frustration of Gar O'Donnell in *Philadelphia, Here I Come!* (1964) provide an obvious equivalent. And Chekhov harbored an ambition to become a beekeeper, a pursuit actively followed by Friel. For both, fishing has an affective place in the mind, in Friel's case famously incorporated into the truth-telling of *Philadelphia* and recounted in his marginalia.[21] Friel, as an avid reader of and about Chekhov, would have known many details of his life; but he was unaware, when writing *Aristocrats*, with its imaginary game of croquet, that Chekhov had a passion for the game, which he played at his estate at Melikhovo, sometimes in the dark.[22] This uncanny echo only serves to underline the extraordinary affinity between the interests of the two men, running parallel to or subliminally in their literary interests.

In their plays the greatest affinity is the dispersal of households, which was an early experience of Chekhov's childhood in Taganrog[23] and which he brought to an apogee in *The Cherry Orchard* (1904). This dramaturgic dispersal is at the core of Friel's *The Gentle Island* (1971), *Living Quarters* (1977), *Aristocrats* (1979) and *Dancing at Lughnasa* (1990). In *Living Quarters*, which explores the lives of "dead souls" with troubling insight, the house is merely a temporary resting place for those seeking and anticipating redeployment of their minds and bodies. *Aristocrats* dramatizes a falling apart of traditions and myths, fueled by fears and anxieties, as the ubiquitous O'Donnell family finally come to terms with their "home" by leaving it. Friel, as a master of the "nostalgia play," pays homage to its literal meaning: *nostos*, the homeward journey; *algos*, pain. Revisiting a troubled household after its dispersal is, in Hannah Arendt's words, a *"retour secret sur moi-même"* (*"a hidden revisiting of oneself"*),[24] which Friel grants with cruel compassion to the two characters in *Afterplay*.

In their personal lives, Chekhov and Friel – and even perhaps Turgenev – might be regarded as writers in search of childhood. The idea of an Arcadian paradise as the location of childhood, and therefore of the place where that childhood could be regained, is certainly embodied in Melikhovo and Glenties. More importantly, the people they portray in their writing, and the anxieties embodied in those people, are evidence of a profound and radical search for childhood. Many of them are adult children, more rooted in wonder and fantasy and a troubled innocence than in the "real" world of responsibilities and achievements.

What are the chief characteristics persuading us that, in the words of the Irish writer George Moore in 1911, "Ireland is a little Russia"?[25] There are the sociological and political givens, such as the prevalence of famine in both countries and the comparability of the emancipation of the Catholic "serfs" in Ireland in 1832 and that of their Russian counterparts in 1861. Behind them lies a psychological terrain of hope and longing, despair, deferral, unease, wonder, sadness, exhaustion and irony. As Emma Polatskaya has written, it is "Russia's inner state [which] shapes people's individual destinies," and this "Russian soul" – in the nineteenth century, at least – had much in common with "Irishness," not least in the dramatists' "sudden awareness of a wasted life."[26] Where Turgenev had written of Russia as "that immense and sombre figure motionless and masked like the Sphinx,"[27] Friel has referred to "inbred claustrophobic Ireland,"[28] and the "romantic ideal we call Kathleen."[29]

Two of these topics were specifically addressed in Friel's 1967 lecture "The Theatre of Hope and Despair," in which he argued that the modern dramatist's only concern is with

> individuals, isolated, separated, sick and disillusioned with their inheritance, existing in the void created by their rejection, waiting without hope for a new social structure that will give a meaning to their lives. [. . .] [When the modern dramatist] depicts man as lost, groping, confused, anxious, disillusioned, he is expressing the secret and half-formed thoughts in all our hearts.[30]

The function of a dramatist, according to Friel, in terms which might have been Chekhov's, is to be "vitally, persistently, and determinedly concerned with one man's insignificant place in the here-and-now world. They have the function to portray that one man's frustrations and hopes and anguishes and joys and miseries and pleasures with all the precision and accuracy and truth that they know."[31] Chekhov said that he discovered his material by looking out of the window, and this is echoed by the Irish actress Susan Fitzgerald who, preparing to play Alice in *Aristocrats*, said: "it's just someone looking out of the window, but it breaks your heart."[32]

As V. S. Pritchett put it in his biography of Turgenev, the gentry whom the writer observed were "a race of failed Hamlets."[33] Perhaps the writing is summed up in a note laid on Chekhov's grave which spoke of his capacity "to express the sad poverty of Russian life."[34] It is significant that Friel states the futility of Russian life much more outspokenly than do previous translators of Chekhov. The earliest and most comprehensive, Constance Garnett, rendered an observation by Vershinin in *Three Sisters* as: "A Russian is peculiarly given to exalted ideas, but why is it he always falls so short in life?"[35] Michael Frayn's version of this line is: "What characterizes the Russian is above all the loftiness of his thinking, but, tell me, why are his aspirations in life so low?"[36] In Friel's "translation," Vershinin refers to "a great void, a great emptiness in man's life,"[37] and poses the dilemma: "We Russians are a people whose aspirations are magnificent; it's just living we can't handle" (43). "Magnificent" is Friel's code word for the inherent irony or pathos in the Russian character. In Act 3 of *Three Sisters*, the drunken Chebutykin addresses his reflection in a passage, the dramatic language and import of which is entirely original to Friel: "Maybe you're the reality. Why not? Maybe this (*body*) is the image.[. . .] I wish you (*reflection*) were the reality, my friend. I wish – oh God, how I wish this (*body*) didn't exist . . . [. . .] Oh you are . . . magnificent" (73).

Perhaps the strongest thematic thread running from Turgenev through Chekhov to Friel is not a specific topic at all, but the palpable presence of irony, which draws together the characteristics common to all three playwrights. Irony is at the heart of both the black and the white humor in their plays, and explains the otherwise inexplicable way in which both Turgenev and Chekhov referred to their works as "comedies." For irony to succeed, it requires a shared referential context, both between the playwright and his subject matter and between playwright and audience. Humor must be as direct as music in communicating to the listener a sense of something intangible yet full of meaning for him or her alone. It is this use of irony that creates and draws together a sense of community among an audience of individual sensitivities.

As in Russia, so in Irish society, especially in the nineteenth century, there is a meeting place of those in possession (the gentry) and the dispossessed (the peasantry). Neither party is able fully to occupy or relinquish its condition, but lives in uneasy symbiosis with the other. This occurs most painfully, in Friel's work, in *The Home Place* (2005). Irony is the condition of this meeting point, a shared predicament with no conceivable solution. There exists only the knowledge of some impending, climactic catastrophe to eradicate the strophe of everyday life and impose a new world order. It was not merely the expectation of some land war or revolution (the Easter Rising of 1916 and the war of independence of 1921–1922 in Ireland; Russia's war with Japan in 1903 and the Revolution of 1917) as of some radical change in mindset which is signaled in *Fathers and Sons*. In the face of a disaster-waiting-to-happen, Turgenev, Chekhov and Friel pose the vapidity of gradual decline. A catastrophe of a different order – the sectarian "Troubles" of Northern Ireland – is addressed in a play by Friel not readily associated with his "Chekhovian" mood, *The Freedom of the City* (1973), with its juxtaposition of hope and wasted lives.

It is as if faith, hope and disillusion constitute a troika, a means by which life is to be lived unsuccessfully and in deferral. No one does any work because, although we are told frequently (in *Uncle Vanya*, for example) that work is the key that will unlock these enervated hopes and energies, some event or non-event takes place to prevent that work being undertaken. Thus, the constant notion that man can endure – articulated most ironically of all in the O'Donnell family motto in *Aristocrats*, "Semper Permanemus" – is cruelly pitted against that of physical, moral and psychological collapse. "We like to think we endure around truths immemorially posited," says Hugh O'Donnell in *Translations*[38]; yet it is his son who – literally – brings home the agents of change. Arkady Kirsanov does the same in *Fathers and*

Sons with the nihilistic Bazarov: "I've brought a friend with me, Father. [. . .] I would like you to make him very welcome" (121–122). When fate knocks on the door, it is an annunciation of both past and future.

Friel's first professional engagement with Chekhov was in 1963, when he observed Tyrone Guthrie at work directing a production of *Three Sisters* at the Guthrie Theater in Minneapolis. Although Chekhov as a writer of short stories can be detected as a presence in Friel's own stories (for example, in "Among the Ruins" and "Foundry House"), his example as an observer of the frailties and challenges of family life did not become manifest in Friel's drama until the later 1970s. *Living Quarters* and *Aristocrats* display the explicit influence of *Three Sisters* with, in each case, three frustrated sisters[39] and an indecisive brother, and the implicit anxieties of the deeply unsatisfying relationships of family life.

Living Quarters, focusing on a longed-for return from the provinces to a Muscovian Dublin, is a threnody on the dispersal of a family. In the background hovers the notion that something dreadful has happened in the past and something equally dreadful is about to happen. The leitmotif, as in so much of Chekhov and so much Friel, is "Do you remember?", memory being the conduit by which one can negotiate and renegotiate the meaning of love. But, while memory can link us to a golden past, there is also a future. The corresponding question for the future is, "What's to become of us?", as we meet it in Friel's versions of *Three Sisters*, *A Month in the Country* and *Uncle Vanya*.[40]

Aristocrats has been called Friel's most "Chekhovian" play because it addresses the questions of absence and of what is not being said. Its setting of Ballybeg Hall (like the settings of *The Seagull* and *The Cherry Orchard*) is more an imagined than a real place, a state of mind for those who experience "the great silence" of the house-as-affect.[41] In what is Friel's first "Big House" play, the hapless son, Casimir, "*gestures towards the house*" and indicates "what it has done to all of us" (311). Irish novelist Molly Keane, in *The Rising Tide* (1937), wrote of the house of the McGraths that it "had its share in the forming and making of that sadness in their natures which so few of the family seemed to escape"; one character says of this "oppression – it belongs to the house. It's a thing we aren't allowed to admit."[42] When writing *Aristocrats*, Friel remarked on the "essence of the play" as "silence," as "the burden of the incommunicable," and that his task was to give "articulacy" to the elements of "*family life*, its quality, its cohesion, its stultifying effects, its affording of opportunities for what we designate 'love' and 'affection' and 'loyalty'."[43] This inability to articulate is due, in the case of the O'Donnell family, to the accumulation of psychic debris in their lives. The characters collectively experience an ongoing condition of bewilderment, of waiting for an indefinable something to enable truths to be told that have always been known but hidden. Knowing that a house holds a secret thought is to acknowledge the *unheimlich*, the "uncanny," which creates inner unease or, in Friel's words, Chekhov's "familiar melancholy [. . .] [b]ecause sadness and melancholy are finally reassuring."[44] The *unheimlich* pervades *Living Quarters* and *Aristocrats* (as it also permeates *The Home Place*), and if there is a *quietus* to be achieved, it is in the laying of ghosts by acting out nodes of anxiety, as the family in *Living Quarters* constantly re-enact and renegotiate the affective transactions of family life.

If it is a commonplace that in every drama the moment is reached at which the truth – individual or collective – must be told, then *Three Sisters* and *Uncle Vanya* provide Friel with opportunities for developing the comparative subtleties with which Chekhov dealt with such admissions. There is in Friel, Turgenev and Chekhov a curious connection between the idea of an acceptable fiction and that of "necessary uncertainty": to arrive at a point where a kind of truth can be told which, although it is not *the* truth, will satisfy one's cravings for narrative. This is also to reach the borders of certainty but to be unable to cross them, essentially remaining on this side of doubt, but perhaps having shed the despair and anxiety that doubt usually carries with it. This condition is embodied in the two sentences which Friel gives to Nikolai Kirsanov in *Fathers and Sons*: "We all have our codes. We all have our masks" (136). It is the task of playwright and audience to challenge this, to decode and to unmask.

Friel's "translation" of *Three Sisters* was both a homage to Chekhov (and Friel's mentor, Guthrie) and a means of coping with some of the tensions which led to the creation of the Field Day Theatre Company and the tensions which that establishment itself engendered. If *Translations* (1980) could be regarded as "a national classic,"[45] and if *The Communication Cord* (1982) was a "vaudeville" deflating some of the hype surrounding *Translations*, then the intervening version of *Three Sisters* was simultaneously an excursion from Ireland and a connection between Irish drama and the drama of the wider world. It allowed Friel to push forward part of the Field Day project by rewriting Chekhov in the medium of Hiberno-English. Seldom could a "translation" achieve the "complete point-to-point mapping of language onto the true substance and shape of things," as George Steiner would have it.[46] This notion was incorporated by Friel directly into *Translations*,[47] the play he wrote during the period when he was working on *Three Sisters*, and which displays his questioning of faith and veracity. Friel has spoken frequently of his "translation" of *Three Sisters* and subsequent projects in a postcolonial context as a means of creating a Hiberno-English which would allow a more accessible and more natural language for Irish ears: "I think that the versions of *Three Sisters* which we see and read in this country always seem to be redolent of either Edwardian England or the Bloomsbury set. Somehow the rhythms of these versions do not match with the rhythms of our own speech patterns. [. . .] This is something about which I feel strongly – in some way we are constantly overshadowed by the sound of the English language."[48] Friel was to define this condition and artistic challenge in the following terms: "The decolonisation process of the imagination is very important if a new Irish personality is to emerge."[49] This is cognate with the Nigerian Chinua Achebe's search for "a new English, still in full communion with its ancestral home but altered to suit new African surroundings . . . able to carry the weight of my African experience,"[50] and K. R. S. Iyengar's embrace of "Indo-Anglian": "our literature which, with all its limitations, still taught us to be a new nation and a new people."[51]

In making Hiberno-English versions, Friel seems to have confirmed something which in 1981 he thought "potentially true":[52] the affinity of Ireland and Chekhov's Russia. The cadences and rhythms which make almost all of his plays redolent of Chekhov establish the eloquent context in which beauty and ugliness find their expression. At the same time, although agreeing that a new version must be subject to the "psychological imperatives" of the original author,[53] Friel maintains that "there are bigger truths beyond that of the literal translation."[54] It is in the qualitative leap towards these truths, beyond the versions of other translators such as Constance Garnett, Richard Freeborn, Elizaveta Fen, Ronald Hingley and Michael Frayn, that Friel, in addition to establishing a new linguistic contour, makes his mark as a playwright refashioning Turgenev's and Chekhov's dramas. Not only does Friel allow his Chekhov-derived characters less space for dramatic silences, he speeds up their language. Cipher-players such as Telegin in *Uncle Vanya* are rounded out by him into a full-blown person with something to contribute. Friel also develops a more interpersonal and Irish relationship between masters and servants than the history of nineteenth-century Russia would bear. Giving people – even insignificant people – more social scope increases their capacity to express themselves, with a consequently greater dynamic from all parts of the stage.

Friel achieved this capacity for his characters to transform or reinvent themselves in *The Yalta Game* (2001), his dramatization of Chekhov's story "Lady with Lapdog." It portrays inactive longing for some kind of livable life while acknowledging the constant hunger, the lack of meaning, the fragmented experience of everyday existence. Friel suppressed many of the details of the story in order to develop the character of the seducer, Dmitry Dmitrich Gurov. The theme, which is the home truth of the play, is that there *is* no home, no truth, and that the various types of delusion through which we lead our melancholy lives are all we have to go on. It is a completely liminal play because the yearning lovers (Gurov and his inamorata, Anna Sergeyevna) are forever at each other's thresholds yet never succeed in consummating their need to be with one another. The denial of the ritual ending means that the arrested moment *is* the play. Again, Friel has taken the germ of Chekhov's text and enlarged it to demonstrate that the "real life" is irrelevant and the "imagined life" is the reality. Chekhov (in David Magarshack's translation) writes:

> By a strange concatenation of circumstances, possibly quite by accident, every-thing that was important, interesting, essential, everything about which he was sincere and did not deceive himself, everything that made up the quintessence of his life, went on in secret, while everything that was a lie, everything that was merely the husk in which he hid himself to conceal the truth, like his work at the bank, for instance, his discussions at the club . . . – all that happened in the sight of all.[55]

Friel's version reads:

> Remember my sly game? Well, it . . . inverted itself. Or else my world did a somersault. Or else all reality turned itself on its head. Because suddenly, for no reason that I was aware of, things that once seemed real now became imagined things. And what was imagined, what I could imagine, what I could recall, that was actual, the only actuality. The bank, colleagues, home, card games, they all subsided into make-believe – they were fictions, weren't they? And the only reality was the reality in my mind.[56]

Friel took this even further in his invention of the afterlife of Sonya Serebriakova and Andrey Prozorov in *Afterplay* (2002). I do not know of any other play in which characters from two other plays constitute the sole inhabitants of the work currently on the stage. Cases in point are Tom Stoppard's *Rosencrantz and Guildenstern are Dead* (1967), in which the lead players are also appearing in a performance of *Hamlet* on another, adjacent stage, or Stoppard's *Travesties* (1974), which involves Joyce, Lenin and Tzara in a production of *The Importance of Being Earnest*. These give cause for vaudevillian confusion of identities and purposes, but beyond emphasizing a truly Russian trait – that the real world is probably taking place in the next room – they don't attempt what Friel is moving towards in *Afterplay*: the afterlife of make-believe, when we discover that we are not characters in someone else's play, but responsible for our own thoughts and deeds.

Afterplay's elegant conceit is so much more than an accidental meeting of two unreal characters. It is a contrived commentary on what happens to people who habitually speak something other than the truth, when they find themselves obliged to admit to reality. In their flights of invention and improvisation, especially in Sonya's astonishing cadences, we witness acts of faith and acts of betrayal, and, as they both call them, "fables," "fictions" and "lies" which are the cries of children waiting to be found. And *Afterplay* bears out the recurrent question of Chekhov's "comedies," because the truth is most piercing when it produces laughter as well as tears. Friel has said that Chekhov creates a state "where one is alive to the word but even more alive to its echoes and resonances" and the imagination "allows itself to move into those uncharted areas where the greater part of our lives is lived."[57] So we have echoes and resonances not only of the two plays in which Sonya and Andrey started off, but of all of Chekhov's work and most of Friel's. In particular, *Afterplay* brings out Friel's overwhelming feeling that "Chekhov is best sensed."

NOTES

1. Graham Greene, introduction to R. K. Narayan, *The Bachelor of Arts* (London: Heinemann, 1978), p. v.
2. Brian Friel, "Seven Notes for a Festival Programme," in Christopher Murray (ed.), *Brian Friel: Essays, Diaries, Interviews: 1964–1999* (London and New York: Faber and Faber, 1999), p. 179.
3. Brian Friel, "Introduction: Ivan Turgenev (1818–1883)," *A Month in the Country – After Turgenev* (Oldcastle, County Meath: Gallery Press, 1992), p. 10.
4. Ibid., p. 11.
5. Rosamund Bartlett (ed.), *Anton Chekhov: A Life in Letters* (London: Penguin Books, 2004), p. 339.
6. Quoted in Isaiah Berlin, "Introductory Note" to Ivan Turgenev, *A Month in the Country* (London: Hogarth Press, 1981), p. 8.
7. In a programme note for *Three Sisters* (Longford Productions at the Gate Theatre, Dublin), 1980.
8. Brian Friel to the author, 2 January 1997.
9. Cf. Irving Wardle, *Independent* (London), 21 October 1990; David Krause, *Irish Literary Supplement* (New York), Spring 1995; Vincent Canby, *New York Times*, 8 January 1996; Nancy Franklin, *New Yorker*, 18 January 1996; Donald Lyons, *Wall Street Journal*, 11 January 1996.
10. Quoted in Avrahm Yarmolinsky, *Turgenev: The Man, His Art and His Age* (New York: Century, 1926), p. 194.
11. Brian Friel, *Fathers and Sons – After the Novel by Ivan Turgenev*, in *Plays Two* (London: Faber and Faber, 1999), p. 131; subsequent references are to this edition and will be incorporated in the text.
12. Brian Friel, "In Interview with Mel Gussow (1991)," in Murray, *Brian Friel*, p. 141.
13. Friel, "Seven Notes," p. 179.
14. Brian Friel to the author, 19 November 2004.
15. Rosamund Bartlett, *Chekhov: Scenes from a Life* (London: Free Press, 2004), p. 238.
16. Friel, "Interview with Mel Gussow," p. 147.

17. Bartlett, *Chekhov*, p. 88.
18. Brian Friel, letter to Ulf Dantanus, quoted in Dantanus, *Brian Friel: A Study* (London and Boston: Faber and Faber, 1988), p. 87.
19. Alexander Chudakov, "Dr. Chekhov: A Biographical Essay," in Vera Gottlieb and Paul Allain (eds.), *The Cambridge Companion to Chekhov* (Cambridge: Cambridge University Press, 2000), p. 5.
20. Bartlett, *Chekhov*, p. 28.
21. See Brian Friel, "Self-Portrait (1972)," in Murray, *Brian Friel*, pp. 38–39.
22. Cf. Donald Rayfield, *Anton Chekhov: A Life* (Evanston, IL: Northwestern University Press, 1997), pp. 222–223.
23. Ibid., p. 42.
24. Hannah Arendt, *The Life of the Mind* (New York: Harcourt Brace Jovanovich, 1978), vol. 1, p. 74.
25. George Moore, *Hail and Farewell* (Gerrards Cross: Colin Smythe, 1976), pp.124–5.
26. Emma Polatskaya, "Chekhov and his Russia," in Gottlieb and Allain, *Cambridge Companion to Chekhov*, pp. 17, 22.
27. Quoted by V. S. Pritchett, *The Gentle Barbarian: The Life of Ivan Turgenev* (London: Faber and Faber, 1977), p. 69.
28. Friel, "Self-Portrait," p. 42.
29. Brian Friel, "Plays Peasant and Unpeasant (1972)," *Times Literary Supplement*, 17 March 1972, p. 222. Also in Murray, *Brian Friel*, p. 56.
30. Brian Friel, "The Theatre of Hope and Despair (1967)," in Murray, *Brian Friel*, pp. 21–23.
31. Ibid., p. 24.
32. *The Irish Times*, 22 May 1991.
33. Pritchett, *The Gentle Barbarian*, p. 88.
34. Bartlett, *Chekhov*, p. 388.
35. Constance Garnett, *Anton Chekhov: Three Plays* (New York: Modern Library, 2001), p. 85.
36. Michael Frayn, *Anton Chekhov: Three Sisters* (London: Methuen, 1983), p. 30.
37. Brian Friel, *Three Sisters by Anton Chekhov: A Translation* (Dublin: Gallery Press, 1981), p. 108; subsequent references are to this edition and will be incorporated in the text.
38. Brian Friel, *Translations*, in *Plays One* (London and Boston: Faber and Faber, 1996), p. 418.
39. Four in *Aristocrats*, if one includes the recorded voice of Anna.
40. Brian Friel, *Uncle Vanya: A Version of the Play by Anton Chekhov* (Oldcastle, County Meath: Gallery Press, 1998), p. 67; subsequent references are to this edition and will be incorporated in the text.
41. Brian Friel, *Aristocrats*, in *Plays One*, p. 295; subsequent references are to this edition and will be incorporated in the text.
42. Molly Keane (as M. J. Farrell), *The Rising Tide* (London: Gollancz, 1937) p. 16, p. 34.
43. Friel, "Extracts from a Sporadic Diary (1976–78): *Aristocrats*," in Murray, *Brian Friel*, pp. 68, 66.
44. Ibid., p. 67.
45. Irving Wardle, *The Times*, quoted on the cover of Brian Friel, *Translations*.

46. George Steiner, *In Bluebeard's Castle* (London: Faber and Faber, 1971), p. 58.

47. See the dialogue between Owen and Yolland in Brian Friel, *Translations*, p. 422.

48. Brian Friel, "In Interview with Paddy Agnew (1980)," in Murray, *Brian Friel*, p. 84. See also Brian Friel, "In Interview with Elgy Gillespie (1981)," in Murray, *Brian Friel*, p. 99; Donal O'Donnell, "Friel and a Tale of Three Sisters" and Eileen Battersby, "Drama of Love: From One Great Master to Another," both in Paul Delaney (ed.), *Brian Friel in Conversation* (Ann Arbor: University of Michigan Press, 2000), pp. 150, 234.

49. Ulick O'Connor, "Friel Takes Derry by Storm (1981)," in Delaney, *Brian Friel in Conversation*, p. 159.

50. Chinua Achebe, *Morning Yet on Creation Day* (London: Heinemann, 1975), p. 62.

51. K. R. S. Iyengar, "Introduction" to *Indian Writing in English*, 3rd edition (New Delhi: Sterling Publishers, 1983), p. 8.

52. O'Donnell, "Friel and a Tale of Three Sisters," p. 150.

53. Battersby, "Drama of Love," p. 233.

54. Friel, "Interview with Elgy Gillespie (1981)," p. 100.

55. Anton Chekhov, *Lady with Lapdog and Other Stories* (Harmondsworth: Penguin, 1964), p. 279.

56. Brian Friel, *The Yalta Game*, in *Three Plays After: The Yalta Game, The Bear, Afterplay* (London and New York: Faber and Faber, 2002), pp. 25–26.

57. Brian Friel, programme note for *Three Sisters* (1981). The concluding quote is from the same source.

11

PATRICK BURKE

Friel and performance history

Any critic of performance history in relation to the works of Brian Friel has, inescapably, to confront the troublesome nature of the relationship between text and performance. The received wisdom among many actors and directors, shared more and more on drama courses in universities, is that the dramatist's text is a means to an end, that of live performance on a stage in the presence of a live audience – hence the multiplicity of courses with titles like "From Page to Stage," and descriptions of play-texts in terms of "scripts," "blueprints" or "scenarios." The debates thus center on what is usually termed the realization of a text for theatrical purposes, often conveyed by obstetric analogy: the writer as parent, the text as fetus, the director as midwife, and the production in all of its aspects (acting, *mise-en-scène*, use of music, etc.) as baby. Mention of directors takes us straight to the plays of Brian Friel and the strength of his passion as to how artistic integrity may best be preserved in their realization.

Over a period of thirty years or more, Friel has been consistently wary of directors and what he views as the inappropriate authority they enjoy in modern theatre. So much was evident as early as the piece he entitled "Self-Portrait," based on a broadcast on the BBC Northern Ireland Home Service in 1971, and what is now seen as its seminal declaration:

> I look on my manuscript as an orchestral score, composed with infinite care and annotated where necessary with precise directions. . . . I look to the director and the actors to interpret that score exactly as it is written. It is not their function to amend, it is not their function to rewrite, or to cut, or to extend. . . . And I use the analogy of the orchestral score with deliberation because I have never known a conductor who would even dream of tampering with the shape of a symphony nor an instrumentalist who would think of rewriting a score before performing it; but I have yet to meet the director or the actor who wouldn't casually paraphrase lines of dialogue or indeed transpose whole scenes.[1]

That manifesto-like statement of principle in relation to the inviolability of his texts has been matched by Friel's intransigence in practice. He threatened legal action in 1966 during the premiere run of *The Loves of Cass McGuire* in the USA when, in his view, the powerful Merrick organization was playing fast and loose with his text. Only under considerable pressure from director Patrick Mason would he agree to alter a few of the concluding lines of *Wonderful Tennessee* during its premiere at the Abbey Theatre in 1993. However, as a possible token of greater amenability in this regard, it was noteworthy that the actor Adrian Dunbar, who directed a production of *Philadelphia, Here I Come!* in 2004 under the auspices of the Association of Regional Theatres in Northern Ireland, appeared to have had little difficulty in negotiating minor alterations to Friel's text.

The clearest practical manifestations of Friel's concern to protect his "manuscript" from directorial intrusion were his decisions to himself direct *Molly Sweeney* at Dublin's Gate Theatre in 1994 and its successor, *Give Me Your Answer, Do!*, at the Abbey in 1997. The decisions were ill-advised. The direction of a notable team of actors in *Give Me Your Answer, Do!* was amateurish, especially in poor blocking and masking and (one assumes) the author's approval of a set design by Frank Hallinan Flood which, in its restrictions on space, inadequately served the dramatic action. The beautifully written *Molly Sweeney* had a small and accomplished cast with Catherine Byrne as Molly, Mark Lambert as her husband, Frank, and veteran T. P. McKenna as her surgeon, Rice. Given this, play direction should have been less onerous; but it was nonetheless notable, especially in the light of Friel's own emphasis on "precise directions," that the relatively static pattern of movement prescribed in the published text was not reflected in the more fussy movement of the stage performance.

But the ostensible severity of Friel's artistic animus towards directors has in fact long been tempered both in statement and in practice. In statement, Friel has expressed admiration for such directors as Konstantin Stanislavsky, Jerzy Grotowski and Peter Brook. Each of them, in Friel's revealingly radical phrase, "turn[ed] upside down the whole practice of theatrical presentation so that we saw it all anew."[2] In practice, Friel *has* worked productively, in a kind of dramaturg capacity, with such directors as Joe Dowling and Patrick Mason. Moreover, in "Self-Portrait," he outlines how for a few months in 1963 he was given an opportunity to observe the Irish director Tyrone Guthrie – whom he described in 1965 as "by far the greatest living producer/director"[3] – at work in a new theatre in Minneapolis. Guthrie was rehearsing productions of *Hamlet* (a play which was to be echoed in Friel's 1975 play, *Volunteers*), Molière's *The Miser* and Chekhov's *Three Sisters* (which Friel was to "translate" for production by Field Day in 1981). While already established as an accomplished short-story writer and with the considerable success of his first major play *The Enemy Within* at the Abbey in 1962 as a source of encouragement, Friel was nonetheless conscious in the presence of Guthrie and his actors of the gaps in his understanding of stagecraft. He became aware of the ways in which he needed to work and in particular of the distinctive languages of theatre:

> I learned about the physical elements of plays, how they are designed, built, landscaped. I learned how actors thought, how they approached a text, their various ways of trying to realize it.[4]

It was surely no accident that the first play he wrote on his return to Ireland should be *Philadelphia, Here I Come!*

It may be critically useful, in resolving the apparent dichotomy in Friel between the dramatist as custodian of his plays and the dramatist as *primus inter pares* among other theatrical artists (directors, actors, designers, etc.) in the realization of the drama, to draw on the analysis provided by Raymond Williams in *Drama in Performance*. There, Williams distinguishes, among other modalities, between drama as "acted speech" and drama as "behaviour." In the former, of which plays as venerable as Sophocles' *Antigone* or the medieval *Everyman* or as recent as Beckett's *Footfalls* are examples, the playwright not only writes the text but the performance:

> [W]hen a text of this kind is set in the known conditions of performance for which the dramatist was writing, the full detail of the performance is seen to be prescribed. Speech and movement are determined by the arrangements of the words, according to the known conventions. . . . Performance here is a physical consummation of a work that is, in its text, dramatically complete.[5]

Hence the apparent paradox that Shakespeare can be less onerous for a beginning director than some seemingly "easier" plays, because his writing indicates a whole dramatic pattern. Hence, from a different perspective, the protectiveness of the Beckett estate in relation to what are unambiguously seen as written performances – no *Waiting For Godot* with women actors! In drama as "behaviour," on the other hand, "the performance . . . is based less on a text than on a response to the text." Citing Chekhov's *The Seagull* as an example, Williams argues that in this model of drama "words and movements have no necessary relation but derive, as it were separately, from a conception of 'probable behaviour' in the circumstances presented. . . . The speech is prescribed, but the 'acting' and 'setting,' and therefore the action as a whole, must often be separately inferred."[6] Such "inferring," logically, would appear to be the domain of the director.

While Friel's deepest allegiances are to the drama of "acted speech" – as *Faith Healer* (1979) so brilliantly demonstrates – many of his plays, or thematically significant features of them, connect to the drama of "behaviour." Questions prompted by the latter could include: What kind of costume should Commandant Frank Butler wear in the relaxed domesticity of the "Portnoo sequence" early in Act 2 of *Living Quarters* (1977)? What kind of incidental music should be used in *Volunteers* (1975) – or should there be any? What degrees of realism should inform the set design of *Dancing at Lughnasa* (1990) and, if elements of the symbolic feature in it, what are the implications for acting style or movement? Does Friel mean it when the lighting in Gar's empty bedroom in Part Two, Episode Three of *Philadelphia, Here I Come!* (1964) seems to be brighter than that of the kitchen? Perhaps he does. Curiously supporting this line of argument, perhaps in a way he never intended, is Friel's "note" to the text of *Faith Healer*, which reads: "In all four parts the director will decide when and where the monologuist sits, walks, stands, etc."[7]

I have seen all of Brian Friel's original plays, translations and adaptations, from *The Enemy Within* in 1962 to *The Home Place* in 2005, twenty-two of them in their premiere productions, two of them (1982's *The Communication Cord* and 1990's *The London Vertigo*) in amateur productions only. I have directed, in semi-professional or student productions, *Living Quarters*, *Faith Healer*, *Philadelphia, Here I Come!*, *The Loves of Cass McGuire*, *Wonderful Tennessee* and the Hungarian premiere of *Translations* at the University of Debrecen in 1996. If the foregoing gives me an adequate basis from which to address the performance history of Friel's plays, I hope in the compass provided to address two categorizations. The first is what I believe to be Friel's masterworks, partly defined as such because of their near-complete congruence of substance with form (always a concern with Friel), of which in my opinion there are seven. The second, much more brief, discussion will be of those plays which are not as fully achieved but which resonate powerfully, sometimes mysteriously, in the theatre. I shall, except where there is good reason to proceed otherwise, concentrate on the first productions of the plays, partly on grounds supplied by Friel himself:

> [I]mmediately before rehearsals begin you have got some kind of ideal sound in your head of what the play is like. Then as rehearsals go on it acquires the authenticity that those particular actors *bring* to it. And then the problem always is that after a first production, those become the definitive sounds of the play.[8]

Masterworks

The first of these has to be *Faith Healer*, aptly described by Thomas Kilroy as "a sublime work of the imagination in which the distinction between theatrical text and literary artefact ceases to be of account."[9] The premiere production – in April 1979, at the Longacre Theatre, New York – was a box-office failure, closing after a mere week. This was the outcome, notwithstanding direction by José Quintero (acclaimed for his productions of Eugene O'Neill) and the superb acting of James Mason in the title role, even though the veteran stage and screen actor played Frank Hardy considerably older than the "middle-aged" character of Friel's script. Neither Clarissa Kaye (married at the time to Mason, and in the cast largely at his behest) as Grace, nor Donal Donnelly as Teddy, could match Mason's level. Reviews were less than enthusiastic, apart from Walter Kerr in the *New York Times* (15 April 1979). The definitive production of *Faith Healer* opened in Dublin at the Abbey on 28 August 1980. It was directed with unshowy sensitivity by Joe Dowling, who, having previously directed the premieres of *Living Quarters* (1977) and *Aristocrats* (1979) at the Abbey, was a director with whom Friel could work well. The theatrical challenge of conveying the mesmeric power of *Faith Healer* made it the most difficult play Dowling had directed up to that point. He was ably assisted by Wendy Shea's economic, uncluttered set design and by Leslie Scott's skillful lighting. What made the production unforgettable, however, was the quality of the acting. Kate Flynn as Grace showed with impressive acting integrity how to distinguish soliloquy from monologue. John Kavanagh, holding the stage alone for almost an hour as Teddy, managed a splendid rapport with the audience, almost (but never quite) going "over the top." And in what has been recognized as one of the greatest characterizations ever seen on the Irish stage, Donal McCann as Frank gave a performance of hypnotic, almost dangerous power. McCann's playing of the ending of the final monologue, where he recounts the dawn confrontation with the cripple McGarvey, will long haunt the memory.

My second choice continues to be one of Friel's best-loved plays, *Philadelphia, Here I Come!* It was first presented at the Gaiety Theatre on 28 September 1964 as part of that year's Dublin Theatre Festival. Against a recurring myth, Friel has consistently denied that it was ever rejected by the Abbey. In fact, from an early stage, and following abortive negotiations with Phyllis Ryan's Gemini Company, the rights were held by Oscar Lewenstein, who agreed the terms of production with Dublin's Gate Theatre Productions. In the early 1960s the Gate was still headed by its founders, actor-writer-designer Micheál MacLiammóir and director-actor Hilton Edwards, an Englishman who was to go on to direct the premiere of *Philadelphia, Here I Come!* and the three following plays. Of the total Friel oeuvre, at least nine plays, including the most recent four, have been premiered at the Gate Theatre or by the Gate Company, which has been under the directorship of Michael Colgan since 1984. Friel has expressed his gratitude for that theatre's founders' early support: "if I had to produce documentation I would be pleased to claim . . . that I came out from under the Edwards–MacLiammoir overcoat."[10] He admired what he termed their "stylishness," which I take to mean a bravura, elegant celebration of the theatrical event in terms of acting, directing and (at a time when it was not the Abbey's strongest point) of lighting and design. *Philadelphia, Here I Come!* proved the hit of that year's Dublin Theatre Festival and was later to run for 326 performances on Broadway and to earn Donal Donnelly a Tony nomination in the role of Gar Private. Edwards's direction was singled out for praise by Dublin reviewers and there was critical acclaim too for Patrick Bedford as Gar Public, Eamon Kelly as Gar's reticent father and for the setting by Alpho O'Reilly. The play spoke powerfully to a new generation of theatregoers. Joe Dowling, then aged 16, and who was later to direct the play more than once himself, went to see the production nineteen times. In the brilliant device of Gar Private the play went beyond the overt issues of lack of communication, loneliness and macho bravado to the existential hunger of youthful consciousness, the need authentically to be. That said, I suspect a modern audience might find the 1964 production rather mannered, externalized, even sentimentalized. The eminent short-story writer Frank O'Connor went so far as to categorize Edwards's directorial approach as having reduced a "beautiful, gentle play" into a "rip-roaring revue"[11] – an opinion firmly dismissed in a letter by Friel to the *Sunday Independent* of 11 October 1964.

Next, perhaps surprisingly, is *Volunteers*, which I have long contended is Friel's most neglected major play. Its focus is on the identities, values and destinies of a group of IRA-like "volunteers" led by Keeney. We never learn the prisoners' forenames because they are socially unappropriated. The men have "volunteered" to work on an archaeological dig, itself ironically soon to be filled in, to make way for a new hotel. Meanwhile, because of alleged treachery, they themselves face death at the hands of their former comrades. When the premiere production of *Volunteers* opened at the Abbey on 5 March 1975, acting, direction and design received quite commendatory comment. But the play itself, directed by Robert Gillespie and with Donal Donnelly as Keeney, was greeted by ignorance and critical myopia. This was so acute that Seamus Heaney felt obliged to defend the play in the *Times Literary Supplement*. With his customary eloquence Heaney identified the heart of the piece:

In *Volunteers* [Friel] has found a form that allows his gift a freer expression. Behind the writing there is an unrelenting despair at what man has made of man, but its expression from moment to moment on the stage is by turns ironic, vicious, farcical, pathetic . . .[12]

Aside from an unsuccessful touring production by Cork Theatre Company in September 1987, it was to be another twenty-three years after its premiere before *Volunteers* was to find adequate realization. This was in the production at London's tiny Gate Theatre on 22 October 1998. London critics united in a virtual chorus of praise for the play, the director Mick Gordon and Patrick O'Kane as Keeney. In his five-star review for the *Guardian* on 27 October, Michael Billington praised the "first-rate performances" of J. D. Kelleher as Keeney's camp sidekick, Pyne; Christopher Whitehouse as Butt; and Colin Farrell as George, the dig foreman. Liz Cook's setting received special praise as "the triumph of Gordon's production."[13] The environmental setting made the audience part of the action by sitting them on concrete seats overlooking the work site, the house lights being left on throughout the play.

My fourth choice, *Translations*, may cause surprise in the opposite direction from *Volunteers*. It is probably Friel's most celebrated play worldwide, seen in so many societies as of central cultural importance. For many fine critics such as Christopher Murray, it is also "surely Friel's masterpiece."[14] My hesitancy relates partly to the play-text and a belief that the second scene of Act 2, principally involving Owen, the Irishman working with the British Ordnance Survey of the 1830s, Yolland, the "romanticized" English lieutenant, and Hugh, the master of the hedge-school, is vitiated in credibility as they engage in linguistic debate (but in that scene only) by an imperfectly absorbed indebtedness on Friel's part to George Steiner's *After Babel*. It relates partly also to what I believe was an uncritically euphoric response to the premiere production by the newly established Field Day Theatre Company at Derry's Guildhall in 1980. The undoubted triumph of that opening night in Derry was not simply a matter of recognizing the artistic worth of a great play. It had much to do also with factors of race memory, the hurt consequent on the loss of a language, political identity in a divided community, as well as cultural aspirations for the city in which the play was being performed. The Field Day production's theatrical strengths were undeniable: the in-depth acting performances of the great Ray McAnally as Hugh, of Liam Neeson as Doalty, Ann Hasson as Sarah, and Roy Hanlon as a memorable Jimmy Jack. With hindsight, however, it is probably fair to say that the dramatic rhythm and ensemble were not always dependably secured by the director, Art O'Briain, that the usually accomplished Stephen

Rea (co-founder of Field Day) was not easy in the role of Owen, possibly because of Field Day "business" demands on his time, and that Consolata Boyle's bark-stripped set design, while interesting visually and spatially, may not have imaged the requisite ambience of a hedge-school, especially in the light of Friel's detailed stage directions.

An early measure of some of the inadequacies of the Field Day premiere was the production of *Translations* seen in London the following year at the Hampstead Theatre Club (12 May 1981), which later transferred to the National Theatre. Here director Donald McWhinnie brought a sense of ease to the play's flow and climaxes, and secured understanding performances from Ian Bannen as Hugh, Bernadette Shortt as Maire, Anna Keaveney as Bridget, Máire Ni Ghráinne as Sarah, Ron Flanagan as Doalty – and Stephen Rea, this time more comfortable in the role of Manus. Eileen Diss designed a serviceable setting of greater realism and three-dimensional solidity. A notable highlight of this production was Tony Doyle's portrayal of Owen, so expertly realized as to extend the overall complexity of the play and remind the audience that Owen's is the largest role. An important consequence of the success of this production of *Translations* in the UK was the entrée it provided, in a long-closed market, both for other plays by Friel and for those of such younger Irish dramatists as Billy Roche and Conor McPherson.

Fifth on my list is a near-perfect production of one of Friel's most achieved texts, the Abbey premiere of *Aristocrats* on 8 March 1979; the play has never, in my experience, been so well realized in any subsequent showing. Director Joe Dowling caught its delicacy to perfection while never losing sight of the play's concern with the degradation of a formerly "Big House" Catholic family. It was selflessly served in exemplary ensemble acting, notably John Kavanagh as Casimir, Stephen Rea as Eamon, Kate Flynn as Judith, Dearbhla Molloy as Alice and Kevin McHugh as Tom Hoffnung. Designer Wendy Shea met Friel's difficult design challenge, wherein must be combined, outdoors downstage, an untidy lawn and an old gazebo, and, indoors upstage, a small room with naturalistic furnishings, all the while allowing space for the actors to move around and sufficient room for an invisible croquet game. An integral element of the play's action, the music of Chopin, was evocatively performed by Veronica McSwiney. *Aristocrats* was a particular beneficiary of the renewed interest in Friel's theatre prompted by the success of *Translations*. Its London production received the *Evening Standard* Drama Award for Best Play in 1988; and its New York production won the Drama Critics' Circle Award for Best New Foreign Play in 1989; both were directed by Robin LeFevre and featured Niall Buggy as Casimir.

My next choice is *The Freedom of the City*, partly because I believe it is better written than Friel's own disclaimer would suggest, partly because of its ongoing broadly defined political relevance. The play had, in a sense, a double premiere: at the Abbey on 20 February 1973, directed by Tomás MacAnna, and in London at the Royal Court Theatre exactly a week later, directed by Albert Finney. *The Freedom of the City* is a finely crafted and unusual combination of two modes of theatre: the movingly naturalistic in the presentation of Lily, Michael and Skinner, who we know from the outset are to be shot by British Army forces, and the Brechtian, in its presentation of a wide range of commenting public agencies – army officers, priests, sociologist, journalist, tribunal judge. Though Friel has regularly insisted that essentially it is a play "about poverty,"[15] and though it can be argued that its defining conflict is that of playfulness versus institutionalized restraint, the ironically titled *The Freedom of the City* was clearly inspired by the appalling events of "Bloody Sunday" in 1972 and the subsequent cover-up in the form of the Widgery Tribunal. This gave it a degree of contemporaneity which engendered official suspicion in Britain, especially in military circles. The *Daily Mail* reported that "the play has angered senior Army officers in Ulster." A similarly hostile response from the English-born Clive Barnes in the *New York Times* contributed to the closure of the play on Broadway after a mere nine nights in February 1974. The Dublin production was cautiously rather than enthusiastically received, with commendation for MacAnna's sympathetic direction, the acting performances of Angela Newman as Lily, Eamonn Morrissey as the enigmatic Skinner, Raymond Hardie as Michael, and John Kavanagh as the Judge. Alan Barlow's setting – an image of Derry's Guildhall, where *Translations* was to premiere seven years later – was very much in accordance with Friel's specifications in the text, and Leslie Scott's lighting, in a play in which lighting is a key component, was also admired. Friel himself preferred the London production, possibly because he was more involved in its preparation. Albert Finney, as a member of the Board of the Royal Court, had insisted from a concern for justice in relation to "Bloody Sunday" that the play be staged as a matter of urgency. Finney directed with commitment, keeping a tight rein on the production, and Stephen Rea made a notable early impression as Skinner. *The Freedom of the City*, which has had far fewer productions than it deserves either in Ireland or abroad, was one of those selected by the Abbey for the 1999 Friel Festival, to celebrate the dramatist's seventieth birthday. That revival (28 April 1999) was directed by the talented Conall Morrison, whose production perhaps could have done more to distinguish the play's two dominant modes, the "warm" naturalistic from the "cool" Brechtian.

As with *Translations*, some readers will argue that my seventh choice, *Dancing at Lughnasa*, deserves a higher placing, not least because of its international reputation. It premiered at the Abbey on 24 April 1990 and was directed by Patrick Mason, the first of at least four productions he was to oversee. Popular all over the world with theatre companies both professional and amateur, *Lughnasa* has garnered many awards, including Play of the Year in the 1991 Olivier Awards in London, three Tony Awards in New York in 1992, and Best Play from the New York Drama Critics' Circle in the same year. Audiences worldwide have been moved by the play's tribute to the human dignity of what the text's dedication describes as "those five brave Glenties women,"[16] modeled on Friel's aunts, together with its resonant plea for adequate healing rituals beyond the available orthodoxies of Christianity. *Dancing at Lughnasa* is one of Friel's best plays, even if there is a slight and perhaps unavoidable blurring of focus between the play as realistic evocation of a certain kind of attenuated living (Donegal in the 1930s) and the play as a drama of consciousness (that of the narrator, Michael). To me that blurring was compounded rather than lessened by designer Joe Vanek's visually beautiful field of corn, which dominated the setting of the premiere production. Intended, in Vanek's revealing phrase, to serve "as several visual metaphors,"[17] it may finally have tried to do too much. In 1990 all five of the sisters' roles were superbly played – Frances Tomelty as the decent teacher Kate, Anita Reeves as the good-humored but keenly aware Maggie, Catherine Byrne as the single mother Chris, Bríd Ní Neachtain as the simple-minded and sympathetic Rose and, in a luminous performance, Bríd Brennan as the quiet Agnes. If Gerard McSorley excelled in delivering the haunting rhythms of Michael's final speech (which he was called on to reprise in the 1998 film version of the play), Paul Herzberg seemed ill at ease as Michael's father, Gerry Evans, and Barry McGovern was over-vocal in the key role of Father Jack. And, while Patrick Mason directed that production with all his characteristic skill and sensitivity, his approach seems in hindsight to have been over-celebratory, especially in the now-famous dance sequence of the sisters in the first act. As Catherine Byrne was shrewdly to observe ten years later:

> *Dancing at Lughnasa* was all golden corn and poppies, beautiful lighting; the women were colour-coordinated. But there's another production of *Dancing at Lughnasa* we haven't seen yet. We haven't seen how dark it is. Ours was the golden production.[18]

A "darker" production of the play was staged at the Gate Theatre in 2004 (24 February). It was directed by Joe Dowling, who by then had become Director of the Guthrie Theatre in Minneapolis, the same one in which Friel had served his playwriting apprenticeship in 1963. Even if the ensemble acting was less impressive than in 1990, one felt the courage of the sisters in the face of exigency and sensed, too, the elements of desperation and frustrated womanhood in their notorious dance.

Of the remaining plays by Friel – excluding the impressive adaptations from Chekhov and Turgenev – a number cry out for attention as undervalued, misunderstood on first production or still in need of outstanding realization. There are the well-made plays, from the early *The Enemy Within* to the much later *Give Me Your Answer, Do! The Gentle Island* has only been produced twice, at the Olympia Theatre in 1971 (directed by Abbey actor Vincent Dowling) and at the Peacock Theatre in 1988 (directed by playwright Frank McGuinness); the play is a grim parable of emotional, material and cultural deprivation and deserves to be more widely known. A revival of *Crystal and Fox* (in the 1968 premiere of which Cyril Cusack was unforgettable) might appeal to our more jaundiced times. *Molly Sweeney*, which has enjoyed considerably more stage success in the USA than in Ireland, seems to me quintessentially a radio play. The unexpected success of Brian Brady's production of *Making History* at the Peacock Theatre during the 1999 Friel Festival, in which Gerard McSorley was a revelation as Hugh O'Neill, provided clear testimony that the Field Day premiere in 1988 did not serve the script adequately. *Wonderful Tennessee*, even if the text strains to endow post-Christian experience with mythological resonance, would benefit from an ensemble-centered revival. *Performances*, first produced at the Gate Theatre in 2003 with direction by Patrick Mason, draws on the experiences of the Czech composer Leos Janáček (memorably performed by the Romanian actor-director Ion Caramitru) to reframe Yeats's classical dilemma of choosing perfection of the life or of the work. *Performances* may be less flawed than the response to its premiere might suggest and proved a fascinating attempt to integrate musical with dramatic form. Towering above all of these, and a favorite of Friel's, is *Living Quarters*, based both on Euripides' *Hippolytus* and Racine's *Phèdre*. The play is that very rare phenomenon, a pure Irish tragedy. Its well-realized premiere at the Abbey in 1977, truthfully directed by Joe Dowling and featuring sensitive performances from a strong "Frielian" ensemble cast (Ray McAnally, Dearbhla Molloy, Clive Geraghty, Fedelma Cullen, Stephen Brennan, Micheál Ó hAonghusa, Niall O'Brien) has been undervalued by theatre historians. A less-achieved interpretation, directed by the creative Jason Byrne, was still the "hit" of the 1999 Festival.

Where some of Friel's plays have had no shortage of productions, others have been insufficiently appreciated from lack of being seen. A wider range of staged works from his extraordinary oeuvre would promote a fuller sense of his achievement as a master dramatist.

NOTES

1. Brian Friel, "Self-Portrait (1972)," in Christopher Murray (ed.), *Brian Friel: Essays, Diaries, Interviews: 1964–1999* (London and New York: Faber and Faber, 1999), pp. 44–45.
2. Brian Friel, "Seven Notes for a Festival Programme (1999)," in Murray, *Brian Friel*, p. 178.
3. Brian Friel, "An Observer in Minneapolis," in Paul Delaney (ed.), *Brian Friel In Conversation* (Ann Arbor: University of Michigan Press, 2000), p. 35.
4. Friel, "Self-Portrait," in Murray, *Brian Friel*, p. 42.
5. Raymond Williams, *Drama in Performance* (Middlesex: Pelican Books, 1972), pp. 173–174.
6. Ibid., p. 173.
7. Brian Friel, *Faith Healer*, in *Plays One* (London and Boston: Faber and Faber 1996), p. 331.
8. Brian Friel, "Brian Friel and Field Day (1983)," in Delaney, *Brian Friel in Conversation*, p. 179.
9. Thomas Kilroy, "Theatrical Text and Literary Text," in Alan Peacock (ed.), *The Achievement of Brian Friel* (Gerrards Cross: Colin Smythe, 1993), p. 99.
10. "Brian Friel," in Peter Luke (ed.), *Enter Certain Players* (Dublin: Dolmen Press, 1968), p. 21.
11. *Guardian*, 8 October 1964, p. 9.
12. Seamus Heaney, "Digging Deeper: Brian Friel's *Volunteers*," in *Preoccupations: Selected Prose 1968–1978* (London and Boston: Faber and Faber, 1980), pp. 215–216.
13. Michael Billington, *Guardian*, 27 October 1998.
14. Christopher Murray, review of published text of *Translations*, *Irish University Review* 11:1 (1981), pp. 238–239.
15. See for example "In Interview with Eavan Boland," in Murray, *Brian Friel*, p. 58.
16. Brian Friel, *Dancing at Lughnasa*, in *Plays Two* (London: Faber and Faber, 1999), p. 1.
17. Joe Vanek, "The Designer," in Tony Coult, *About Friel: The Playwright and the Work* (London and New York: Faber and Faber, 2003), p. 207. (Editor's note: for a more detailed and positive account of Vanek's set design, see Derek West's in Coult, *About Friel*, pp. 208–210.)
18. In "Voices and Documents," in Coult, *About Friel*, p. 156.

12

RICHARD ALLEN CAVE

Friel's dramaturgy: the visual dimension

The advent of electric light within theatre effected over the twentieth century a series of radical innovations in stage practice. Electricity exposed the falsities of pictorial scenery, the painted shadows, the games with perspective, showed them for what they were: illusions, tricks of the eye. The new lighting system put an end to a centuries-long tradition of scenic representation, which came patently to seem what had long been implicit within the turn-of-the-century term for stage design: decoration (deriving from the French, *décor*, the arranging, furnishing, color choice and tonal balance of a room, significantly an interior space, to reflect the taste, status and income of the resident). Electricity made possible a whole new approach to stage design, allowing a focus on volume and space. There were the architectural settings of Appia and Craig, constructivist settings chiefly in Russia, and Expressionist settings in Germany (often exploring power structures through the dynamic use of varying stage levels, especially in the stagings of Leopold Jessner), the presentational (as distinct from the representational), which frankly admitted its theatricality, and in time the permanent setting, where changes of location were achievable by changes to the lighting state. All to varying degrees required a major input from lighting; and electricity was discovered to be a highly flexible medium available for coloring in far subtler ways than had ever been possible with candle power or gas, and for soft, almost imperceptible gradations of intensity towards extremes of brilliance or of darkness.

Lighting such as this made space "elastic, emotional and mobile." The epithets are Pamela Howard's, made (while writing about her own and her contemporaries' practice as designers) in a monograph that poses by way of its title the question: *What is Scenography?* Of the aspects of her artistry she discusses in detail, it is surely of note that the one to which she gives the privileged position of opening chapter is Space.[1] As a preface to her study (by way of giving the reader a "World View"), Howard invited some forty-four contemporary designers of international standing to answer her question in no more than a sentence; more than two-thirds make some reference to space. Joseph Svoboda of the Czech Republic, arguably the most influential of postwar European scenographers, replied succinctly: "The interplay of space, time, movement and light on stage."[2] Even the term Howard selects to define her profession, "scenography," positions her decidedly apart from all that is implicit in the term "designer." The former alludes to a geography of the scene, to a mapping ("graph") of the territory of the stage, which determines its given appearance for a particular production; where "designer" suggests the creation of a flat image that still has to be realized in three dimensions. Twentieth-century designers have often seen their work as allied either to architecture (Erich Mendelsohn, Emil Pirchan, Robert Edmund Jones, Doria Paston) or to sculpture (Caspar Neher, Jocelyn Herbert) not to fine art and easel painting, the like of their nineteenth-century predecessors (and their forebears, too), who tended to think in terms of a "stage picture." Architecture and sculpture both take on a solidity, dynamism and character ("have life") within the ever-shifting play of light. Electricity enabled that "play of light" within theatre.

It may seem strange (even wayward) to begin a discussion of Brian Friel's stagecraft with a schematized history of twentieth-century stage design, but it is quite deliberate. Even a cursory study of commentaries on Friel's work shows an unyielding tendency to focus on him as wordsmith and the literary qualities of his writing: forms, themes, characterizations, influences, styles of dialogue or monologue, the precision of his matching of words to psychological or emotional nuance. Even two excellent essays by Christopher Murray and Anthony Roche, respectively analyzing Friel's debts to Yeats and Synge, noticeably ignore the visual dimension.[3] This is not to devalue such criticism but to point to a serious omission; one which may best be understood in the context of a confusion that seems currently to obtain among theatre practitioners about Friel's attitude to elements of design in staging his plays. There are those like Joe Dowling and Joe Vanek, director and designer respectively, who appear to consider Friel's attitude to design as dated. Vanek refers to the "almost Shavian details of windows, doors, furniture and domestic utensils," which suggest for him a studied, detailed realism "bound by conventional stage imagery," out of sympathy with the expectations of contemporary audiences. These comments come from an essay about designing *Dancing at Lughnasa* (1990).[4] It may be that Vanek was taking this line to justify his inclusion of a stylized cornfield in his design for *Lughnasa*, for which there is no direct sanction in Friel's stage directions.

Dowling pursues a similar line of argument in justifying his claim that Friel demonstrates a "lack of concern for the visual environment":

> In spite of his early apprenticeship with Tyrone Guthrie, one of the most inno-
> vative and visually exciting directors of this century, Friel never really developed
> a sense of the possibilities of stage design as a way of expressing the imagery
> of his plays. He is usually very literal in his demands for the physical environ-
> ment, describing in detail exactly the type of setting he requires. This rarely
> allows for an imaginative approach from the designer and demands a clear
> naturalism [. . .].[5]

The reference to Guthrie relates to the period in 1963 when he invited Friel to
observe the rehearsals for his opening productions at the newly built theatre
in Minneapolis. The attempted contrast here is factitious: Friel attended
rehearsals, while Dowling is referring to finished *productions*; and there
is a significant difference between the two processes of staging. As will be
argued later, Friel was a shrewd and responsive observer, learning more from
Guthrie's practice than Dowling allows.

Dowling's conclusion is that "essentially [Friel's] plays demand productions which concentrate on the performances without much emphasis on the
externals."[6] Vanek and Dowling seem to be judging the issue from a pictorial standpoint, itself now decidedly dated, as shown above; both see the
designer as needing latitude ("an imaginative approach") to make some kind
of "imagistic" statement. Ironically, Dowling elsewhere in his essay under-
cuts the force of his comments when he warns potential directors against
seeing "Friel's work as a way of making their own theatrical statements."[7]
Why, then, does he insist on a latitude for designers which he would deny
directors? One might counter-argue that the visual dimension can relate
to other factors onstage than a bold pictorial or imagistic statement; and
that such statements can well prove intrusive or, by offering an overly powerful interpretation, easily effect a closure of spectators' own imaginative
responses to the action.

The director, Patrick Mason, offers a view wholly opposed to Dowling's:

> I think he [Friel] has an extraordinary precision, not only obviously of lan-
> guage, of expression, but also a precision of gesture. And a precision of, if
> you like, *position*. A physical sense of positioning on the stage [. . .]. But I
> would argue that all the best playwrights have an acute sense of the physical
> dimension of theatre as well of course as its music, its power of language.[8]

"Positioning," of course, relates to space. (One recalls Brecht's relish at seeing
Caspar Neher at work: ". . . with what care he selects a chair, and with what
thought he places it! And it all helps the playing."[9]) Much of Guthrie's
brilliance as a director came from his mastery of placing actors within the
playing space such that their arrangement had the power of a Brechtian
gestus (though Guthrie would not have used the term). I would argue that

what Friel most likely registered in Minneapolis as "innovative and visually exciting" were just this sensitive spatial awareness and its function within Guthrie's style of directing. But crucially he did this while observing Guthrie *in the rehearsal room*; and in that situation none of the trappings to do with a set would be present.[10] To argue that an acute spatial awareness is the key to the visual dynamic of Friel's dramaturgy is to suggest he is more up-to-date than his critics: with Friel we must think not in terms of scenery, but of scenography.

Innovations in dramatic form usually demand equally innovative methods in their staging (Yeats, O'Casey and Beckett within the Irish theatrical tradition validate that claim); and Friel is no exception here. In one of his earliest plays, *The Enemy Within* (1962), one finds Friel returning in his setting for Columba's cell to what for its time was the highly innovative design scheme that Sturge Moore and Robert Gregory created to Yeats's specifications for *The Hour Glass* as staged by the Irish National Theatre Society in 1903 and its later adaptation for the staging of Yeats's *On Baile's Strand* at the Abbey Theatre in 1904: a simple box set with one entrance centre-back in the plainest of colors to foreground the actors and emphasize a pertinent contrast between action onstage and off.[11] The monks have a uniform habit, which allows them to function both as individuals and, when occasion demands, as chorus. That Columba has an identical habit in a different color emphasizes his place within the order but as their leader; and the simplicity of this design scheme draws an immediate contrast with the various, more colorfully attired visitors to Iona, coming to tempt Columba back to a life of social and familial duties in Ireland. As the title implies, the action is to be viewed less as historical than as psychological drama, as an exploration of the inner costs of the renunciations required by a pursuit of the ascetic ideal: all the figures (Brian, Eoghan, Aedh) who come from *without* that space constitute a challenge and a threat to Columba's commitment and equanimity to his order and its principles; they are temptations disturbing his soul's peace. Friel stresses this concept in distinctly spatial terms towards the close of Act 1, where the directions require a symbolic grouping: "COLUMBA *is in the centre*, GRILLAAN [Columba's spiritual adviser] *on one side of him*, BRIAN *on the other. He is torn between the two.*"[12] The design features of the staging prescribed by Friel are subtle correlatives of the thematic life of the drama, directing the sensitively attuned spectator to a particular reading of the action. That the visual conception relates inter-textually to the staging of several of Yeats's plays situates Friel's play within a specific Irish genre and tradition, which again directs the informed audience to specific modes of interpretation. Use of the term "directs" implies that the design conveys a manipulative, rhetorical intent, and to some extent this is true. Significantly it was a line of experiment that Friel chose not to pursue. Instead his next plays show him seeking ways to leave spectator response open, flexible or, to use Friel's preferred epithet, "fluid."

Friel first applies this term within the direction (headed "Set") that precedes the text of *Philadelphia, Here I Come!* (1964). The main stage space is to be divided between the spartan kitchen and Gar's equally austere bedroom; both are conceived in the tradition of stage realism. One might in consequence have expected this divided setting to be framed directly by the proscenium arch but Friel asks instead that this occupy the rear "two-thirds of the stage" to leave a substantial apron or forestage. This isolates the traditional setting at a distance from the spectator and so breaks the dramatic conventions that such a setting usually invites. The staging thus neatly anticipates how the division of the central role between two actors playing Gar's public and private selves will disrupt the conventions of dramaturgical realism. Significantly, Friel concludes: "The remaining portion [of the playing space] is fluid."[13] That forestage will be put to many uses, chiefly for the enactment of sequences which are Gar's processes of recall, for the staging of memory which, given its particular proximity to the audience (the lack of distancing which obtains with the rest of the setting), endows all that takes place on it with a vivid immediacy. Gar has not yet left Ballybeg for America, but already his psyche is setting up the conditions for homesickness. The play ends with the two Gars watching Madge, the housekeeper and Gar's surrogate mother, shuffling off to bed, receding out of the space:

> PRIVATE: Watch her carefully, every movement, every gesture, every little peculiarity: keep the camera whirring; for this is a film you'll run over and over again [. . .].　　　　　　　　　　　　　　　　　　　　　(99)

Gar is divided within himself because of the emotional conflict he is experiencing at the prospect of leaving. But the whole play through its processes of distancing represents his alienation from everything that has shaped his identity till now. In the Brechtian sense of alienation, the familiar is being rendered strange, as Gar faces an emotional crisis. Everything we experience in the play is a film in the making, as in the above scene, where Gar patently recognizes Madge's exit from his life; it is all becoming material to be played in future on the forestage of his imagination. Friel's deployment of stage space is meticulously conceived to prepare the audience for the final lines: "God, Boy, why do you have to leave? Why? Why?" (99). This is not stage design in its dated sense, but an exact and exacting focus on space demanding a designer's respect. What impresses here is that the more Friel conceives the role of design in his plays as a means through a careful deployment of space to engage with his audience's imaginations, the more he circumscribes a designer's potential for latitude. The apron is notably an empty space, shaped into meaningfulness by the work of the actors and to some degree by that of the lighting designer.

Once Friel embraced the potential of fluidity made possible by a creative response to space as distinct from design, it was perhaps inevitable he should push that potential to an ambitious extreme. This is demonstrated by his directions for *The Loves of Cass McGuire* (1966). Here, the setting largely comprises an arrangement of chairs and table mostly situated near a fireplace and a raised dais, upstage left, supporting a bed consciously balanced, downstage right, by a large winged armchair. These at Cass's command may configure a lounge in either her brother's house or an old folks' home, her private room in that home, or a place to find a protected inner dreamscape. While the conventions of realism may obtain within any of the first three locations, those conventions are limited by a spectator's awareness that the situations are summoned into being and changed as Cass dictates while she tells her story. There are times for her when the only "real" relation is between her as narrator and the theatre audience, whom she peers at and directly addresses. Whatever elements of stage design are present onstage have in consequence a decidedly tenuous hold on realism (their signification is never precise but continually in a state of flux). The one concession to pictorial imagery (a formal garden with a statue of Cupid) is marginalized to a distantly seen backdrop and then rendered disturbingly quixotic, since the statue is to seem "frozen in an absurd and impossible contortion."[14] If this is an imagistic commentary on Cass's life history, it is noticeable that Friel never requires his character to enter the territory of the garden, unlike other inmates in the home. Cass is a survivor, a joyous free-wheeler who refuses to be contained by her prissy brother: a *playing space* is her rightful home, defining her indefatigable resilience and creativity. Not for Friel the attendant artifice of the Noh; but the imaginative release offered by a (relatively) bare stage is for him as for Yeats the prerequisite for a theatrical journey into what the latter would call the "deeps of the mind." One is reminded in this context of Fox Melarkey in *Crystal and Fox* (1968), whose world is an embodiment of impermanence in being situated within a fit-up theatre, forever broken up, moved on and recreated. But even that fails to content Fox eventually, as he casts off all his relationships and responsibilities and is last seen alone at a crossroads in a bare rural terrain facing a choice of possible destinations. The play enacts Fox's process of shedding contingencies and responsibilities, which seem to him increasingly intrusive, to embrace a core of self where anything becomes possible. Perhaps the play has the status of parable?

The experimenting with space has continued unabated throughout Friel's career, producing a wide range of styles in design. There is the house situated in its characterizing landscape, where the realistic portrayal of a central room (usually kitchen or lounge) is rendered strange because one or more of the outer walls has been removed. This began with *The Gentle Island* (1971) and has continued through *Living Quarters* (1977) and *Dancing at Lughnasa* (1990). There is a practical consideration affecting such a setting: the need for clear sightlines into the room on display. Strategically raising and lowering a wall into the theatre flies might have achieved this. But that technique smacks of gimmickry and loses the connotation that, far from being divided spaces, interior and exterior are fluid and interconnected, even if "within" tends to be a place of inhibition and claustrophobia while "without" offers respite or release (especially in *Dancing at Lughnasa*, where the garden is the site for dancing and ritual as expressions of selfhood, otherwise forcefully repressed inside the social space). This concept of a setting admirably supports the communication of the respective plays as structured processes of recall, in which place is occasioned more by a controlling mood than a literal geography, and where constituent elements (details of furnishing, the grouping of objects in relation to means of entrance and exit) are selected as contributing to the prevailing atmosphere and its movement towards change (be it guilt shading towards atonement in *Living Quarters*, or anger at a private loss moving into compassionate insight in *Dancing at Lughnasa*).

If little comment has been offered on *The Gentle Island* in analyzing this style of setting, it is because it is the least successful (perhaps because the earliest) attempt. However, the grounds for that relative failure in design terms help explain the excellence of the later two works. In *The Gentle Island* a kitchen gives access to a street and view of the island, but there are to be no walls separating these areas. However, in this play far more of the dramatic action takes place within the kitchen than without. Initially the street allows for varying images of the mass emigration from the place, which defines the complete isolation of Manus Sweeney and his family, the islanders who remain; and subsequently the action shows the bringing out into the light of hidden but primal tensions within the triangular relationship of father, son and daughter-in-law. But this play does not achieve the concentration and intensity of the other two, where the action is filtered through memory so that a coming-to-terms with the past enacts a decided change in the present. *The Gentle Island* hovers precariously on the edge of melodrama, where the other plays contain and displace it in favor of psychological subtleties discovered through a concern with the consequences of engaging with a past that is potentially disabling.

A variation of this type of setting defines the playing space as chiefly a garden backed by a house, where an exposed interior is raised somewhat above the main stage level on a kind of dais approached up two steps. *Aristocrats* (1979) and *Give Me Your Answer, Do!* (1997) follow this pattern, where the house seems now deliberately a place apart, even if it lies open to view. Both plays explore dispossession. The former sees the onetime inhabitants of a "Big House" facing exile because political and social change have placed them beyond the means of its upkeep. The action involves a parent's death, and the ensuing wake extends to the house and its way of life, viewed by the surviving generation with responses varying between fear at its disciplines and comic affection for its eccentricity. There are times when the garden becomes like that downstage space in *The Loves of Cass McGuire*, where characters retreat into their private rhapsodies; and this play might have been an exercise in nostalgia haunted by melodies from Chopin. But what impresses is the clear-eyed efficiency with which the characters accept change and the need to depart, now garden as well as house have grown derelict and alien. The house is occupied by the dead, and its history is now of interest only to an American academic; sentiment suddenly has no place here. The dilapidated garden of *Give Me Your Answer, Do!* and the seedy house beyond it have a chance of renewal and redefinition as a home, if Tom would agree to sell the manuscripts that constitute his life's work as novelist to an American library; but the recognition brought by the money would be an enshrining, an entombment of his talents in his wife's view. Tom's artistry builds alternative worlds in the imagination (we twice see him playing with a reckless fantasy, trying to build an imaginative and emotional bridge to his hospitalized, autistic daughter); his talent thrives in the uncertainty of seemingly waste spaces. The characters' rejection of the temptations of the space in both plays (one hardly needs to stress the Edenic connotations of the garden) is a measure of their profound courage.

A further line of experiment deploys a creative way with margins and the periphery, the all-but-offstage. Most of the action in *The Freedom of the City* (1973) is seemingly in the realist mode, set within a traditional box set representing the Mayor of Derry's parlour in the Guildhall. In a Brechtian manner, however, that setting does not extend beyond the proscenium, but is exposed as a theatrical construct within a surrounding black space (the margins of a spectator's sightlines), where in sharply angled spotlights characters appear who inhabit different narratives and time frames from that being enacted in the main playing space. A realist play is circumscribed by another in the Expressionist political mode; the values, tone, dramatic conventions and expectations of the first are challenged, judged, forcibly changed and determined by the second. Space here is at its most elastic and fluid, and in consequence, so too are an audience's responses, making it difficult to extrapolate any secure interpretation. The result of this theatrical *tour de force* is not confusion but a searing awareness of the power of ideologies to shape distinct perceptions of events and to transform those biased perspectives in time ineluctably into myth, when the context is one of political struggle. Use of space here defines and determines a maturity of political insight.

The Home Place (2005) is worth discussing in the context of margins, though it is a difficult play to categorize because of a significant disparity between the expectations of the playwright and those expectations as realized by the designer of the inaugural production. Friel's directions as printed in the Faber edition require a setting akin to *Aristocrats* and *Give Me Your Answer, Do!* comprising an extensive *"unkempt lawn,"*[15] backed to one side by the opened-out breakfast room of a "Big House" and a crescent of trees to the other. The designer for the initial production at the Gate Theatre, Dublin, Peter McKintosh, actually ignored these instructions and created what was a politically more charged space. The breakfast room occupied the forestage with windows opening fully to the sides to reveal the lawn backed all round by the trees. (The result was a further framing device within the theatre's proscenium.) Much of the action takes place on the lawn and is the subject of varying moral and political interpretations within the play. Characters secretly watch the house from the security of the trees; others view the trees from the house, enjoying what their maturity implies about the stability of the family and political structures that have protected their planting. The watchers from within the trees, Con Doherty and Johnny MacLoone, encroach on the lawn and in time control what may or may not take place there; and the owner of the house is finally left pondering what further "invasions" might be imminent. The lawn in the production became a contested space, which the initially marginalized took possession of, threatening in their turn to marginalize the original owners of the place within the confines of the house or into exile. That a degree of latitude has been taken with Friel's prescriptions is undeniable, yet in this instance the latitude actually strengthens the political strategies within Friel's conception by finding visual strategies to complement them. This is decidedly different from asserting the right to use the play to make a personal visual statement, which Joe Vanek clearly sees as a designer's prerogative. Through his sophisticated exploration of margins, McKintosh rendered the play more akin to *The Freedom of the City* than to *Aristocrats*.

Volunteers (1975), *Translations* (1980) and *Wonderful Tennessee* (1993) appear to resort to a traditional (Shavian-type) realism, which expertly defines a precise location by chiefly pictorial means. If one considers a

Shavian setting in this context, one sees that its function is limited to offering a fitting visual support to the action, generally by defining a specific social (class) milieu; and that function does not appreciably change. This factor distinguishes such settings from Friel's usage, where one continually discovers new levels of significance to their construction, as the plays develop. The setting may remain fixed, but an audience's response to it is flexible. That for *Volunteers* is a building site, an archaeological dig, a Viking settlement, graveyard and place of sacrifice, a community project employing criminals on day release, while its envisaged future life is as the foundations of an international hotel, all glass and steel. Its form suggests both a giant cauldron where past, present and future coalesce in the shaping of heritage and a vortex where (as in Yeats's gyres) time is replayed in cycles in which repeatedly outcasts are scapegoated and victimized. The setting conjures forth an intricate vision of history as questionably determinist for lacking a responsible sense of what constitutes progress. The hedge-school of *Translations* is valued increasingly as a site of cultural discovery even as its existence is threatened into extinction; it is an image of loss to the ravages wrought by another materially driven concept of progress. The pier and jetty of *Wonderful Tennessee* are a liminal space, caught between land and sea, as is learned in the depths of self by the characters who come brashly to party but find themselves privately undergoing a pilgrimage, in which all the constituent features of the set (the lifebelt stand, the puddles, stones and catwalk) come to take on ritual, indeed sacramental significance. Setting in these instances is more than support for the action; it exists in synergy with the thematic life of the drama as a stage metaphor. As such, it demands varying levels of translation by the spectator as it undergoes continual transformation, becoming ever richer as it becomes estranged from its immediate material significance. Nothing in these plays is simply what it seems.

Finally there are the plays demanding virtually no setting whatever. *Faith Healer* (1979) occupies metaphysical space after death, where only fragmentary objects that define a lost life are to hand. Frank's first monologue is accompanied by his promotional banner and the scattering of chairs that denote his status as performer; Gracie's by the banner, one stark chair and a table top bearing numerous ashtrays, packets of cigarettes, whiskey and a glass; Teddy's by the banner, a more comfortable chair, the table, an empty dog basket and a small cupboard containing a seemingly endless supply of beer. When Frank delivers his second monologue there is finally nothing but the one chair bearing the coat and hat that come to emblematize his stoic acceptance of death. Given the length of time in performance that we see these largely unchanging arrangements of objects within an otherwise black void, they severally take on a status akin to a still life, connoting the ultimately defining qualities of each speaker's existence. *Molly Sweeney* (1994) inhabits an even starker place, defining the dark spaces known by the blind. (The setting requires merely three chairs for the three characters.) In both plays an audience focuses on the characters' verbal evocations of place; the space they inhabit is given density, volume, atmosphere, by the play of light. We are denied an optical perspective the better to concentrate imaginatively in performance on each character's modes of seeing and defining experience; we cannot *place* them (with all the judgmental connotations of that word) because we cannot situate them within any defining conception of space.

This brings into consideration another remarkable feature of Friel's scenographic artistry. Pamela Howard comments: "Every space has a line of power, reaching from the acting area to the spectator, that the scenographer has to reveal and explore."[16] The chief line of power with pictorial, especially perspectival, scenery is from center-back to center-front, everything taking its required place in relation to that line. Friel continually frustrates that expectation. His divided settings often situate the dividing wall along that central axis and so disempower it, destabilizing what constitutes a periphery by creating a choice of points of focus, as in *Philadelphia, Here I Come!* and *Living Quarters*. Deploying an apron forestage disturbs that axis before it connects with the audience; so too does the tendency to prescribe two architectural structures to right and left at the back of the stage, leaving the center pictorially vacant.[17] This is the case in *Aristocrats*, where Friel then has the character, Casimir, create a "wide arc" of seating traversing roughly the middle and forefront of the stage where most of the action takes place; the semicircle breaks and is reformed, then shaped to allow finally for three distinct pairings of characters. Psychological nuances impel these changing patterns; the movement of characters within or beyond the arc creates new, continually shifting power lines that invite the spectator to focus optically where the psychological movement is most intense. *The Freedom of the City* continually denies the existence of one centralizing axis, while in *The Loves of Cass McGuire* the line of power is largely where Cass dictates it should be. In *Volunteers* the only feature that permanently occupies a place close to (though noticeably not at) stage-center is the unearthed skeleton; nothing modern is given such prominence. And the skeleton is the key to the patterns of victimization that the play examines, as is the centrally placed (but "*listing and rotting*") cruciform lifebelt stand in *Wonderful Tennessee* which, though similarly ignored for much of the action, becomes the centralizing metaphor for it all.[18]

It is the actors (as Howard implies they should) who control the power lines in Friel's plays in performance. Even those centralizing metaphors gain

RICHARD ALLEN CAVE

their significance only from the way the characters are required to relate to them. No scenic arrangement dictates one controlling axis. That Friel in his monologue plays should have abandoned all conventional determinants of space would seem a logical development. His scenographic experimenting has invariably worked to privilege the actor. Consequently, space in his plays is experienced precisely as Howard describes it, as "elastic, emotional and mobile," because "constantly changed by the performers themselves."[19] Perhaps it would be fitting to add a further epithet, "democratic," since achieving that elasticity demands sensitive ensemble playing and direction of the highest order. That term better reflects Friel's seeming understanding of the performance process as fundamentally collaborative. It may appear that this conclusion is perversely joining Dowling when he states (as quoted above) that "essentially the plays demand productions which concentrate on the performances without much emphasis on the externals."[20] But this is not so. Friel's deployment of the visual possibilities of stage space, it has been argued, is not a matter of trivial "externals," but of central (and thematically centralizing) importance. Perhaps it would more accurately reflect Friel's practice if Dowling's words were rephrased to read: "Essentially Friel's plays demand productions which concentrate on the performances [actors] and their precise relation to space". This is to situate Friel's visual creativity where it properly belongs: with the scenographers, not the designers.

NOTES

1. Pamela Howard, *What is Scenography?* (London: Routledge, 2002), p. 15.
2. Ibid., p. xiv.
3. See Christopher Murray, "Friel's Emblems of Adversity and the Yeatsian Example," in Alan Peacock (ed.), *The Achievement of Brian Friel* (Gerrards Cross: Colin Smythe, 1993), pp. 69–90; Anthony Roche, "Friel and Synge: Towards a Theatrical Language," in Anthony Roche (ed.), *Irish University Review* (Special Issue: Brian Friel) 29:1 (1999), pp. 145–161. Murray also contributed a similar exercise entitled "Friel and O'Casey Juxtaposed" to that issue of *IUR*, pp. 16–29.
4. See Tony Coult, *About Friel: The Playwright and the Work* (London and New York: Faber and Faber, 2003), p. 205. The essay (one of several by Vanek on designing this play) was originally published in *Sightline* (January 1991).
5. Joe Dowling, "Staging Friel," in Peacock, *The Achievement of Brian Friel*, p. 187. The essay is anthologized in Coult, *About Friel*; quotation p. 183.
6. Dowling, "Staging Friel," p. 187 (Coult, *About Friel*, p. 184).
7. Dowling, "Staging Friel," p. 183 (Coult, *About Friel*, p. 178). Interestingly, Rosaleen Linehan made a distinctively similar remark, though couched in terms of her own profession as actress when she observed that, because the dialogue has many of the qualities of a musical score, "I don't think his plays attract selfish playing." The comment was made during a forum-discussion, entitled "The

140

Road to Ballybeg" held at the Abbey Theatre as part of the Friel Festival in 1999. It is transcribed in Coult, *About Friel*, p. 144.

8. Mason's comment was made during the Abbey forum in 1999, mentioned above; ibid., p. 141.

9. Quoted from Brecht's *Messingkauf Dialogues* in John Willett's translation by Pamela Howard as the epigraph to *What is Scenography?*, p. v.

10. For a highly informative account of Guthrie's techniques in rehearsal, which is pertinent to the argument offered here, see Michael Blakemore, *Arguments with England: A Memoir* (London and New York: Faber and Faber, 2004), especially pp. 200–213.

11. For a detailed account of the evolution of this type of functional setting and its subsequent deployment by Yeats and Synge, see Richard Allen Cave, "On the Siting of Doors and Windows: Aesthetics, Ideology and Irish Stage Design," in Shaun Richards (ed.), *The Cambridge Companion to Twentieth-Century Irish Drama* (Cambridge: Cambridge University Press, 2004), pp. 93–108; and "Robert Gregory: Artist and Stage Designer," in Ann Saddlemyer and Colin Smythe (eds.), *Lady Gregory: Fifty Years After* (Gerrards Cross: Colin Smythe, 1987), pp. 347–400, 428–439.

12. Brian Friel, *The Enemy Within* (Dublin: Gallery Press, 1979), p. 33.

13. Brian Friel, *Philadelphia, Here I Come!*, in *Plays One* (London and Boston: Faber and Faber, 1996), pp. 26–27. Subsequent references to the play are from this edition and will be incorporated within the text.

14. Brian Friel, *The Loves of Cass McGuire* (Oldcastle, County Meath: Gallery Books, 1984), p. 9.

15. Brian Friel, *The Home Place* (London: Faber and Faber, 2005), p. 2.

16. Howard, *What is Scenography?*, p. 2.

17. See *Give Me Your Answer, Do!* Note too how the directions for *Translations*, by situating the main entrance to stage left with a stairway rising upwards across the back wall, aim to achieve a similar effect.

18. Brian Friel, *Wonderful Tennessee*, in *Plays Two* (London: Faber and Faber, 1999), p. 344.

19. Howard, *What is Scenography?*, p. 15.

20. Coult, *About Friel*, p. 184.

13

ANNA McMULLAN

Performativity, unruly bodies and gender in Brian Friel's drama

Friel's drama frequently features unruly bodies which flout the corporeal regime of their particular community, social environment and historical moment, perhaps most hauntingly enacted by the Mundy sisters' defiant and desperate dance in *Dancing at Lughnasa* (1990). This chapter will explore the tension between such unruly bodies or performances and their suppression or marginalization within Friel's fictional worlds. My title draws on the work of Judith Butler, whose concept of gender as "performative" has become highly influential in both gender and theatre criticism.[1] Butler formulates "performativity" as a regulatory force: it indicates a "reiteration of norms, which precede, constrain and exceed the performer."[2] However, she also articulates a resistant performativity, located in the disruption and reappropriation of normative gender patterns: "the possibility of a different sort of repeating."[3] Taking these terms as a starting point, I will consider how particular characters in Friel's drama either submit to or subvert the social and gender conditioning of their world. My argument will come to focus on *The Loves of Cass McGuire* (1966),[4] a relatively early play in which Cass struggles with the forces of normalizing performativity in 1960s Ireland.

The stage directions of *The Loves of Cass McGuire* indicate that the play is set in *"the present in Ireland."*[5] Although the 1960s was a period of rapid change in Irish economic and social structures, when the foundations of Ireland's dependence on foreign, especially American, investment (satirized by Friel in 1969's *The Mundy Scheme*) were laid, Friel also focuses on the continuing control of conservative social and religious forces. Elmer Andrews notes that "in the plays of the 1960s, the emphasis falls on 'subjection' rather than 'transformation,'" and underlines "Friel's sense of the individual as subject to the forces of control in his or her society."[6] These forces of control included the religious hierarchy and clergy, who had had a strong influence in De Valera's Constitution of 1937, in the economic policies of the new State, and in family and educational structures, including the definition and supervision of gender roles in accordance with Catholic and nationalist ideologies. Women were categorized as either domestic, maternal guardians of the nation's morals and traditions or as figures of sexual temptation and betrayal. However, the 1960s saw the emergence of the value system of the "new Ireland" which, according to Terence Brown, "was prepared to abandon much of its past in the interests of swift growth in the context of the modern British and western European economies."[7] The Friel Papers in the National Library of Ireland include notes that Friel took in preparation for *The Loves of Cass McGuire* in which he observes that "the new Irish" are concerned primarily with the "pursuit of material things and the treadmill of the social ladder."[8]

Friel's drama certainly critiques post-independence Ireland as a society stifled by reified patriarchal authority and an economic, class and gender system reinforced and reproduced through the performative injunctions of "respectability" and status. Unruly bodies, like that of Cass, are marginalized and stigmatized. I will argue that the tension in Friel's drama between regulatory discipline and subversive modes of performance on the part of his characters is played out also in Friel's exploitation of the contradictory logic of mimesis: on the one hand, authoritative mirror of "how it is"; on the other, a masquerade or mimicry that can expose and destabilize the mechanisms through which both dramatic and social or state authority is performed on and through the bodies of others.[9] To what extent, though, does Friel's revelation of masquerade (metatheatrical or social) depend on and indeed reproduce the structures of authority it exposes? And what role does gender play, not only in the dynamics of subjection and resistance within the "Ireland" of the plays, but also within the drama of symbolic authority where the power to reveal the operation of masquerade and illusion is performed?

In the patriarchal world of Friel's plays where mothers are often absent – for example, in *Philadelphia, Here I Come!* (1964), *The Gentle Island* (1971), *Translations* (1980) and *Molly Sweeney* (1994) – the most subjected are either younger men who occupy a subaltern status in terms of age, class, sexuality or situation (such as the Republican prisoners on the archaeological dig in 1975's *Volunteers*), or women. While Friel's male subalterns do not just suffer subjection, but turn the mimetic mirror back on the structures and individuals who subject or limit them, mocking or mimicking them, Friel's women may occasionally flout authority, but they rarely perform it.

Friel's male trickster or joker figures often reveal the internalized mythology that sustains a particular social order or community. In *The Gentle Island* (1971), the myth of island life, however bleak or harsh, as the true home of the real Irish is punctured by the arrival of a male couple to an island which has already been depopulated of all but one remaining family: Manus Sweeney, who continues to believe in the viability and authenticity of life on the island, his two sons, Joe and Philly, and Philly's wife, Sarah. The younger visitor, Shane, is constructed as unruly "other" to the world of the patriarch, Manus Sweeney, on various levels: orphan born out of wedlock, homosexual, joker and dancer. His impersonation of Manus reveals the latter's clinging to the "authentic" performance of island/peasant life as self-deluding masquerade:

> SHANE: Be Jaysus, Shane boy, you're a quare comedian. You should be on the stage. Like me. Look at the act I have – the simple, upright, hardworking island peasant holding on manfully to the *real* values in life, sustained by a thousand-year-old culture, preserving for my people a really worthwhile inheritance.[10]

In *Volunteers* (1975) Keeney is the joker, with his irreverent limericks. His jokes do not change his subaltern status: as Republican internee, like the other four prisoners he has encouraged to join him, he is about to be executed by a court of his fellow internees for volunteering to work on an archaeological project against their orders, and as manual worker on the dig. However, Keeney's linguistic mastery and mockery of the middle-class mores of the non-prisoners on the site expose the deep class divisions in Irish society (as the archaeological site is carefully labeled into different sections and eras). They also reveal his awareness that those who control symbolic authority generate the dominant version of social or historical reality or "truth," which has material effects on individual bodies which may oppose, contradict or simply not conform to that version (as 1973's *The Freedom of the City* fatally demonstrates).

Both male and female bodies in Friel's theatre are subjected to the rules or norms of their particular environment. Shane, Keeney and faith healer Frank Hardy are destroyed by the community they enter or return to, which cannot accommodate their protean and unsettling otherness. In the case of Shane, it is not Manus but Sarah, the subaltern woman, repressed and unfulfilled, who shoots him, telling Manus that she saw him making love to her husband, and Shane's wounded body is removed from the island. Yet Friel's subaltern jokers achieve a measure of symbolic authority through appropriating the power of mimicry – hence, Keeney's references to, and identification with, Hamlet's "antic imagination."[11]

The symbolic or linguistic authority of mimetic destabilization is rarely wielded by women in Friel's drama, even though they may be very perceptive about their own subjection (and there are such exceptions as the witty and irreverent Maggie in *Dancing at Lughnasa*). Women also perform, and indeed create, moments of resistance to the discursive and regulatory codes of their environment, but their bodies function increasingly in the later work as conduits to the unconscious or to repressed areas of individual or cultural history. These female performances may provide liberation from confining gender roles, but they often reproduce uncritically the gendered construction of women as the non-rational and corporeal "other" to both social and symbolic authority.

The dance of the Mundy sisters in *Dancing at Lughnasa* (1990) defies the corporeal codes of respectable female behavior. It performs a moment of interconnection not only between the sisters (though the eldest, Kate, keeps to her own space), but also with an earlier time in Irish pagan history when the festival of Lughnasa was an active community ritual, and with other cultures, such as the leper colony of Ryanga, whose public rituals Father Jack praises. However, the symbolic interpretation of the sisters' dance is defined by the narrator, Michael (and by the audience), even though Friel acknowledges, as he does in many of his plays, that discursive, interpretative frameworks always fail to account for or to explain the corporeal energy of live performance.

Molly Sweeney (1994) directly stages the performance of male authority on the female body. Molly Sweeney's blindness represents an alternative mode of interaction with the world, based on the intimacy of touch or smell and corporeal immersion, figured especially by swimming: "every pore open and eager for that world of pure sensation, of sensation alone."[12] However, Molly is persuaded into having an operation to restore her sight by her autodidact husband with an obsession for lost causes, and an alcoholic eye surgeon hoping to restore his reputation by one more performance. Molly sees this clearly: "Why am I going for this operation? None of this is my choosing. Then why is this happening to me? I am being used" (473). Yet she submits, and cannot survive the ensuing dislocation. Initially presented as self-possessed, independent and highly resourceful, her integrity is destroyed by instrumental masculine authority, and, as Karen Moloney has argued, citing several references to Molly's pagan namesake, mad Buile Suibhne, at an allegorical or tropological level she becomes a symbol of Ireland "astray."[13] Molly's corporeal subjection and role as symbol, rather than agent or author, may have the performative force of naturalizing what it purports to critique.[14]

The Loves of Cass McGuire both conforms to and departs from this gender repertoire. Cass is presented as an unruly presence not only in her excessive corporeal performances (her drinking and her brash dress and manners) but also in her self-conscious appropriation of authority in her initial attempts to take control of her own narrative and its staging. I will be suggesting that in *The Loves of Cass McGuire* Friel exposes the pedagogic and performative mechanisms through which social norms and corporeal (including sexual) regimes are inscribed on individuals in order to reproduce disciplined or "docile"[15] bodies, or to marginalize those who do not conform. Cass is gradually subjected to such a disciplining process. Yet does such rendering visible of regulatory structures, which ultimately destroy any possibility of performing otherwise, also reinforce their deterministic power? What is the effect of Friel's framing of mimetic illusion on his own authority to expose and define the failures of the society which emerged after independence?

The Loves of Cass McGuire was conceived initially as a counterpoint to *Philadelphia, Here I Come!*, featuring Gar O'Donnell's return to Ireland from America after twenty years.[16] But Friel's play evolved into the story of Cass, who has been working as a waitress among the roughest inhabitants of New York's Lower East Side for fifty-two years, and now returns to her family to find that they are in much more comfortable circumstances than she ever imagined. Cass's story questions both the myths of traditional Irish identity and the myth of the American dream. After fifty years in the United States, her social and economic status is lower than that of her family, who stayed in Ireland and profited from the economic boom of the 1960s.

The play opens with a set which represents a *"spacious, high-ceilinged room"* (9), a mimetic representation of a middle-class family home. However, Friel gradually undermines the apparent "reality" of this structure without dismantling it. For example, the new Ireland is represented from the outset as unstable and uneasily located between the older and younger generations: Cass and Harry's mother, and his son, Dom. The stage directions present the Mother as a senile and infirm Mother Ireland or Cathleen Ni Houlihan living in a totally anachronistic world: *"Were she able to walk around she would have the authority and self-possession of a queen; but because she is invalided she just looks monumental"* (11). She is one of the few appearances in Friel's drama of Irish matriarchal authority, here shown as guardian and reproducer of the patriarchal, religious social order. However, she now lives entirely in the past (when she was a school teacher) and is oblivious of any contemporary reality: "Hands up any child who can tell me the name of the new cardinal" (11). While her presence is pervasive, in practical terms everyone ignores her. Her grandson Dom dwells in a fictional world of detective comics and sexual fantasy: he envisages the local community as a brothel, with Mother as the madam (12). The domestic space therefore becomes both a pedagogic space of religious instruction and its "other," the brothel, reproducing even as it merges the polarized gender roles of mother and prostitute. The present moment seems curiously suspended between the atrophied authority of the past and a frenzied adolescent fantasy of the future.

After this prelude,[17] Friel brings on Alice, who re-establishes order and is presented as the epitome of a middle-class housewife in her appearance, occupation and manners. Harry enters shortly after, wearing a "[g]ood *black coat, soft hat, carrying a paper*" (13). The couple perform the conventional gender roles of the time for a middle-class professional couple. Cass, however, shatters the norms of this affluent and respectable world. She is introduced before she enters the stage, through descriptions by the rest of her family: "singing at the top of her voice half the night" (12) or creating mayhem in Sweeney's pub, where Harry had to pay for her breakages. She is specifically presented as "breaking in," as her entrance performs a rupture of the world that has been presented: "*The subdued domestic atmosphere is suddenly and violently shattered by CASS's shouts. She charges on stage (either from the wings or from the auditorium) shouting in her raucous Irish-American voice*" (14). The stage directions pay particular attention to her appearance and behavior:

CASS *is a tall, bulky woman of seventy. She wears a gaudy jacket (because of the cold weather) over gaudy clothes; rings; earrings; two voluminous handbags which never leave her. She smokes incessantly and talks loudly and coarsely (deliberately at times).* (14)

Cass's entrance not only disturbs the middle-class propriety of Harry's living room, but the parameters of dramatic illusion, and the narrative coherence of realist mimesis. In *Cass*, Friel was "praying to Pirandello"[18] and his juxtaposition of different dramatic codes is integral to the play's performance of social and dramatic authority. Harry wishes to represent Cass's story in a linear fashion, explaining and therefore justifying his decision to send her away to a rest home: "It must be shown slowly and in sequence why you went to Eden House" (15). Cass, however, disrupts the middle-class/realist script (or gives the illusion of disrupting it, since, as in Pirandello, the mimetic ruptures are themselves scripted), breaks the fourth wall, and establishes a direct connection with the audience: "Who's Cass McGuire? Me! Me! And they'll see what happens in the order *I* want them to see it" (16). She both talks and looks back critically at the middle-class masquerade of the world of her family, and later that of the rest home, Eden House.

At the beginning, Cass's resistance is figured through her ability to see and address the audience. She is very aware of her disruptive effect as the antithesis of the contemporary respectable Ireland embodied by her brother and his wife, and she sometimes deliberately and ironically plays on this, though their distaste evidently distresses her. She announces to Dom: "The less you see of your old Auntie Cass the better, because she ain't got no money, and we suspect she doesn't go to church, and we're not too sure if she's a maiden aunt at all" (16). She identifies the regulatory mechanisms of the middle-class Ireland of the 1960s as money, religion and the surveillance of sexuality, especially female sexuality. Cass's relationships do not conform to the middle-class norm of marriage and the economic order it represents and supports.

Her increasing assimilation into the fantasy world of Eden House is emphasized by the fading of this critical vision. Cass becomes increasingly unable to distinguish between fact and illusion, and loses her ability to see the audience, existing only within the fictional world of the rest home. Her resistance to seeing herself through the middle-class eyes of her family is shored by her stories and mimicry of the regulars of her Bowery café, whom she also refuses to identify with: "deadbeats, drags, washouts, living in the past!" (19). In the end, neither the sanitized middle-class world of Harry and his wife, nor the materially and emotionally deprived world of her New York past, can provide Cass McGuire with the emotional or cultural resources to remake herself or her past symbolically, or to deal with the disappointments and losses of her history: her father, her Irish and New York lovers and, finally, her family.

After her family reject Cass and ask her to move into Eden House, she gradually submits to the performative seduction of the mythologizing processes taught her by Trilbe and Ingram, two of the other inhabitants. When the reality of their everyday existence depresses them, they sit in a special "winged chair" isolated within the space of the stage, and recite an idealized and mythologized version of their past. The pair appropriate symbolic authority and cultural resources to rewrite their own histories. Having been excluded from the more "swank" Trilbe and Ingram's references to literature or opera, which she always takes on a literal level, Cass assumes that their reference to "Wagner" is to a well-known New York mayor of the 1920s and remarks that the Tristan in the opera should have taken out accident insurance. She now retells a version of her history where she becomes fabulously wealthy in New York, marries her employer and returns home surrounded by all her loved ones. Ingram recites the final tragic reunion of Tristan and Isolde as she speaks. Cass's story is therefore dignified and transformed through the musical and narrative language of Wagner's opera.[19]

Cass's rhapsody can also be seen as re-narration of her heterogenous past into a comforting narrative which represses and conceals her history of manual work, disappointment and selfless generosity. Her ribald stories of the world of Skid Row are transformed into a private fantasy of wealth, legitimate marriage, and a successful homecoming where all losses and sufferings are redeemed. Cass is thereby reintegrated into the social, cultural and gender norms of middle-class Ireland, emphasized by Trilbe's rechristening of her as "Catherine" (another Cathleen, retired to a rest home and consumed by dreams of upward mobility!). When Cass enters the stage, she is interested only in the present moment, and avoids confronting her past. However, by imitating Trilbe and Ingram, she learns to perform a less painful, more "docile" narration of her history. Yet Friel maintains a tension between his own pedagogic, diagnostic revelation of the truth of the new Ireland, and a questioning of the mimetic materials employed in that very revelation of truth. Is Cass's masquerade a triumph or a failure? Is her transformation of her own history into myth a personal rewriting of her own script, or a delusion? To what extent is Eden House on the margins of the new materialist Ireland, or its mirror?

If we follow the spatial fluidity created by the lack of boundaries in the fictional spaces of home/rest home,[20] Cass's mythologizing may not only represent a private fantasy to comfort her when she has been rejected by her family and lost all her loves, but a macrocosmic cultural addiction to a paradisal myth which refutes loss, labor and suffering, concocted from a mixture of Yeats, Wagner, romantic fiction and the American Dream. Most people in the world of the play construct fictional versions or myths of reality. Alice is unable to confront the disintegration of her apparently ideal family: after Harry has revealed to Alice that the children are not happy and are not coming back for Christmas, she performs for Cass an idealized fiction of a happy Christmas family reunion, as she has always avoided the truth of her own father's behavior with young women. Cass therefore trades the contestatory authority of her Act 1 entrance for admission to the world of private illusion as the only way she can perform in the world of Eden House. The play vividly evokes the recurrent sense in Friel's drama of potentially regenerative energies which have been dissipated, repressed or normalized by the dominant social order.

Aristocrats (1979), however, offers a different ending, which accommodates new possibilities, however limited. It specifically dramatizes the inscription on subjected bodies of familial and institutional authority, that of the father/district judge, and that of the Big House itself, a materialization of the history and mythology of the Catholic aristocracy. The house is no longer economically viable and its culture is politically irrelevant, but it is still dominated by the father, now senile, incontinent and confined to bed. His four daughters and one son all bear the embodied traces of their subjection or resistance to the father's authority. The absent daughter, Anna, has entered the religious discipline of a convent in Africa. Claire, the youngest, suffers from depression and anxiety, finding escape and relief only in piano playing. She is about to marry an older man in order to secure her future as the play opens. The eldest, Judith, disobeyed the authority of her father by becoming involved with the civil-rights protests across the border in the 1960s, described by her father as a "great betrayal."[21] She gave birth to an illegitimate child by a Dutch reporter but gave it up for adoption, and in the world of the play she is entirely absorbed in the daily discipline of running the house and caring for the father. Alice and Casimir have both left Ireland and the family home. Alice has married a local villager, Eamon, and resists the decorum of the home in her speech and her drunkenness. Casimir has settled in Germany with a German wife and family (whom we never see). From the patriarchal perspective, Casimir has failed to learn the manly gender code expected of him: his German children refer to him as the "*kinder mädchen*" or "children's maid" (278). On hearing his father's voice, Casimir falls to his knees and sobs like an infant. Uncle George has given up speech and wanders aimlessly about the house. Yet the force of the father's authority within the fictional world is almost entirely divorced from his corporeal presence. As is clear in Anna's tape sent from Africa, it is the myth of the father and the culture of the aristocratic house which sustains its performative repetitions.

The father's voice, which occasionally issues commands and judgments as if in the past, is conveyed to the household through the device of a baby alarm, described by Eamon, husband of one of the daughters, Alice, and one of Friel's jokers, as a "Judas hole" (279), the hole in a prison through which the inmates are spied upon, but which can also, Eamon suggests, work both ways. Act 2 climaxes with the onstage spectacle of the father's vulnerable and sick body. Summoned by the voice of his absent daughter speaking on a tape recorder and her evocation of a long-gone past, he appears onstage and howls with inarticulate frustration. This grotesque scene exposes the elaborate illusion which has denied the decay of his authority and the myth of "the life of the quality" which the family have struggled to uphold in spite of occasional rebellions. After the father's death and the acceptance of the sale of the house, the inmates begin gradual transformations: Uncle George rediscovers his voice and decides to move to London with Alice and Eamon; Judith decides to reclaim her daughter who is in an orphanage and Casimir confesses to Eamon that his discovery of his own limitations enabled him to achieve a sphere of agency within those "confined territories" (310). It may be that the escape from the double authority of the father and the Big House signals a possible way out of the performative economy of repetition: once the spatial determinism of home and place is removed,[22] the world of the characters is available to be remade within achievable parameters, and they survive in new, albeit compromised configurations.

Aristocrats is one of the few Friel plays which contemplates an open-ended future in which the imprint of history and the past might be "transformed." Often, Friel exposes rather the internalization of the historical script, particularly evident in *Living Quarters* (1977), where the family repeat the history of the past over and over again, stuck in a performative moment of failed authority which determines the world of the play. Like the authority structures of the fictional world which signifies modern Ireland, Friel displays and even parodies his own authority through this device but, like that of Sir, ultimately it must be adhered to exactly: "I look to the director and the actors to interpret that score exactly as it is written."[23] Friel is exposing the material conditions and symbolic mechanisms which prevent transformation. But to what extent are the performance acts within the fictional world of the plays condemned to subjection by the dependence of the dramaturgy on the very mimetic model of truth and authority which it exposes as illusion? Or is this an invitation to the directors, performers and creative team to focus on exactly these contradictions in Friel's drama? As Elin Diamond suggests, "Theater itself may be understood as the drama's unruly body, its material other, a site where the performer's and the spectator's desire may resignify elements of a constrictive social script."[24] Claudia Harris draws attention to the moments of corporeal resistance in Friel's drama, where the performer can appropriate that "unruly body"[25] of theatre, such as the dance of the Mundy sisters, or Cass's final exit, which Siobhán McKenna accompanied with a raucous version of "Yankee Doodle Dandy," suggesting that Cass's spirit is not entirely tamed.[26] Yet his dramaturgy also depends on the ambivalence of this tension between unruly performance, including liberation from restrictive gender scripts, and the restoration of the social norms and internalized discursive, symbolic or mythical frameworks which contain and control it.

Friel's staging of a society in transition has spoken to diverse audiences across the globe. How will twenty-first-century performances of Friel's plays resonate in contemporary Irish society (or societies which are modeling themselves on Ireland), which is now a success story at least in terms of global economic indices? How will Friel's drama speak to contemporary mechanisms of regulation, exclusion and performativity whose power remains strong, even if their authority is more carefully disguised and circulated through global technologies? The dramatic dynamic of his theatre seems to lie in the explosive moments of tension when the script is destabilized, when the masquerade is exposed and the possibility of performing otherwise is glimpsed. Perhaps this is the particular challenge of the unruly body of theatre: to operate in the gap or rupture between the masquerade of performative identity and the performance of becoming.

NOTES

1. See Judith Butler, "Performative Acts and Gender Constitution: An Essay in Phenomenology and Feminist Theory," in Sue-Ellen Case (ed.), *Performing Feminisms: Feminist Critical Theory and Theatre* (Baltimore, MD: Johns Hopkins University Press, 1990), pp. 270–282.
2. Judith Butler, *Bodies That Matter: On the Discursive Limits of "Sex"* (London: Routledge, 1993), p. 234.
3. Ibid. p. 271.
4. *The Loves of Cass McGuire* is Friel's fifth play, and the first to feature an eponymous central female character. The play premiered on Broadway in 1966, with the American actress Ruth Gordon in the title role, but closed after twenty performances. It achieved a much warmer critical reception when it was presented on the Abbey stage of the National Theatre in Dublin in 1967, directed by Tomás MacAnna, with Siobhán McKenna in the title role. Since then, the role has been interpreted by some of Ireland's leading actresses: Marie Keane (Ulster Theatre Company, Belfast 1968), Maureen Toal (Abbey, Dublin 1978), and Marie Mullen (Druid Theatre Company, Galway, 1975 and 1996).
5. Brian Friel, *The Loves of Cass McGuire* (Dublin: Gallery Press, 1984), p. 8. All future references to the play are to this edition and will be incorporated in the text.
6. Elmer Andrews, *The Art of Brian Friel: Neither Reality Nor Dreams* (Basingstoke and London: Macmillan, 1995), p. 77.
7. Terence Brown, *Ireland: A Social and Cultural History 1922–1979* (Glasgow: Fontana, 1981), p. 244.
8. The Brian Friel Papers, National Library of Ireland, MS 37052, p. 2. Further references to this collection will be indicated by manuscript number.
9. See Elin Diamond, *Unmaking Mimesis* (London: Routledge, 1997).
10. Brian Friel, *The Gentle Island* (Oldcastle, County Meath: Gallery Press, 1993), p. 40.
11. Brian Friel, *Volunteers* (Oldcastle, County Meath: Gallery Press, 1989), p. 71.
12. Brian Friel, *Molly Sweeney*, in *Plays Two* (London: Faber and Faber, 1999), p. 466. Future references are to this edition and will be incorporated in the text.
13. Karen Moloney, "Molly Astray: Revisioning Ireland in Brian Friel's *Molly Sweeney*," *Twentieth Century Literature* 46:3 (2000), pp. 285–311.
14. See Claudia Harris, "The Engendered Space: Performing Friel's Women from Cass McGuire to Molly Sweeney," in William Kerwin (ed.), *Brian Friel: A Casebook* (New York and London: Garland Press, 1997), pp. 43–75.
15. In *Discipline and Punish: The Birth of the Prison* (Harmondsworth: Peregrine Books, 1977), Michel Foucault analyses the technologies of knowledge and surveillance developed in early capitalist regimes during the eighteenth century, in order to produce a "docile body that may be subjected, used, transformed and improved" (p. 198).
16. Friel Papers, MS 37052, p. 2.
17. In his Author's Note, Friel emphasizes that he conceived the play in musical terms: "I consider this play to be a concerto in which Cass McGuire is the soloist" (p. 7).
18. Friel Papers, MS 37052, p. 1. Note to Hilton Edwards, director of the 1966 New York premiere, April 1965.

19. On the particular significance of the choices of Wagnerian music to accompany each of the rhapsodies, see Elmer Andrews, *Art of Brian Friel*, pp. 99–101.
20. I am grateful to Tomás MacAnna for sharing his memories of, and providing me with a detailed stage plan for, his 1967 Abbey production of *The Loves of Cass McGuire*. My thanks also to Mairéad Delaney, Archivist of the Irish National Theatre Society, Ltd, for her assistance.
21. Brian Friel, *Aristocrats*, in *Plays One* (London and Boston: Faber and Faber, 1996), p. 257. All future references to the play are to this edition and will be incorporated in the text.
22. See Una Chaudhuri, *Staging Place: The Geography of Modern Drama* (Ann Arbor: University of Michigan Press, 1995), for an exploration of the particular complexity of the trope of home as desired origin and as prison in realist drama.
23. Brian Friel, "Self-Portrait," in Christopher Murray (ed.), *Brian Friel: Essays, Diaries, Interviews: 1964–1999* (London and New York: Faber and Faber, 1999), p. 44.
24. Diamond, *Unmaking Mimesis*, p. iii.
25. Harris, "The Engendered Space," p. 50.
26. My thanks to Tomás MacAnna for this information.

14

CSILLA BERTHA

Brian Friel as postcolonial playwright

Brian Friel wrote postcolonial drama before the term was coined or theoreticians and critics discovered its potential. The question with which he begins *The Mundy Scheme* (1969) points to the core of postcolonial discourse: "What happens to an emerging country after it has emerged?"[1] He is postcolonial in the sense that, feeling in his nerves the responsibility for the community he comes from, and worrying about the survival not only of individual but also of cultural values in the value-free modern/postmodern world, Friel continually faces the consequences of colonization, the experience that so deeply determined the formation of modern Irish history, society and identity. His writing has been concerned with the nuances of both personal and cultural-national identity and its relation to colonial dispossession and confusion, issues of home, language, tradition, the workings of private and public memory – all issues that inform postcolonial consciousness. Apart from thematic considerations, Friel has also experimented with the techniques of fragmenting, subverting and destabilizing conventional stage realism favored by postcolonial drama.

Brought up in Northern Ireland, Friel personally experienced from childhood the dividedness of country and culture. Deeply aware that political tensions in Northern Ireland are exacerbated by the presence of the English, he also acknowledges that "if England were to go tomorrow morning, that wouldn't solve it. We still have got to find a *modus vivendi* for ourselves within the country."[2] His plays dramatize moments of this search for a *modus vivendi*, on both sides of the border, showing a constant cultural awareness that keeps the individual and the community conflated. Reflecting the twentieth-century-long tension in Ireland between tradition and (post)modernity, Friel takes a position between the role of the ancient *file* (poet) and the postmodern artist; between the "diviner" – his own (early) metaphor for the artist[3] – or faith healer of magic, prophetic, healing power and self-reflective, self-ironic, disillusioned observer.

Whether Ireland can be considered postcolonial, and in what sense or to what extent, has been a crucial issue in Irish cultural debate for the last twenty years or so. On the basis of Ireland's location in Europe, the Irish being white, and the country sometimes benefiting from British rule, some critics have contested the very fact of Ireland's once being a colony. For instance, Steven Ellis argues that Ireland's colonial relationship with Britain "is a matter of opinion, since colonialism as a concept was developed by its modern opponents and constitutes a value-judgement."[4] Clearly, the colonial relationship itself was not invented by postcolonial discourse and, in Richard Kearney's apt judgment, "omitting reference to the historical injustices of British colonialism and unionism amounts to a tacit apologia of the latter."[5] However politicized all cultural debate may be, by now the postcolonial approach has gained dominance in Irish Studies.

Postcolonialism is primarily a discourse and not only a period. Nevertheless, it might be fruitful to distinguish anti-colonial literature – reflecting resistance to a still-existing foreign power – from postcolonial, which contends with the effects, the long-term internalized consequences of colonization. The once-oppressed, if they do not fully regain cultural, psychological, moral and emotional autonomy, easily fall prey to neo-colonization, and the literature of resistance to that might be called anti-neocolonial, if the term itself were not so awkward. Besides the many overlapping features in the literature of the various phases of decolonization, one essential difference concerns the problem of identity. Anti-colonial literature tends to reflect a less confused identity than postcolonial, since it often proves easier to define the self against the "other" of the colonizer. Postcolonialism (and anti-neocolonialism), on the other hand, involve less immediately recognizable psychological distortions originating from an inferiority complex occasioned by the emphasized superiority of the colonizer, uncertainty about the "native" value system complicated by incomplete interiorizing of the colonial other's values. It also causes divided, split character, self-debasement, self-hatred or other psychological damage.

While most of Friel's plays fall into the postcolonial (and anti-neocolonial) category, a few are closer, at least thematically, to anti-colonial attitudes. *The Freedom of the City* (1973) focuses on the workings of colonial institutional politics and representation. Its three Irish Catholic civil-rights marchers, who unwittingly stumble into Derry's Guildhall – the symbolic center of Protestant supremacy – and become victims of the British Army's shooting, are not shaped by the alien power, nor do they show any symptoms of hybridization in their identities. Rather they share a remarkable independence and ability to subvert through play, mockery, laughter – the carnivalesque – the symbols of authority that will destroy them. The structure of the play, foregrounding fragmentation and discontinuities, does, however, deploy strategies typical of postcolonial drama. It ruptures chronology and renders the action in center-stage in a totally different theatrical space, convention and register from that around it. The spatial arrangement of the realistically drawn individualized characters, surrounded by the representatives of authority of Brechtian styl-ization, projects the discrepancies between reality, facts and their interpreta-tions. Acknowledging the postmodern notion that truth cannot be accessed from outside, the play at the same time shows that there *is* a truth, which then becomes distorted as the English Judge dismisses the army's responsibil-ity for the murder of unarmed civil-rights marchers on evidence that clearly does not match the facts as the audience witnesses them. The Irish balladeer, who forms an alternative discourse when he equally strongly changes the facts by making heroes out of the unheroic victims, also exemplifies how discourse alone is ineffective unless backed by institutional forms of power.

In most other plays Friel concentrates more on the identities, the inter-nalized colonial losses, confusions, uncertainties and consequences of those losses the Irish have had to come to terms with. Identity, both personal and cultural, is closely related to the idea of home. There is an ontological need for people to feel at home in their own place, country, village, as Áron Tamási, the Hungarian-Transylvanian writer, sums up: "we are in the world so that we should be at home in it in some place."[6] Similarly, Seamus Heaney famously demanded the right "[t]o be at home/In my own place and dwell within/Its proper name."[7] That the necessity of being at home in their own place and own name is disproportionately enlarged for a once-colonized, physically and spiritually dispossessed people, is stating the obvious. But home, belonging to some place, also provides a position of security in the face of globalization in the present and future.

Friel emphasized the need for home, particularly in Northern Ireland, in 1982: "we aspire to a home condition in some way. [. . .] And what's con-stantly being offered to us, particularly in the North, [. . . is] the English home and we have been pigmented by an English home."[8] In *Philadelphia, Here I Come!* (1964), he created an Irish home for most of his charac-ters, the fictitious village of Baile Beag that, due to British colonization, becomes Ballybeg – a metonym for, or a microcosm of, Ireland. It is Friel's Archimedic fixed point from which he can observe (if not change) the world. It is the physical and spiritual home of both the individual and the com-munity as Friel masterfully connects the most private and secret places of individual life with the plight of the whole culture. As such, Ballybeg itself is a multifaceted place, now empowering, now incarcerating, usu-ally on the threshold of crucial change, which more often than not brings a loss. Yet it also indicates remnants of an earlier form of culture, some authenticity, that might (have) enrich(ed) its inhabitants if incorporated in their lives. Through simultaneously establishing and destabilizing its features as home, Friel makes Ballybeg correspond to the postcolonial situation and consciousness that are positioned on the fault lines between cultures, a space which is at one and the same time center and marginality, authenticity and change. Imaging what Homi Bhabha calls the "third place," between colonizer and colonized, old and new culture, where "an interstitial future [. . .] emerges *in-between* the claims of the past and the needs of the present," this is where the "incommensurable elements – the stubborn chunks – as the basis of cultural identification" are still to be found.[9] But unlike the Bhabha-formulated hybridity, "where the past is not originary,"[10] the incommensurable elements in Ballybeg do show continuity from an originary past. The plays posit these elements as elusive, half-hidden, evokable in memory even if no longer in practice and sometimes, even in their absence, holding the promise of renewing spiritual life. In his constantly seeking contact points between authenticity and contemporary life, Friel dramatizes that "[o]ne can never go back to the old culture, but it could extend to the present day."[11]

The Ballybeg plays taken together present a fragmented yet still continuous history, with recognizable features of sameness and change. Put together in the chronology not of their writing but of the time they are set in, they delineate the story of Ireland from the turn of the sixteenth to the seventeenth centuries (1988's *Making History*, although here Ballybeg is only alluded to), through the pre-Famine early nineteenth century, when the Irish-speaking population is threatened with the prospect of losing their language (1980's *Translations*), to late nineteenth-century stirrings on the eve of the Land War (2005's *The Home Place*), then abandoning old traditions under the strictures of the Catholic Church in the Free State (1990's *Dancing at Lughnasa*) and on to the silenced, split protagonist of Gar in *Philadelphia, Here I Come!* in the 1960s and further, to the contemporary urban Irish who, like tourists in their own country, visit the now-deserted Ballybeg area (1993's *Wonderful Tennessee*). Ballybeg Hall, the Big House, owned by English landlords in the nineteenth century (*The Home Place*) became the property of an Irish lawyer in the twentieth, whose heirs, however, lack the finances to hold on to it (1979's *Aristocrats*) and finally the dishevelled home of the impoverished contemporary writer in 1997's *Give Me Your Answer, Do!* In this "history" the idea of home itself is transformed from a physically defined location into a sublimated and metaphoricized space, from the obvious place of belonging threatened by eviction (*Translations*) to a site of nostalgic remembering (*Lughnasa, Aristocrats*), then to a place more coercive than enabling

(*Philadelphia*). Similarly, the notion of dispossession changes from physical to metaphysical exile (*Faith Healer, Wonderful Tennessee, Molly Sweeney*). Home increasingly has become a loss, a lack, where the desired homecoming entails death and destruction (*Faith Healer, Molly Sweeney*), but also a location of origin and source of some (indefinite) faith. This spiritual dwelling, made up of personal, psychological and cultural meanings, even though missing, can still be conjured up through ritual, song, dance and the magic power of words. In *Wonderful Tennessee* what has remained of Ballybeg is only its name, yet the visitors, having lost language and tradition, still find some spiritually enriching experience in its vicinity in their yearning "[t]o be in touch again."[12] Friel, in the course of over four decades, has developed Ballybeg into a place at once well-defined, concrete and spiritualized, a "Fifth Province"[13] – the non-physical center of Ireland above borders, political, cultural, sectarian divisions.

Friel's insistence on setting his plays in the same village, and often naming his characters by the same names (many of his protagonists are called O'Donnell), offers a way of showing how certain elements of culture need to remain fixed in order to allow for, and absorb, changes in the always complex tension between tradition and modernity. Both tradition and modernity are problematized through the moving, shifting boundaries and proportions of their coexistence. The past is never idealized. Nor is it depicted as something "pure," exclusively Gaelic, untouched by other cultures. In *Translations*, for instance, while all the Irish speak Gaelic, they seem to know more about classical mythology and culture than their own. In *The Gentle Island* (1971), *Lughnasa* and *Tennessee*, the past is darkened by crime, violence, transgression. Yet modernity is not hailed either. The discourse of modernity in Ireland (and other colonized countries) is complicated by its being related to foreign intervention claiming to bring enlightenment. Such is the introduction of "order and prosperity" by the Queen's Marshal in *Making History*, to which Mabel, his daughter who has "gone native," retorts that "there is a mode of life here that is at least as honourable and as cultivated as the life I've left behind."[14] Such is the new, "national" (that is, English national) school system and the "standardizing" of place names through the map-making in *Translations*. Between *Translations*, Friel's most obviously postcolonial play, and *The Home Place*, in which he revisits *Translations* a quarter of a century later, in play after play, with subtlety and elegance, he shows a hesitation between embracing new values and preserving the old, the danger of looking backward but also the risk of forgetting the past, the impossibility of going back but also the necessity to preserve or revive some of its "incommensurable elements" to face the (post)modern world of neo-colonization.

In *Philadelphia, Here I Come!* Ballybeg proves too parochial, too lacking in opportunities for its young people. The protagonist Gar, doubled into Private and Public, corresponds to what Anthony Roche identifies as the "anti-hierarchical nature of a postcolonial Irish drama," where the lead role is divided between two equally important characters so "every pronouncement by the one is likely to be countered or questioned by the other."[15] While this division ensures dynamic tension in the drama, it also points to the fatal lack of integrity in the silenced native, who is able to express himself only within himself. Seamus Deane, speaking about the language issue in Ireland in general, could be describing Gar's split condition: "the language of the real, in all its rigour, is Irish – and that emerges as silence; and the language of the possible is English – and that emerges in eloquence. [...] The condition of dumbness, aphasia, or silence is the repressed condition of non-modernity."[16] In Gar's experience of his valueless environment, only his mother's memory stands for vitality, a connection with past cultural values. Shaun Richards suggests that she, with her love of dance, coming from "beyond the mountains" barefoot, embodies an alternative to the "two material cultures of the play,"[17] the Ireland of Ballybeg and the new world of "[i]mpermanence and anonymity" of America.[18]

Friel said about *Translations* that it "has to do with language and only language,"[19] but he is of course only too aware of the political weight language carries in Ireland. The question of language always opens colonial wounds of loss and ambiguous feelings towards English. Among the anomalies of Irish cultural changes, Deane points out that the Famine Irish tended to see the retention of the Irish language as if it were responsible for all the tragedy, poverty, death, exile.[20] But if it is true that the Irish themselves abandoned their language,[21] it must never be forgotten either that the circumstances leading to that abandonment were constructed by their colonial position.

Language, especially naming or renaming, is one of the most ancient forms of taking something or someone into possession. Highlighting the process of renaming – that is, Anglicizing – Irish place names in the process of English map-making, parallel with the introduction of English national schools replacing Irish-language schools, *Translations* identifies a moment when the loss of the Irish language accelerated. The consequences of the action are built into the play's technique. On the stage everybody speaks English – apart from the Greek and Latin quotations – which stands for both Gaelic and English, demonstrating that by the time the play is acted out the only spoken language is English. Friel dramatizes the "conceit" of two languages in one, in a process of "palimpsest," by superimposing one language, one name, one translation, over another.[22] Cultural values enclosed in language can only partly be translated, leaving all the untranslatable elements unavailable to the next generation. Even though old meanings, stories, associations accompanying names do wear off and corrode in any language – as the Tobair Vree story in the play exemplifies – this does not justify abolishing the name itself in the service of an intruding foreign power. Much critical attention has rightly been paid to Friel's applying George Steiner's thoughts in *After Babel* on human communication as inevitably involving translation and interpretation, even within the same language. But that does not dim the parallel truth that a forced replacement of one language by another is not an effort for communication but an act of appropriation. Hostile or reductive critical readings of *Translations* interpreted it as a purely nationalistic lament for the loss of Gaelic language and culture, a dramatization of the contemporary Northern Catholic situation, or a depiction of the failure of a potential (innocent) union with another culture – without taking into account that the other culture is not an equal partner but the dominant military power. Friel's manifold ironies depict greater complexities. The loss is everybody's: the colonial intervention reduces partakers on both sides. Names, those Irish place names doomed to disappear, help to communicate love between the Irish Maire and the English Yolland, yet the political situation does not allow the individual relationship to flourish. Owen, the mediator between natives and English soldiers, comes to rebel and demand that he be called his own name by the English, and goes to join the guerrilla fighters more as a "gesture" of returning to his own than in any real hope of successful resistance. Hugh's resignation to making the new names their home in the silenced community on the brink of eviction may lead to new confusions. Confusion, he says, is "not an ignoble condition."[23] Neither is it empowering.

The Home Place changes the focus from the natives' to the settlers' disintegration. The idea of home is questioned, destabilized throughout, beginning with the title, since the "home place" (family seat, origins) and "home" (where one lives and feels at home) do not coincide in the play. The English landlord of the Big House loves Ballybeg as his home, yet he feels homesick for his home place in Kent. Neither fully identifying with the more arrogant members of his "tribe" nor with the native rebels, Christopher Gore remains in an in-between position with "[n]o home, no country, a life of isolation and resentment."[24]

Ballybeg House also becomes a liminal place, a place of "exile" for Margaret, his Irish housekeeper. Like Owen in *Translations*, she hesitates between the two worlds. In intercultural relationships such as Maire and Yolland in *Translations* and Mabel and Hugh O'Neill in *Making History*, Friel probes into the possibilities of crossing borders, yet rarely does he allow someone to succeed. Mabel provides a unique case, since, in this

figure of an English woman of high colonial position who comes to identify fully with her Irish husband, Friel reverses the expected identification of
the colonial with gender oppression. In other cases, the union is thwarted
by the rift between the groups each partner comes from, not so much due
to cultural differences or lack of communication as to the power relations.
Romantic Yolland, in love with the country and an Irish woman embodying
it with all of Orientalism's attraction, has become reincarnated in *The Home
Place* and split into father and son, Christopher and David Gore, who still
have not penetrated into "the private core" of the natives. Hence they both
remain insensitive to the humiliations Christopher's cousin Richard causes
when he starts measuring the local people's heads. Eventually, both landlords become "doomed" – the heavily charged word refers both to trees
to be cut down (native trees overshadowing the imported ones) and to the
"doomed nexus of those who believe themselves the possessors and those
who believe they're dispossessed" (71). Unhomeliness, "a paradigmatic colonial and post-colonial condition," replaces the homeliness of the beginning,
in which the "recesses of the domestic space become sites for history's most
intricate invasions."[25]

Kevin Whelan has written that "[m]emory is a necessary stay against the
annihilating force of time and its erosion of traces," necessary to recreate
the past with its "lost opportunities and betrayed possibilities" and thereby
"reactivate unkept promises to create a better future," at least in "the utopian
instinct."[26] In many of Friel's plays, memory mediates between home and
displacement, gives meaning to meaningless moments. Whole relationships
might hinge on it. If the father in *Philadelphia* were able to engage with
Gar's memory of their moment of happiness together in the past, instead of
meticulously searching for the "facts" as to whether the boat was blue or
brown, then Gar might stay at home. The most extensive exploration of the
way memory works occurs in the extraordinary play *Faith Healer*, where the
three characters each gives the audience his or her version of the same story
and, through that, deep insights into their psyche. In many other Friel plays
memory is also dramatized as a mixture of fact and fiction, formed by emotional and psychological needs to create or recreate the self. Seamus Heaney
identifies the double nature of memory in the early *The Enemy Within*
(1962), suggesting that what may look like a "disabling nostalgia" represents
rather "an enabling pilgrimage to the sources of [. . .] emotional stamina,"
memory as "an element where energy and vision are given new sharpness
and confirmation."[27] In *Aristocrats* many of Casimir's stories prove to be
such "pilgrimages." Those about the house's glorious past and its visitors,
including Chesterton, Hopkins and Yeats, turn out to be inventions. Similarly, his description of his father's funeral in grandiose terms soon becomes

contradicted by his sister's account of the same event. Casimir's translating of facts into an acceptable form enables him to enhance self-respect, to balance unbearable "truths," most especially what he was told in his childhood: that, had he been born among ordinary people, he would be the village idiot. As another character says in encouragement, "There are certain things, certain truths, Casimir, that are beyond Tom's [the fact-hunting 'chronicler''s] kind of scrutiny."[28] These truths are both private and part of a whole culture, a whole value system, which (although disappearing) can still sustain those who remember them. As Casimir does not need physical mallets to play an imaginary croquet game with his sister, so his memories do not have to be justified by factual evidence to be true.

Although set in Ballybeg, the blind *Molly Sweeney*'s entirely inner landscape of "home" is composed of memories of childhood bliss, fragrance of flowers, the embrace of water while swimming. The kind of "improvement" forced upon her – the eye operation to gain partial sight – corresponds to the paradigm of colonialism, based on the assumption that the colonial "other" is less developed. That this intervention destroys the integrity and the possibilities of life moving on at a different pace, relying on its own resources, is never a consideration. Molly becomes evicted from her familiar world, loses her self-confidence and freedom and is never able to fit into the new world. In the process of assimilating her "otherness," her husband Frank and the ophthalmologist Dr. Rice manage to "other" her to herself, to rob her of the "dignity of particularity" – to borrow the Hungarian András Sütő's phrase. The parable of the dislocated badgers (which Frank and his friend inadvertently damage when trying to save them by removing them from their old habitat) or Frank's imported Iranian goats, which never become acclimatized to Ireland but remain forever on Iranian time, reiterate the feeling of dispossession. Deprived of an organic growth according to her own inner laws, Molly cannot build the future on the values of her past, so she loses both future and past. At the close of the play, in her "borderline country" she feels "at home," but on reflection she corrects herself – "Well . . . at ease there"[29] – underlining the shift from home to a place of resignation. F. C. McGrath's relating Molly's "borderline country" to the Northern Irish experience of the ongoing "colliding historical narratives" and "different discourses" that construct reality[30] sounds too direct. Nevertheless, his postcolonial reading of *Molly Sweeney* helps to identify the dangers and mechanisms of neocolonization which, instead of military or political pressure, relies on the participation of the victim.

Shaun Richards convincingly maintains that Irish drama is postcolonial primarily in content and not in form, since it does not deploy any specific precolonial indigenous theatrical forms.[31] I would argue, however, that certain forms of self-expression can be traced back to old Irish practices (being aware that much of what is assumed to be "traditionally" Irish is often a mixture of native and foreign influences). One such is the *dinnseanchas* tradition, the mythic lore of places embedded in the names, deployed most obviously in *Translations* and *Faith Healer*. Indeed, the creation of Ballybeg and its stories is itself a process of *dinnseanchas*. Storytelling, looking back at a long tradition in Irish culture, has become a major form of self-expression and self-reflection and even a structuring element in *Faith Healer, Dancing at Lughnasa* and *Wonderful Tennessee*. In Friel's recent plays, music, dance and ritual carry meaning significantly, in addition to words. Even though frequently Irish and non-Irish forms of music, dance and ritual appear together, the indigenous Lughnasa celebrations or the cairn-building and circling the "beds" in *Wonderful Tennessee* – however deformed they are, and with however much self-irony and self-mockery they are performed – create a spiritual and emotional contact with a part of their heritage. That most of the rituals appear in the language rather than being acted out onstage confirms their distance yet also their existence, at least within memory. In *Lughnasa*, memory conveyed in language – as the narrator, Michael, relates his childhood memories – embraces everything in a "golden" mist as opposed to the dire facts of poverty, deprivation and destitute death in exile. Friel's mastery makes it possible that the golden mist does not deny stark reality; memory and fact can be embraced together. The Ryangan commingling of religious and secular celebrations that Father Jack seeks in vain in Ballybeg, finds an echo in (the dying) George's accordion playing in *Wonderful Tennessee*. George frequently switches "between sacred and secular music, [. . .] so the sacred intrudes on the secular, and the secular encroaches on the sacred."[32] Secularized and impoverished the rituals of the contemporary urban Irish may be, yet participating in them revives cultural memory. Cultural memory, mediated through "ceremonial communication," preserves and reproduces knowledge that ensures identity.[33] As Patrick Mason, who directed *Wonderful Tennessee* at the Abbey in 1993, testifies, "When the characters lift those stones, when they touch those cloths, there are generations stirring in the air of this theatre. [. . .] I feel it every night. People know it in their bones."[34]

Brian Friel worried as early as 1972 that "[w]e are rapidly losing our identity as a people. [. . .] We are no longer even West Britons; we are East Americans.'[35] In his plays he grasps moments when the source culture from which the Irish were evicted still lurks in the background, and attempts to salvage something of that culture that could still sustain the emptied-out present. In 1970 he described his hope "to write a play that would capture the peculiar spiritual and indeed material flux that this country is in at the moment. This has got to be done, for me anyway, and I think it has got to be done at a local parochial level, and hopefully this will have meaning for other people in other countries."³⁶ Postcolonial readings testify to the ample success of his endeavor, as Edward Said, among others, asserts: "Brian Friel's immensely resonant play *Translations* [. . .] immediately calls forth many echoes and parallels in an Indian, Algerian, or Palestinian reader [. . .] for whom the silencing of their voices, the renaming of places and replacement of languages by the imperial outsider, the creation of colonial maps and divisions also implied the attempted reshaping of societies, the imposition of foreign languages" and other forms of dispossession.³⁷ Cultural memory, embedded in Ballybeg, Friel's at once realistic and mythic image of Ireland, helps to resist new imperial reshaping and to defend its inhabitants from spiritual homelessness.

NOTES

1. Brian Friel, *Crystal and Fox and The Mundy Scheme* (New York: Farrar Straus and Giroux, 1970), p. 157.
2. Brian Friel, "In Interview with Mel Gibson (1991)," in Christopher Murray (ed.), *Brian Friel: Essays, Diaries, Interviews: 1964–1999* (London and New York: Faber and Faber, 1999), p. 142.
3. Richard Pine aptly entitled his extensive study *The Diviner: The Art of Brian Friel*, emphasizing Friel's shamanic position and power (Dublin: University College Dublin Press, 1999).
4. Steven G. Ellis, "Writing Irish History: Revisionism, Colonialism, and the British Isles," in *Irish Review* 19 (1996), p. 9.
5. Richard Kearney, *Postnationalist Ireland* (London: Routledge, 1997), p. 58.
6. Áron Tamási, *Ábel* (Budapest: Szépirodalmi Könyvkiadó, 1984), p. 560.
7. Seamus Heaney, "An Open Letter," in *Ireland's Field Day* (London: Hutchinson, 1985), p. 26.
8. Brian Friel, "In Interview with Fintan O'Toole (1982)," in Murray, *Brian Friel*, p. 112.
9. Homi Bhabha, *The Location of Culture* (London: Routledge, 1994), p. 219. For discussion of Bhabha's concept of "incommensurable elements" in Friel's drama, see Shaun Richards, "Brian Friel: Seizing the Moment of Flux," *Irish University Review* 30:2 (2000), p. 257.
10. Ibid., p. 219.
11. Brian Friel, "In Interview with Desmond Rushe (1970)," in Murray, *Brian Friel*, p. 27.
12. Brian Friel, *Wonderful Tennessee*, in *Plays Two* (London: Faber and Faber, 1999), p. 372.
13. For a definition and discussion of this term as it applies to Field Day and Friel, see, among others, Elmer Andrews, *The Art of Brian Friel: Neither Dreams nor Reality* (London: Macmillan, 1995), p. 165; and Richard Pine, *The Diviner: The Art of Brian Friel* (Dublin: University College Dublin Press, 1999), p. 25.
14. Brian Friel, *Making History*, in *Plays Two*, p. 279.

15. Anthony Roche, *Contemporary Irish Drama: From Beckett to McGuinness* (Dublin: Gill and Macmillan, 1994), pp. 59–60.
16. Seamus Deane, "'Dumbness and Eloquence,' A Note on English as We Write It in Ireland," in Clare Carroll and Patricia King (eds.), *Ireland and Postcolonial Theory* (Cork: Cork University Press, 2003), p. 118.
17. Richards, "Brian Friel," p. 259.
18. Brian Friel, *Philadelphia, Here I Come!*, in *Plays One* (London and Boston: Faber and Faber, 1996), p. 52.
19. Brian Friel, "Extracts from a Sporadic Diary (1979): *Translations*," in Murray, *Brian Friel*, p. 75.
20. Deane, "'Dumbness and Eloquence,'" p. 114.
21. Declan Kiberd similarly argues that in the nineteenth century "an entire generation of the Irish themselves decided no longer to speak it." See *Inventing Ireland* (London: Jonathan Cape, 1995), pp. 615–616.
22. Christopher Murray, "Palimpsest," *Hungarian Journal of English and American Studies* 5:1 (1999), pp. 91–92.
23. Brian Friel, *Translations*, in *Plays One*, p. 446.
24. Brian Friel, *The Home Place* (London: Faber and Faber, 2005), p. 71. All future references are to this edition and will be incorporated in the text.
25. Bhabha, *The Location of Culture*, p. 9.
26. Kevin Whelan, "Between Filiation and Affiliation: The Politics of Postcolonial Memory," in Carroll and King, *Ireland and Postcolonial Theory*, p. 93.
27. Seamus Heaney, "For Liberation: Brian Friel and the Use of Memory," in Alan Peacock (ed.), *The Achievement of Brian Friel* (Gerrards Cross: Colin Smythe, 1993), p. 232.
28. Brian Friel, *Aristocrats*, in *Plays One*, pp. 309–310.
29. Brian Friel, *Molly Sweeney*, in *Plays Two*, p. 509.
30. F. C. McGrath, *Brian Friel's (Post)Colonial Drama: Language, Illusion, and Politics* (Syracuse, NY: Syracuse University Press, 1999), p. 278.
31. Shaun Richards, "Throwing Theory at Ireland? The Field Day Theatre Company and Postcolonial Theatre Criticism," *Modern Drama* 47:4 (2004), p. 614.
32. Tony Corbett, *Brian Friel: Decoding the Language of the Tribe* (Dublin: The Liffey Press, 2002), p. 98.
33. Ian Assmann, *A kulturális emlékezet* (Budapest: Atlantisz könyvkiadó, 2004), p. 142.
34. Quoted in John Lahr, "Sight Unseen," *New Yorker* 69 (19 July 1993), p. 83.
35. Brian Friel, "In Interview with Des Hickey and Gus Smith (1972)," in Murray, *Brian Friel*, p. 49.
36. Brian Friel, "In Discussion with Fergus Linehan, Hugh Leonard and John B. Keáne (1970)," in Murray, *Brian Friel*, pp. 35–36.
37. Edward Said, Afterword, in Carroll and King, *Ireland and Postcolonial Theory*, p. 178.

SELECT BIBLIOGRAPHY

Primary works

First UK, Irish and US editions, in chronological order

Individual plays

Philadelphia, Here I Come! (London: Faber and Faber, 1965; New York: Farrar, Straus and Giroux, 1966).

The Loves of Cass McGuire (New York: Farrar, Straus and Giroux, 1966; London: Faber and Faber, 1967; Dublin: Gallery Press, 1984).

Lovers (Winners/Losers) (New York: Farrar, Straus and Giroux, 1968; London: Faber and Faber, 1969; Dublin: Gallery Press, 1984).

Crystal and Fox (London: Faber and Faber, 1969; New York: Farrar, Straus and Giroux [with *The Mundy Scheme*], 1970; Dublin: Gallery Press, 1984.)

The Mundy Scheme (New York: Farrar, Straus and Giroux [with *Crystal and Fox*], 1970).

The Gentle Island (London: Davis-Poynter, 1973; Oldcastle, County Meath: Gallery Press, 1993).

The Freedom of the City (London: Faber and Faber, 1974; Oldcastle, County Meath: Gallery Press, 1992).

The Enemy Within (Newark, DE: Proscenium Press, 1975; Dublin: Gallery Press, 1979).

Living Quarters (London and Boston: Faber and Faber, 1978; Oldcastle, County Meath: Gallery Press, 1992).

Volunteers (London and Boston: Faber and Faber, 1979; Dublin: Gallery Press, 1989).

Aristocrats (Dublin: Gallery Press, 1980).

Faith Healer (London and Boston: Faber and Faber, 1980; Oldcastle, County Meath: Gallery Press, 1991).

Translations (London and Boston: Faber and Faber, 1981).

Three Sisters by Anton Chekhov (Dublin: Gallery Press, 1981).

American Welcome, in Stanley Richards (ed.), *Best Short Plays 1981* (Radnor, PA: Chilton Books, 1981).

The Communication Cord (London and Boston, 1983; Dublin: Gallery Press, 1989).

Fathers and Sons: After the Novel by Ivan Turgenev (London and Boston: Faber and Faber, 1987).
Making History (London and Boston: Faber and Faber, 1989).
Dancing at Lughnasa (London and Boston: Faber and Faber, 1990).
The London Vertigo: Based on a Play "The True Born Irishman" or "The Irish Fine Lady" by Charles Macklin (Oldcastle, County Meath: Gallery Press, 1990).
A Month in the Country: After Turgenev (Oldcastle, County Meath: Gallery Press, 1992).
Wonderful Tennessee (London and Boston: Faber and Faber, 1993; Oldcastle, County Meath: Gallery Press, 1993).
Molly Sweeney (London and New York: Penguin, 1994; Oldcastle, County Meath: Gallery Press, 1994).
Give Me Your Answer, Do! (London and New York: Penguin, 1997; Oldcastle, County Meath: Gallery Press, 1997).
Uncle Vanya: A Version of the Play by Anton Chekhov (Oldcastle, County Meath: Gallery Press, 1998).
The Yalta Game: After Chekhov (Oldcastle, County Meath: Gallery Press, 2001).
Three Plays After: The Yalta Game, The Bear, Afterplay (Oldcastle, County Meath: Gallery Press, 2002; London: Faber and Faber, 2004).
Performances (Oldcastle, County Meath: Gallery Press, 2003; London: Faber and Faber, 2005).
The Home Place (Oldcastle, County Meath: Gallery Press, 2005; London: Faber and Faber, 2005).

Collected plays

Brian Friel: Plays One [formerly *Selected Plays*] (London and Boston: Faber and Faber, 1996; Washington, DC: Catholic University of America Press, 1984); includes *Philadelphia, Here I Come!*, *The Freedom of the City*, *Living Quarters*, *Aristocrats*, *Faith Healer* and *Translations*.
Brian Friel: Plays Two (London: Faber and Faber, 1999); includes *Dancing at Lughnasa*, *Fathers and Sons*, *Making History*, *Wonderful Tennessee* and *Molly Sweeney*.

Short stories

The Saucer of Larks (London: Victor Gollancz, 1962; New York: Doubleday, 1962).
The Gold in the Sea (London: Victor Gollancz, 1962; New York: Doubleday, 1966).
The Diviner: The Best Stories of Brian Friel [formerly *Selected Stories*] (Dublin: Gallery Press, 1979; Dublin: O'Brien Press, 1983; London: Alison and Busby, 1983; Old Greenwich, CT: Devin-Adair, 1983).

Interviews, etc.

Delaney, Paul (ed.), *Brian Friel in Conversation* (Ann Arbor: University of Michigan Press, 2000).
Murray, Christopher (ed.), *Brian Friel: Essays, Diaries, Interviews: 1964–1999* (London and New York: Faber and Faber, 1999).

Archive

The Brian Friel Papers are located in the National Library of Ireland, Dublin. They comprise 130 boxes dating from 1959 to 2001, covering the writing and production of 30 radio and stage plays and his early days as a short-story writer. They include manuscripts of the plays and documents concerning the establishment and administration of the Field Day Theatre Company, correspondence with actors, directors, producers and writers and academics and theses on Friel and his work.

Secondary works

Books on Brian Friel

Andrews, Elmer, *The Art of Brian Friel: Neither Reality Nor Dreams* (Basingstoke and London: Macmillan, 1995; New York: St. Martin's Press, 1995).

Corbett, Tony, *Brian Friel: Decoding the Language of the Tribe* (Dublin: The Liffey Press, 2002).

Coult, Tony, *About Friel: The Playwright and the Work* (London and New York: Faber and Faber, 2003).

Dantanus, Ulf, *Brian Friel: The Growth of an Irish Dramatist* (Göteborg, Sweden: Acta Universitatis Gothoburgenisis, 1985).

Brian Friel: A Study (London and Boston: Faber and Faber, 1988).

Dean, Joan FitzPatrick, *Dancing at Lughnasa: Ireland into Film* (Cork: Cork University Press, in association with the Film Institute of Ireland, 2003).

Grant, David, *The Stagecraft of Brian Friel* (London: Greenwich Exchange, 2004).

Jones, Nesta, *Brian Friel: Faber Critical Guides* (London: Faber and Faber, 2000).

McGrath, F. C., *Brian Friel's (Post)Colonial Drama: Language, Illusion, and Politics* (Syracuse, NY: Syracuse University Press, 1999).

Maxwell, D. E. S., *Brian Friel* (Lewisburg, PA: Bucknell University Press, 1973).

O'Brien, George, *Brian Friel* (Dublin: Gill and Macmillan, 1989; Boston, MA: Twayne Publishers, 1989).

Brian Friel: A Reference Guide 1962–1992 (New York: G. K. Hall and Co., 1995).

O'Connor, Ulick, *Brian Friel: Crisis and Commitment: The Writer and Commitment* (Dublin: Elo Press, 1989).

Pine, Richard, *Brian Friel and Ireland's Drama* (London and New York: Routledge, 1990).

The Diviner: The Art of Brian Friel (Dublin: University College Dublin Press, 1999).

Essay collections

Duncan, Dawn, John C. Countryman and Susan C. Harris (eds.), *Studies in the Plays of Brian Friel* (Fort Lauderdale, FL: Nove Southeastern University, Department of Liberal Arts, 1994).

Harp, Richard and Robert C. Evans (eds.), *A Companion to Brian Friel* (West Cornwell, CT: Locust Hill, 2002).

SELECT BIBLIOGRAPHY

Kerwin, William (ed.), *Brian Friel: A Casebook* (New York and London: Garland Press, 1997).

Morse, Donald E., Csilla Bertha and Maria Kurdi (eds.), *Brian Friel's Dramatic Artistry* (Dublin: Carysfort Press, 2006).

Peacock, Alan (ed.), *The Achievement of Brian Friel* (Gerrards Cross: Colin Smythe, 1993).

Roche, Anthony (ed.), *Irish University Review* (Special Brian Friel Issue) 29:1 (1999).

Books with material on Brian Friel

Deane, Seamus, *Celtic Revivals* (London and Boston: Faber and Faber, 1985).

Etherton, Michael, *Contemporary Irish Dramatists* (Houndmills: Macmillan, 1989).

Grene, Nicholas, *The Politics of Irish Drama: Plays in Context from Boucicault to Friel* (Cambridge: Cambridge University Press, 1999).

Kiberd, Declan, *Inventing Ireland* (London: Jonathan Cape, 1995).

McCarthy, Conor, *Modernisation: Crisis and Culture in Ireland 1969–1992* (Dublin: Four Courts Press, 2000).

Maxwell, D. E. S., *A Critical History of Modern Irish Drama 1891–1980* (Cambridge: Cambridge University Press, 1984).

Morash, Christopher, *A History of Irish Theatre 1601–2000* (Cambridge: Cambridge University Press, 2002).

Murray, Christopher, *Twentieth-Century Irish Drama: Mirror up to Nation* (Manchester: Manchester University Press, 1997).

Pilkington, Lionel, *Theatre and the State in Twentieth-Century Ireland: Cultivating the People* (London and New York: Routledge, 2001).

Richtarik, Marilynn J., *Acting Between the Lines: The Field Day Theatre Company and Irish Cultural Politics 1980–1984* (Oxford and New York: Clarendon Press, 1994).

Roche, Anthony, *Contemporary Irish Drama: From Beckett to McGuinness* (Dublin: Gill and Macmillan, 1994: New York: St. Martin's Press, 1995).

Welch, Robert. *Changing States: Transformations in Modern Irish Writing* (London and New York: Routledge, 1993).

The Abbey Theatre 1899–1999: Form and Pressure (Oxford and New York: Oxford University Press, 1999).

Selected essays on Brian Friel

Arkins, Brian, "The Role of Greek and Latin in Brian Friel's *Translations*," *Colby Quarterly* 27:4 (1991), pp. 202–209.

Bertha, Csilla and Maria Kurdi, "Hungarian Perspectives on Brian Friel's Theatre after *Dancing at Lughnasa*," in Dermot Bolger (ed.), *Druids, Dudes and Beauty Queens: The Changing Face of Irish Theatre* (Dublin: New Island, 2001), pp. 173–195.

Burke, Patrick, "'Both Heard and Imagined': Music as Structuring Principle in the Plays of Brian Friel," in Donald E. Morse, Csilla Bertha and Istvan Palffy (eds.), *A Small Nation's Contribution to the World: Essays on Anglo-Irish Literature and Language* (Gerrards Cross: Colin Smythe, 1993), pp. 43–52.

Cullingford, Elizabeth Butler, "British Romans and Irish Carthaginians: Anti-Colonial Metaphor in Heaney, Friel and McGuinness," *PMLA* 111:2 (1996), pp. 222–239.

Germanou, Maria, "Brian Friel and the Scene of Writing: Reading *Give Me Your Answer, Do!*," *Modern Drama* 46:3 (2003), pp. 470–481.

Hughes, George, "Ghosts and Ritual in Brian Friel's *Faith Healer*," *Irish University Review* 24:2 (1994), pp. 175–185.

Kiberd, Declan, "Fathers and Sons: Irish Style," in Michael Kenneally (ed.), *Irish Literature and Culture* (Gerrards Cross: Colin Smythe, 1992), pp. 127–146.

"*Dancing at Lughnasa*," in Enda McDonagh (guest ed.), *The Irish Review* 27 (2001), pp. 18–39.

Lanters, José, "Gender and Identity in Brian Friel's *Faith Healer* and Tom Murphy's *The Gigli Concert*," *Irish University Review* 22:2 (1992), pp. 278–290.

"Violence and Sacrifice in Brian Friel's *The Gentle Island* and *Wonderful Tennessee*," *Irish University Review* 26:1 (1996), pp. 163–176.

Lojek, Helen, "Brian Friel's Sense of Place," in Shaun Richards (ed.), *The Cambridge Companion to Twentieth-Century Irish Drama* (Cambridge: Cambridge University Press, 2004), pp.177–190.

McGrath, F. C., "Irish Babel: Brian Friel's *Translations* and George Steiner's *After Babel*," *Comparative Drama* 23:1 (1989), pp. 31–49.

Moloney, Karen, "Molly Astray: Revisioning Ireland in Brian Friel's *Molly Sweeney*," *Twentieth Century Literature* 46:3 (2000), pp. 285–311.

Murray, Christopher, "Brian Friel's *Making History* and the Problem of Historical Accuracy," in Geert Lernout (ed.), *The Crows Behind the Plough: History and Violence in Anglo-Irish Poetry and Drama* (Amsterdam: Rodopi, 1991), pp. 61–77.

"Brian Friel's *Molly Sweeney* and its Sources," *Études Irlandaises* 23:2 (1998), pp. 81–97.

Neil, Ruth, "Non-Realistic Techniques in the Plays of Brian Friel," in Wolfgang Zach and Heinz Kosok (eds.), *Literary Interrelations: Ireland, England and the World*, Vol. II (Tübingen: G. Narr, 1987), pp. 349–359.

Pine, Richard, "Brian Friel and Contemporary Irish Drama," *Colby Quarterly* 27:4 (1991), pp.190–201.

Richards, Shaun, "Brian Friel: Seizing the Moment of Flux," *Irish University Review* 30:2 (2000), pp. 254–271.

"Throwing Theory at Ireland? The Field Day Theatre Company and Postcolonial Theatre Criticism," *Modern Drama* 47:4 (2004), pp. 610–623.

"Irish Studies and the Adequacy of Theory: The Case of Brian Friel," in Ronan McDonald (guest ed.), *Irish Writing Since 1950*, special issue of *The Yearbook of English Studies* 35 (2005), pp. 264–278.

Robinson, Paul N., "Brian Friel's *Faith Healer*: An Irishman Comes Back Home," in Wolfgang Zach and Heinz Kosok (eds.), *Literary Interrelations: Ireland, England and the World*, vol. III, *National Images and Stereotypes* (Tübingen: Gunter Narr Verlag, 1987), pp. 223–227.

Strain, Margaret M., "'Renouncing Chance': Salvation and the Sacred in Brian Friel's *Faith Healer*," *Renascence* 57:1 (2004), pp. 63–83.

Upton, Carole-Anne, "Visions of the Sightless in Friel's *Molly Sweeney* and Synge's *The Well of the Saints*," *Modern Drama* 40:3 (1997), pp. 347–358.

White, Harry, "Brian Friel, Thomas Murphy and the Use of Music in Contemporary Irish Drama," *Modern Drama* 33:4 (1990), pp. 553–562.

Winkler, Elizabeth Hale, "Brian Friel's *The Freedom of the City*: Historical Actuality and Dramatic Imagination," *Canadian Journal of Irish Studies* 7:1 (1981), pp. 12–31.

Worth, Katharine, "Translations of History: Story-telling in Brian Friel's Theatre," in James Acheson (ed.), *British and Irish Drama Since 1960* (Houndmills: Macmillan; New York: St. Martin's Press, 1993), pp. 73–87.

Zach, Wolfgang, "Criticism, Theatre and Politics: Brian Friel's *The Freedom of the City* and Its Early Reception," in Michael Kenneally (ed.), *Irish Literature and Culture* (Gerrards Cross: Colin Smythe, 1992), pp. 112–126.

INDEX

WORKS

PLAYS

TRANSLATION/VERSIONS/ADAPTATIONS

SHORT STORIES

OTHER WORKS

CAMBRIDGE COMPANIONS TO LITERATURE

CAMBRIDGE COMPANIONS TO CULTURE